YOUTH SOCCER

Youth Soccer: From Science to Performance provides the first comprehensive guide to the science behind the development of young players. Each chapter in this innovative collection by world leading specialists demonstrates how sport science research can, and should, directly inform coaching practice.

The book includes:

- growth of young physiological systems
- development of children's motor and perceptive skills
- paediatric environmental physiology
- prevention of injury in young players
- diet and nutrition
- youth fitness and soccer skills training
- effective teaching and coaching of junior players
- the role of football academies.

Youth Soccer: From Science to Performance is an essential resource for students and academics. It will also be an invaluable guide for professionals involved in youth soccer, including coaches at all levels, PE teachers and physiotherapists.

Gareth Stratton is Reader of Paediatric Exercise Science and Chairs the REACH (Research into Exercise Activity and Children's Health) Group at Liverpool John Moores University. **Thomas Reilly** is Professor of Sports Science and Director of the Research Institute for Sport and Exercise Sciences at Liverpool John Moores University. **A. Mark Williams** is Professor of Motor Behaviour in the Research Institute for Sport and Exercise Sciences at Liverpool John Moores University. **Dave Richardson** is Senior Lecturer in Sport Management and Development at Liverpool John Moores University.

YOUTH SOCCER

From Science to Performance

**GARETH STRATTON, THOMAS REILLY,
A. MARK WILLIAMS AND DAVE RICHARDSON**

Routledge
Taylor & Francis Group

LONDON AND NEW YORK

First published 2004
by Routledge
2 Park Square, Milton Park, Abingdon, Oxon OX14 4RN

Simultaneously published in the USA and Canada
by Routledge
270 Madison Ave, New York, NY 10016

Routledge is an imprint of the Taylor & Francis Group

Typeset in Zapf Humanist and Eras by
Keystroke, Jacaranda Lodge, Wolverhampton, West Midlands
Printed and bound in Great Britain by
TJ International Ltd, Padstow, Cornwall

British Library Cataloguing in Publication Data
A catalogue record for this book is available from the British Library

Library of Congress Cataloging in Publication Data
A catalog record for this book has been requested

ISBN 0–415–28661–1 (hbk)
ISBN 0–415–28662–X (pbk)

CONTENTS

12 THE ROLE OF THE SOCCER ACADEMY 199

ILLUSTRATIONS

FIGURES

TABLES

CHAPTER ONE

AN INTRODUCTION TO THE SCIENCE OF YOUTH SOCCER

Association football, otherwise known as soccer, is the most popular global sport with millions of males and females participating in the game. The production line of young footballers operates non-stop with each individual having dreams and aspirations of 'making it to the top' and emulating his/her superheroes. Many youngsters have their bedroom walls and rooms plastered with memorabilia and the expectations for success at all levels of competition are high. Furthermore, greater emphasis has been placed on boosting the production line at the start with a playground to podium approach. The focus on youth soccer has grown since the huge financial implications of 'spotting a future star' together with increased professional approaches to training and education have encouraged coaches, parents and administrators to support soccer development programmes. These approaches have emerged since the early 1980s and development programmes and structures are highly sophisticated and well funded in the new millennium. It is against this backdrop that a book considering essential scientific aspects of youth soccer is required. Over the years, there have been various texts covering the principles of youth soccer coaching and training. These texts include playing principles and practices with an almost infinite number of soccer activities, skill practices and strategic approaches described. Soccer coaching material is now readily available at the end of a computer terminal and thousands of web sites dedicated to soccer reflect the global demand. Surprisingly, therefore, there are few if any dedicated texts on the science of youth soccer. Given the emphasis on this sector of the playing population the need to fill this gap in the literature is important.

Since its inception in 1987, the World Congress of Science and Football has been held once every four years. The first Congress included a theme titled 'strain in adolescent footballers' reflecting the concerns about youth football at that time. Over subsequent congresses, scientific reports on varied aspects of paediatric sports and exercise science and youth soccer have been presented. Other

1

professional and scientific conferences have also included papers on youth soccer. However, relative to other areas the number of scientific communications on youth soccer has been small. This mirrors the fact that interest in paediatric sports and exercise science has lagged behind the development of sports science overall.

Nevertheless, there has been increasing interest and research momentum in the field of paediatric exercise science since the early 1990s. Much discussion has revolved around identifying talented players, then perfecting this talent. As there is no consensus on exact procedures for identifying sports talent, this text concentrates mainly on the development and perfection of youth soccer players. The measurement of fitness in age-group populations has increased in sophistication from methods used in large epidemiological studies carried out in North America in the 1960s to more consistent and validated tests in the new millennium. Furthermore, laboratory equipment and tests specifically designed for youngsters of various ages and stages are now more widely available for assessment of both physiological and psychological performance. As scientific support for potentially elite sports girls and boys becomes more widespread, robust scientific data will be more consistent and informative. At present scientific data on the performance of elite young sports performers are sketchy. Even sketchier are studies of the effects of training programmes on the development of fitness and skill in young sports performers.

This text incorporates a survey of the available literature and data pertinent to the understanding of scientific study in youth soccer. From this survey, essential scientific concepts and issues important for effective youth soccer coaching programmes are outlined. This text aims to provide students and coaches of soccer with a synthesis of the most important concepts from a multidimensional perspective. Psychological, physiological, pedagogical and sociological themes related to fitness, injury, growth, skill, learning, teaching, coaching and administration in soccer are considered. The contents of this text should arm the youth coach or student of soccer with the important principles to instil excellence in coaching practice. The core aspects are principles of growth and development, age specific scientific data and differences between children and adults. So important are these principles to the long-term well-being of the game that it can be argued that top quality and highly paid coaches should be recruited to work in youth soccer. Currently the financial reward for coaching lies in professional football management at the elite adult side of the game. As professional soccer is the 'shop window' for the game, this situation is unlikely to change. Therefore, the best-paid coaches are usually employed at this level.

Development programmes for soccer have two major goals: the first is to engage players in lifelong participation in the sport; and the second is to maintain a professional outlook that continues to inspire and motivate youngsters to participate. The 'art' of the soccer coach is to use all the tools available in a manner that is appropriate for the child and motivates the child to keep practising and improving. Even if players do not make the professional ranks, appropriate coaching programmes should motivate players to develop lengthy careers in the sport, through playing, coaching or administrating. However, combining appropriate and effective training approaches and structures is a complex task for coaches of individuals who are growing, developing and maturing at different rates and at different stages. Being able to match training intensity and competition to the stage of development of youngsters requires a detailed multidisciplinary awareness of psychology, physiology and sociology as well as a clear under-standing of the processes of growth and development. It is particularly difficult to gather all these special skills, knowledge and competencies together and to use them effectively and relatively few coaches are blessed with such an array of talents.

Coaches working in groups or teams best serve the needs of a developing group of young soccer players. Teams of coaches are also more likely to have the range of skills, knowledge and competence to enable gifted young players to reach their potential. Coaches in the so-called 'football academies' have most experience in this field and understand the particular needs and demands of individual players. The organisation of 'academies' represents part of the sophisticated structures set up to support youth soccer. Personnel in these academies have the specific responsibility to detect, select and perfect young soccer players who are potentially elite. The likely benefits of getting these processes right are enormous; on the other hand the ethical and moral consequences of getting it wrong by implementing soccer-centred rather than child-centred programmes could be catastrophic. Very few children realise their sporting aspirations to become elite, professional soccer players. The vast majority who do not achieve professional status in soccer also deserve a sound, professional and caring soccer education.

The concept of 'readiness' is central to this book. Coaches need to apply the principle of readiness when considering the progress of young players. Readiness may be defined as a player's ability to meet the challenges set within a planned long-term soccer development programme. Sometimes readiness does not run in synchrony with chronological age (age in years). This is especially the case during the circumpubertal period when players delayed or advanced in maturity status may be of the same chronological age but different maturational age. Consequently, issues surrounding maturation are covered throughout this text. For example, what are the key factors required before an adolescent progresses from participation in youth to adult soccer? Young soccer players should be progressively exposed to increased training and competitive demands. This may

3

mean moving up to a higher level of performance or following an exit route to a lower level of participation. Each level of decision-making by coaches is dictated by a player's readiness to cope with the physical, mental and social demands required at that level. A player may be deemed 'ready' or not for that level by coaches who decide whether the individual would benefit from the coaching and teaching processes and the demands of competition and training. These issues of readiness and maturity are particular to the individual and the chapter on growth and development highlights the varied tempo and intensity of these aspects of physical performance. Soccer players will develop optimally when training programmes are commensurate with their psychological, physiological and sociological needs. Furthermore, if able players are exposed for significant amounts of time to the correct environment set up by expert junior coaches then their skill and technique will develop. In addition, there are explicit differences in skill and technique between novice and expert performers and these differences are reviewed in this text.

To help soccer educators develop an understanding of growth-related performance a number of youth development models that have been proposed for training, coaching, fitness and skill development, and injury avoidance are reviewed. The most popular model to date in the United Kingdom (UK) is the long-term athlete development model (LTADM). This model outlines essential goals for each of the four stages of athlete development. Between the ages of 5 and 11 years, fundamentals of movement should be developed. Fundamental movements such as running, jumping, throwing, kicking, catching, rolling, skipping, striking and so on are best developed through multiple activities and not just soccer alone. The second 'training to train' stage represents the key goal for 11–14-year-olds. At this stage it is suggested that coaches should aim to educate players about how to improve through training not just during organised sessions but also on their own. This recommendation fits with the theories on expertise outlined in the chapters on acquisition of skill and perceptual and cognitive expertise. Becoming elite requires a substantial amount of practice and preparation time. Up to 7000 hours are reported in this text for the time invested by youth soccer players in becoming expert, whilst other authorities have suggested that 10,000 hours of practice are required to reach an elite level. This commitment amounts to 3 hours a day for 10 years and clearly not all this time can be spent in organised coaching. Therefore educating players about principles and practices of training is essential and represents the major aim of the 'training to train' stage. The third stage for 14–16-year-olds increases the emphasis on training to compete, and these years represent the stage where the particular emphasis on individual performance within competition is highlighted. The final 'training to win' stage sets out the key criteria for winning. It is not until 16 years of age that winning is emphasised. This does not mean that winning is not important during any of the stages: it is simply

4

that the goal of the final stage is met through activities and coaching that emphasise winning. The LTADM is discussed in more detail in the training and fitness and coaching and pedagogy chapters in this text. Other models and approaches to training young soccer players have also been identified. These include the soccer development model, identification of sensitive periods for training, and the content of training for potentially elite athletes. These models and guides are included to help coaches and students of soccer to identify priorities for training at each age and stage of development.

This text covers not only scientific issues surrounding readiness to train and perform but also environmental concepts such as climate, travel, altitude, and heat and cold stress. With travel to foreign parts becoming cheaper and more accessible these are essential topics for coaches who may take players to soccer tournaments and tours in countries with other climatic conditions. The importance of safety is also discussed in the chapter on injury where common injuries to youth soccer players are reviewed and preventative measures discussed. The exponential increase in the number of female soccer players warrants a chapter on the female performer with particular emphasis on the menstrual cycle, the female athlete triad and their relationship with sports performance. The chapter on the female soccer player also complements that on growth and development.

A substantial body of research has been generated in the area of sports nutrition over the past 25 years and Chapter 7 provides clear guidance for health nutrition practices and principles in the growing child. Generally, children's diets include excess amounts of refined sugar, sweet carbonated drinks, snacks and fatty foods. Basic dietary practice and sound principles of rehydration need to be promoted by coaches to whole families. In terms of families, social aspects are discussed in the chapter on psychosocial issues. This chapter clearly identifies the support mechanisms required if young soccer players are to develop into potentially elite players. Key concepts and principles about the development of expertise in young soccer players and differences between elite and average players in motor skill and performance provide important reading for those concerned with the development of skilled performance and game understanding. Chapters on skill acquisition coupled with detailed models of pedagogy and coaching draw on key concepts discussed in other chapters in the text. Principles of coaching, teaching, learning and assessment are covered in detail in these chapters and cutting edge research is used to support training and coaching theory. Original research comparing skill acquisition, game understanding and perception between expert and novice players provides novel insights into the development of elite soccer players. Data on expert and novice performers are combined with examples of models for developmentally appropriate soccer coaching and the LTADM is used as an example of a graded approach to developing junior and youth soccer players in the four stages. Finally, the role of the Football Academy in the development of young footballers is reviewed, and empirical research from processes and practices of soccer academies is presented.

This text aims to provide coaches and students of soccer with a vision towards the future and discusses the potential of stronger scientific evidence on the development of youth soccer players. This future should involve effecting a stronger marriage between soccer and science. In order for sustainable collaborations between sport and exercise science, youth soccer structures should make strategic use of applied soccer science. By studying this text students and coaches should become more knowledgeable and their developmental structures and programmes and coaching and training approaches should be better informed, more professional and ultimately enlightened.

CHAPTER TWO

THE GROWTH OF THE
PHYSIOLOGICAL SYSTEMS

INTRODUCTION

An understanding of growth and maturation is important for any aspiring youth soccer coach. Tanner's works are seminal in this field and these have provided most data using globally recognised methodological approaches. Some of these concepts have been used to assess youth soccer players. Furthermore, over the past 10 years developments in technology such as dual-energy x-ray absorptiometry (DEXA), magnetic resonance imaging (MRI) and near infrared spectroscopy (NIRS) have led to an upsurge in scientific advancement. New technologies are enabling scientists to develop a better understanding of factors that affect growth and performance. Sport and exercise scientists interested in how growth affects performance are beginning to use these technologies to help sports coaches and teachers apply sound scientific principles in their practice.

The aim of this chapter is to help develop an understanding of how physiological and anatomical systems affect skill and performance. Knowledge of these processes should aid coaches of youth football players to maximise player potential. Data from studies on young soccer players are used where they are available. Data from general populations are also used as reference material because of the scarcity of growth studies on soccer playing boys, and girls in particular.

FUNDAMENTALS OF GROWTH, DEVELOPMENT AND MATURATION

From conception through to physical maturity, growth represents the dominant biological process of the first 20 years of life. Growth itself has a particular definition and although sometimes used interchangeably with development, growth is represented by an increase in size or quantity. In biological terms the increase in number of cells (hyperplasia) occurs mainly before birth (prenatal)

7

whereas the increase in size of cells (hypertrophy) occurs after birth. A combination of hyperplasia, hypertrophy and accretion (increase in intercellular substances) results in growth. Development on the other hand represents qualitative changes that can be psychological, physiological or social. Maturation is also difficult to describe, as it represents the process of becoming mature. The path to the mature state may involve biological progress in sexual, skeletal or morphological characteristics. The process of maturation is highly complex and has been the central focus of research scientists in their attempts to unravel the many interactions of growth, maturation and training in young people. The physiological processes involved in growth and maturation are closely interrelated but involve large individual differences in tempo and intensity.

Being active is important for the health of all young people, none more than the soccer player. During childhood, fundamental motor skills such as kicking, throwing, catching, jumping, running, rolling, balancing and so forth (Haywood and Getchell, 2001) are developed and refined in preparation for entry into specialist sporting activities such as soccer. Regular engagement in physical activities increases the potential for refined motor behaviour and an optimal level of development. The interaction of the young person with the environment has been described as biosocial since growth and maturation do not proceed independently of it (Malina and Bouchard, 1991). The interaction of these factors shapes an individual's progress from 'foetus to man' (Tanner, 1984) or, using sporting metaphors, 'playground to podium', or 'cradle to cup'. Coaching this highly complex, developing, growing and maturing soccer player needs careful consideration by football educators. The investment of time and money into football academies where young players are trained from 8 years onwards needs a realistic return. Professionals with a detailed understanding of growth, development and maturation are better placed to support young footballers in their quest for stardom.

GROWTH CURVES

In 1930 the anatomist Richard Scammon summarised the postnatal growth of tissues in four curves that are relative to each other. The *general* curve is characteristic of most systems of the body such as weight, cardiorespiratory, skeletal and digestive systems. This curve is S (sigmoid) shaped representing two rapid periods of growth during infancy and puberty. The *neural* curve reflects the growth of the brain and nervous system, the majority of which occurs in the first seven years of life. Once formed a nerve cell can increase its mass 200,000 times. Furthermore, the diameters of myelinated fibres in the periphery increase to about 90 per cent of their adult size in the first 5–6 years whereas growth of the neural system slows from age 12–13 years. The cranium follows the neural pathway of growth unlike the lower face and jaw that follow the general curve. The *genital* curve represents the growth of primary and secondary sexual characteristics. These tissues undergo slight growth during infancy followed by rapid growth during adolescence. The *lymphoid* curve is indicative of the capacity of children's immune systems. At age 11 children have relatively twice as much lymphoid tissue as adults. This decline of the curve to adulthood is a result of a reduction in size of the thymus and tonsils. These curves are shown together in Figure 2.1.

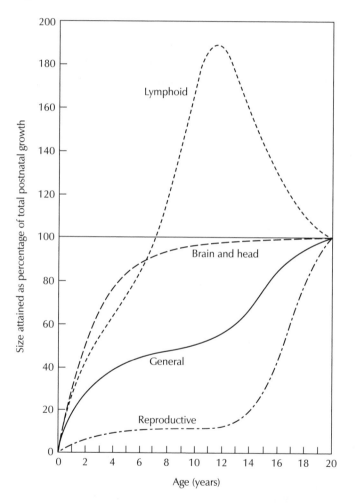

Figure 2.1 A summary of Scammon's growth curves
Source: Tanner, 1984.

Scammon's curves provide an illustration of the structural and functional changes that occur as a result of growth. These changes are complex and not fully understood. The processes are slow and are not obvious on a daily basis. Therefore, soccer coaches need to understand the general pathway that youngsters will follow from child to adulthood.

GROWTH OF BODY SYSTEMS

Morphological (somatic) growth

Perhaps the most widely recognised growth charts are those used for height (stature) and weight (mass). These charts map out morphological growth curves for height and weight and essentially follow Scammon's general growth curve (Figure 2.1).

Figures 2.2a–2.2d are commonly used to assess a child's growth status. The central line on graphics a and c represents the 50th percentile or average line. Percentile lines above and below this average line refer to larger and smaller than average scores respectively. Curves b and d only include the 50th percentile line for clarity. Curves b and d illustrate the 'rate' of growth and are described as growth 'velocity' curves.

Growth curves for height and weight

Figures 2.2a and 2.2c represent growth curves for height and weight respectively. These curves are described as sigmoid because of their stretched 'S' shape. The slightly concave parts of the curve represent accelerated periods of growth during the early years and during puberty whereas the convex sections represent slower periods of growth. The range of normal heights and weights for girls and boys of various ages is easily assessed using these growth charts. The normal range is wide and depicted by the percentile lines to be described later.

Growth velocity curves

Figures 2.2b and 2.2d represent height and weight velocity curves respectively. Puberty represents the time when key changes occur in the growth of body tissues of boys and girls. Between 8 and 14 years of age, girls gain weight more rapidly than boys. Girls increase their weight four times as much between 10 and 14

10

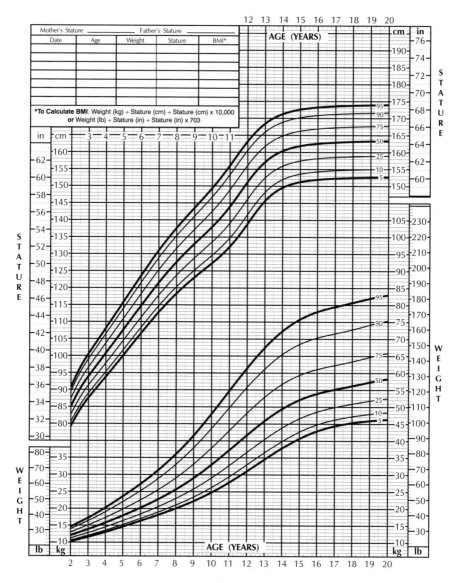

Figure 2.2a Height and weight growth curve, girls

Source: Childgrowth foundation, Kids Health Website, accessed 1/9/03.

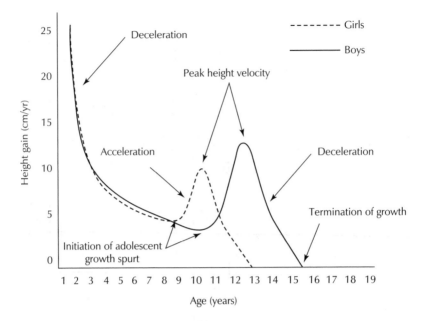

Figure 2.2b Height velocity curves for girls and boys
Source: Author.

years of age as between 16 and 20 years of age (20 kg compared to 5 kg). After 14 years of age the rate of increase in weight slows. Boys on the other hand experience their growth spurt approximately two years later than girls. The maximum rate of weight gain of 20–25 kg for boys occurs between 12 and 16 years of age whilst about 10 kg is gained between 16 and 20 years of age.

Rates of increase in stature are similar between girls and boys up to 10 years of age. At the age of 10, the weights of girls and boys are similar at the 50th percentile after which girls grow at a faster rate compared to boys until about 13 years of age. After 13 years of age the rate of increase in height slows whereas the height spurt in boys is in its early phase. By 14 years of age, boys are on average taller than girls. Girls generally gain no more than 5 cm in stature after the menarche compared to boys who may continue to grow in height in their early twenties. By the time adult stature is reached, the 50th percentile for stature-for-age is about 15 cm higher for males than for females. Thus, the average adult Caucasian male is about 1.8 m tall, and the average adult female is about 1.65 m tall.

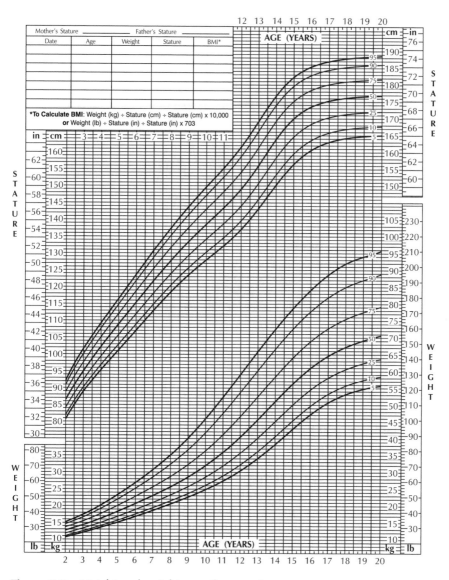

Figure 2.2c Height and weight growth curve, boys
Source: Childgrowth foundation, Kids Health Website, accessed 1/9/03.

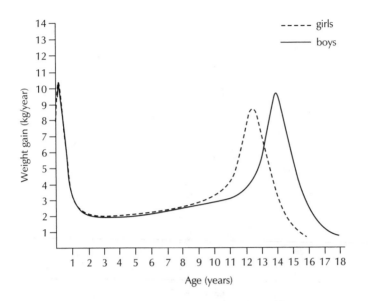

Figure 2.2d Weight velocity curves for girls and boys

Source: Author.

The use of growth curves in soccer

Growth curves provide invaluable information for coaches who wish to compare their players' height and weight compared to the average (50th percentile). One of the most straightforward aspects for a coach to analyse is the relationship between height and weight. For example, a 10-year-old midfielder is on the 25th percentile for height, and 75th for weight. The coach of this child needs to consider the possible causes and consequences of this 'heavy for height' scenario and whether this could carry through to adulthood. It is appropriate here to introduce the principle of *tracking*. Tracking relates to the stability of a variable over time. For example, if the same 10-year-old boy remained on the 25th percentile for height between 10 and 18 years of age, he would have maintained his percentile position through to adulthood, and scientists would state that his height 'tracked'. Another term for tracking is 'canalisation'. If the same boy stayed within the 25th and 50th percentile lines (these represent a canal) on the growth curve from childhood to adulthood, then using this criterion his height would also have tracked. The degree of tracking depends on the criteria used and is open to interpretation depending on the 'width' of canals used. Weight does not track quite as well due to environmental influences such as physical activity and dietary behaviour. Fluctuations in weight are less likely to occur in young soccer players who are generally leaner than the average young person (Baxter-Jones and Helms, 1996; Hansen et al., 1999). Furthermore, elite young soccer players have similar somatotypes to their adult counterparts suggesting that these are observable during childhood (Peyna Reyes et al., 1994). Janssens and colleagues (2002) revealed that level 1, 12-year-old soccer players were significantly leaner than average Flemish children and level 2 and 3 soccer players. These ecto-mesomorphic somatotypes were similar to Cuban and Brazilian soccer players of similar age. In a detailed review Malina (2003) plotted the height and weight of male soccer players from Europe and the Americas onto United States reference data (see Figures 2.3a and 2.3b).

According to these plots height and weight were normal and lay between the 25th and 75th percentile lines. Only one result lay above the 75th and 11 lay below the 25th percentile line. Height fluctuated above and below the median reference line until late adolescence when the majority of mean values fell below the median reference value. For weight the mean scores approximated the median until later adolescence when they moved above the median. The weight and height for soccer players tracked the normal population up to late adolescence after which players' weight increased more than height. This trend was probably a result of increases in lean body tissue.

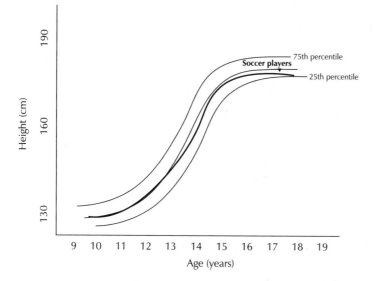

Figure 2.3a Mean heights of soccer players from Europe and Americas plotted against normal growth curves

Source: Malina, 2003.

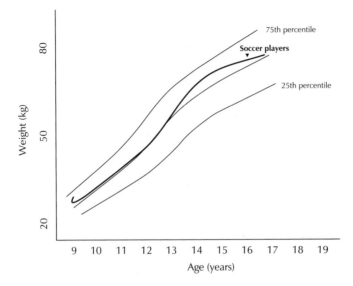

Figure 2.3b Mean weights of soccer players from Europe and Americas plotted against normal growth curves

Source: Malina, 2003.

The range of heights and weights of young soccer players also varied globally with national level Japanese players being relatively heavy for their height compared to similar Chinese players who were the opposite. Growth related data are difficult to compare internationally and reflect cultural diversity. Data from this report (Malina, 2003) are cross-sectional and derived from various countries. Robust data would be longitudinal and taken over similar age ranges; unfortunately data over the age span are not available. Even fewer data are available on young female soccer players. Although there are fluctuations in weight, both height and weight in young soccer players track well from childhood to adolescence but less well from adolescence to adulthood. Many problems with accurately tracking players occur because of the tempo and intensity of the adolescent growth spurt.

MATURATION AND YOUNG SOCCER PLAYERS

The growth of the body's systems is mainly consistent pre-puberty and post-puberty. However, puberty (average age of onset: 11.5 years for girls and 13.5 years for boys) represents a time when predictions of height and weight become extremely difficult. The intensity and timing of the adolescent growth spurt are

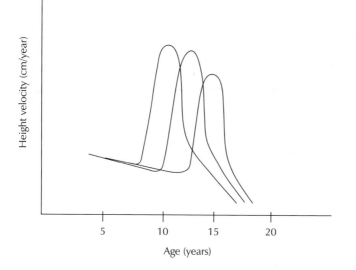

Figure 2.4 Early, average and late maturing growth velocity curves
Source: Tanner, 1984.

highly individual and variable but identifying the spurt is useful for detecting early, average or late maturing girls and boys. A number of methods have been used to assess the onset of puberty. Age at menarche is an established method and girls recall this particular lifetime event with some accuracy. There is no parallel lifetime event in boys and the assessment of maturation status by measuring testicular volume has both ethical and technical difficulties. Assessing skeletal age by x-raying the left wrist is very reliable although ethically questionable because of its use of radiation (Roche et al., 1988). The most difficult measure to obtain is age at peak height velocity (PHV). This approach requires a longitudinal methodology (repeated measures on the same person). In this method, height is measured twice yearly and permits a PHV curve to be constructed (Figure 2.2c). Maturity is then described as the number of years before or after PHV. Other velocities such as peak weight velocity or peak velocity of vertical jump may be described in similar fashion. Fluctuations in growth, particularly around puberty, cause difficulty in organising coaching sessions appropriate for age and stage of development. The peaks and troughs illustrate the increases and decreases in height velocity between 5 and 18 years of age. This particular group of growth curves could well be those of members of a football academy. The question of dealing with a variety of footballers at the same chronological age but different biological age will be discussed later in this chapter. The two methods most commonly used to assess maturation are Tanner's indices of maturation, and percentage stature of adult or morphological age. Tanner's indices include rating breast and pubic hair development in girls and genitalia and pubic hair development in boys (Tanner, 1984). These indices are used regularly in practice by paediatricians and paediatric nurses. More recently, youngsters have used these scales to assess themselves. Morphological age is recorded as the percentage of predicted adult height and requires accurate records from the biological parents of the youngster as well as a measure of his or her height. For example, if a 12-year-old female footballer was predicted to reach 1.7 metres by maturity from her mid-parent height and she had reached 1.36 metres she would be 80 per cent of her predicted value (1.36/1.7 × 100). Another method reported recently for assessing maturation status uses sitting height (from rump to crown), height and leg length to predict maturation stage (Mirwald et al., 2002). This method provides the first real practical and ethical solution for matching adolescent athletes such as soccer players by maturation age.

Maturity in young soccer players has been assessed in a number of studies. Studies confirm the classical results in that some players are delayed, others on time, or advanced in maturity (Malina, 2003). However, cross-sectional studies reveal that with increasing age boys with advanced maturity status are more common than expected especially in elite groups. Other data from longitudinal research indicate that age at PHV in sub-elite subjects varies from 14.2 years in Welsh and Danish to 13.8 years in Belgian players. Only the Belgian group was advanced in maturity status when the data were compared to PHV data from European adolescents. Overall, data on the adolescent growth spurt of young soccer players are inconsistent. It is only during late adolescence that players are advanced in maturity. This is a key issue as maturity status may also affect the selection process. Panfil and colleagues (1997) found that coaches favour players who are more advanced in morphological growth during the selection process. Richardson and Stratton (1999) also found that the majority of players selected for England's World Cup squads between 1986 and 1998 were born between September and December. Early maturers seem to be selected into elite groups more often than their late maturing peers. However, size represents only one item of the criteria for selection and other factors such as skill and practice time also have large influences on performance.

GROWTH OF BODY TISSUES

Body composition

Between the ages of 5 and 20 years body density in boys (1.078–1.099 g/ccm) is always greater than that of girls (1.073–1.095 g/ccm) (Malina and Bouchard, 1991: 94). These sex differences are to do with girls possessing a higher percentage of body water (girls 5–20 years: 77.6–74.8 per cent; boys 5–10 years: 76.6–74.0 per cent), but lower percentages of protein (18.0–19.2 per cent; 18.5–19.4 per cent) and minerals (3.7–6.0 per cent; 4.3–6.6 per cent) than boys. Body density in females decreases just prior to puberty, increasing slightly through puberty to a plateau in early adulthood. Body density in boys decreases during late childhood, then increases linearly from about 10 to 18 years of age when it reaches a plateau.

Fat free mass

Measures of fat free mass (FFM) are derived from body density and as such follow similar trends to those described above. Differences in FFM are small until late adolescence when females possess 70 per cent of the FFM of their male counterparts. This difference is a result of females' FFM reaching a plateau at 15 years compared to a continuous increase in males' through to 20 years. According to Malina and Bouchard (1991) these changes result in young adult males possessing 0.36 kg/cm of FFM compared to 0.26 kg/cm of FFM in similar age females. Sex differences in FFM of 32.5 kg in males before and after puberty

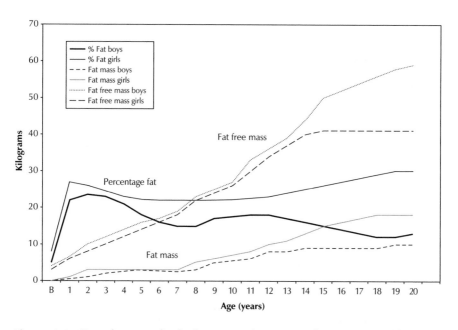

Figure 2.5 Growth curves for fat free mass, fat mass and percentage of fat
Source: Based on Malina, 2003.

compared to 17.3 kg in females significantly affect running performance. Conversely, girls have a greater percentage of body fat from early childhood than boys and this difference increases during the adolescent growth spurt. Through this period females accrue twice as much fat mass as males. There is also growing evidence that adiposity tracks from child to adulthood.

Skeletal

Skeletal weight increases in parallel with height and weight growth curves from about 15 per cent of total weight in childhood to 17 per cent in young adulthood. From birth boys have a larger percentage of bone mineral than girls; black Americans have greater amounts of bone mineral than their white peers (Malina and Bouchard, 1991). As bone matures, calcium infiltrates collagen and ossifies to produce bone. During the ossification (bone forming) process water stored in collagen is also displaced. The combination of these two processes results in an increased length and width of bone in adulthood.

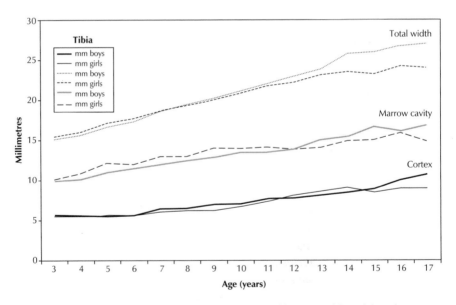

Figure 2.6 Changes in marrow cavity and cortical bone widths of the tibia in 3- to 18-year-old girls and boys

Source: Based on Tanner et al., 1981.

20

Muscle

There are three types of muscle: involuntary (smooth), cardiac and skeletal. Cardiac and skeletal muscles are most closely related to growth development and performance. The microstructure of all 500 skeletal muscles in the body consists of three fibre types – type I (slow twitch; ST, SO), type IIa (intermediate twitch; FOG) and type IIb (fast twitch; FT, FG). There are limited data available on the effects of growth and training on muscle structure during childhood and adolescence. This deficiency is much to do with the problems of using invasive procedures. To date, relatively little difference in fibre distribution between children and adults has been found. However, muscle fibre size is dependent on the load placed upon it during growth and increases dramatically with age. Between childhood and adulthood, the increase in fibre diameter is 14-fold in boys compared to 10-fold in girls. From childhood to adulthood, the relative muscle mass to body weight of males increases from 40 to 50 per cent compared to 40 per cent in females over the same period. Similar differences are found in muscle width in the arms and legs.

Table 2.1 Changes in the muscle width of the calf and arm in 3- to 18-year-old girls and boys

Age (yrs)	Arm		Age	Calf	
	Boys	Girls		Boys	Girls
3	35	31	3	43	42
4	36	33	4	46	45
5	37	34.8	5	47	47
6	38	34	6	50	50
7	40	37	7	52	51
8	41	39	8	54	53
9	42	40	9	55	54
10	44	40	10	57	56
11	46	43	11	58	58
12	47	46	12	59	61
13	48	47	13	61	65
14	52	49	14	66	67
15	56	52	15	71	69
16	61	53	16	74	70
17	65	54	17	75	71
18	66	50	18	76	70

Source: Tanner et al., 1981.

21

Longitudinal studies provide little evidence of changes in body composition in youth soccer players. Data from Baxter-Jones and Helms (1996) and Hansen et al. (1999) suggest that elite soccer players are leaner, taller and maturer than counterparts at a lower level of play. Malina (2003) reported that Japanese players were taller and heavier than Chinese players who had less weight for height. These data demonstrated that weight and height are generally indicative of the normal weight and height of the corresponding age group population.

GROWTH OF THE CARDIOPULMONARY SYSTEM

The heart increases in size in parallel with weight from 40 cm³ at birth to 600–800 cm³ at adulthood, although these volumes remain relative at about 10 cubic centimetres per kilogram weight throughout growth. Studies using echocardiography have revealed that left ventricular mass (LVM) correlates with body surface area (BSA) during the growing years (Rowland, 1996). Basal heart rates reduce from about 65 beats per minute for boys and 73 beats per minute for girls, to 57 beats per minute for young men and 62 beats per minute for young women (Stratton, 1996). Basal heart rates are normally attained during sleep and are lower than resting heart rates (boys 72 beats per minute; girls 76 beats per minute) which are obtained in quiet surroundings whilst awake (Malina and Bouchard, 1991). Electrocardiograms reveal a longer QRS interval in adults compared to children whilst stabilisation of the autonomic nervous system, heart position and other haemodynamic factors all serve to bring more regularity to the heart beat with age. Stroke volume on the other hand increases from 3–4 ml during infancy to about 40 ml in late childhood. In boys, this value increases rapidly during the adolescent growth spurt to about 60 ml. Cardiac output increases from about 0.5 litres in the new-born to 5 litres in the young adult male in similar fashion to blood volume. Factors that increase the power of the heart muscle during growth such as circulating androgens and increased vascular resistance combine to allow the cardiorespiratory system to cope with progressively greater workloads. Blood composition also changes during this period. Haematocrit (the ratio of the volume occupied by packed red blood cells to the volume of the whole blood) increases progressively from 30 per cent in the infant to 40–45 per cent in adult males. Haematocrit in females increases in similar fashion to boys during childhood after which it levels off to 38–42 per cent of red cell volume. These changes are related to changes in FFM. Red blood cell count increases linearly with age from 4–4.6 million in females and 4–5.5 million in males. Haemoglobin (Hb) increases in a linear fashion from about 10 g dl⁻¹ in the first year to 14 and 16 g dl⁻¹ in adult females and males respectively. These differences have significant implications for male and female exercise performance as total body Hb and $\dot{V}O_{2max}$ (maximum volume of oxygen used per minute) are closely related. As with cardiac tissue the lungs grow rapidly from around 65 g after birth to 1.3 kg at maturity. However, growth of lung tissue is most closely related to height. The alveoli number increases from 20 million at birth to their peak of 300 million at age 8. Furthermore, adults are three times as efficient at breathing – 10 ml air per gram of tissue compared to 3 ml in the new-born. Little is known about the regulation of breathing during the developmental stages although breathing frequency decreases from about 22 breaths per minute at age 5 to 16–17 breaths per minute at maturity. As with height, dynamic lung volumes track into adulthood in healthy individuals. As a result maximal voluntary ventilation increases from 50 litres at age 5 to 110 litres at maturity.

GROWTH OF FITNESS PARAMETERS

The fundamentals of growth and development of body size and constituent tissues have been discussed. In the next section, the aim is to review the growth of physical performance from childhood through to adulthood.

Accounting for size

Physical performance can be related positively or negatively to body size. This section considers how performance is related to body size while Chapter 6 considers the problems of separating growth effects from training-related increases in performance. Accounting for increases in physical performance during the growing years represents a significant challenge to the paediatric exercise specialist. Consider the scenario of a group of 12-year-old soccer players in a football academy. Over a season of football practice and competition, their aerobic power increased from 2.2 to 2.5 litres per minute. The important question here is what caused the large increase in aerobic fitness? Was it the fact that players were engaged in football four times per week? Or was it mainly a result of growth-related increases in body and heart size and increases in Hb, muscle mass and a more stable autonomic nervous system? The same kind of question applies when different age groups are compared. The problem with defining 'normal' is that youngsters are in a constant state of dimensional change. The difficulty that exercise scientists have is agreeing on the most effective way of interpreting growth-related data. Most data are expressed relative to weight or surface area, and these are known as ratio standards. Whilst evidence is still equivocal on the validity of using ratio standards as a linear dimension most studies report fitness data relative to weight. Data reported relative to weight are easier to interpret especially when the activity involves translocation of the body (Rowland, 1996). Most of the data used in the following section have been drawn from field tests of physical fitness tests and motor performance. Field tests (see Chapter 6 for a description) have commonly been used in longitudinal growth studies to measure gross motor developments such as running, jumping and throwing.

Strength

Strength may be measured through quantification of peak force or torque during maximal voluntary contraction, or electrically evoked muscle contractions. For males strength is strongly correlated with chronological age through mid-childhood and adolescence. In contrast only moderate positive correlation coefficients between strength and age are found in girls during childhood (Blimkie, 1989). Correlations are weak for females during adolescence and early adulthood. Isometric grip strength represents the most robust set of data available and trends in these data clearly demonstrate the growth in strength from child to adulthood.

For boys the curvilinear increase in strength occurs from childhood until puberty followed by acceleration through to early adulthood. The pattern is similar for girls until the onset of puberty when the increase in strength slows dramatically to age 15. Females possess 90 per cent of the strength of males until age 7 compared to 60 per cent at age 18. Similar trends are found in composite (a combination of strength measures) and handgrip strength although it is also recognised that handgrip is only weakly correlated with other measures of strength in youngsters (see Figure 2.7).

Changes in strength are attributed to increases in weight, FFM, and developments in the neuromuscular and neuroendocrine systems. These differences are mirrored in motor performance tests such as the standing broad jump and counter-movement jump (see Figure 2.8).

Although boys on average always jump further than girls the pattern of development is similar between 5 and 12 years of age when the broad jumping capability of females reaches a plateau. It then slightly decreases compared to an exponential increase in jumping distance achieved by boys. Similar to differences in muscle mass girls manage to jump approximately 70 per cent of the distance of boys by age 17 (counter-movement jumps – 80 per cent or greater).

Similar patterns of development exist for running speed and other activities that engage the leg muscles. Differences between girls and boys are larger in motor performance of the upper limbs. Throwing the softball for distance involves

24

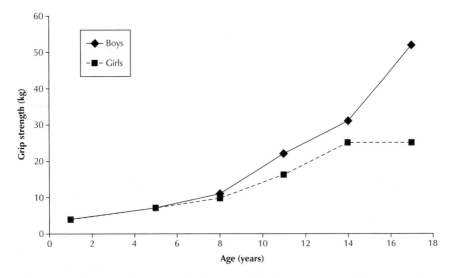

Figure 2.7 The development of grip strength in 2- to 17-year-old girls and boys
Source: Based on Blimkie *et al.*, 1989.

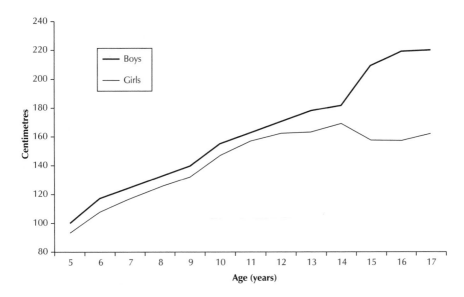

Figure 2.8 The development of standing long jump in 5- to 18-year-old girls and boys
Source: Based on Blimkie *et al.*, 1989.

dynamic performance of the whole body as well as coordination of the upper limb and trunk. Throwing distance is also reliant upon shoulder girdle strength. Girls throw about 60 per cent of the distance achieved by boys at age 6, falling to about 50 per cent at age 12 and 30 per cent at age 17. Wild and Stratton (1992) revealed that the best predictor of throwing distance was arm strength in girls and whole-body coordination in boys.

Flexibility

Flexibility has been described as the forgotten part of fitness or the overlooked sibling of strength endurance and speed. Flexibility is defined as the range of movement around a joint or series of joints. This definition reflects the approaches used to measure flexibility. The sit-and-reach test measures flexibility around a range of joints whereas the use of goniometers or 'flexometers' allows the exercise scientist to measure flexibility (joint angle) at single joints. Field tests indicate that girls are more flexible than boys at all ages. Boys' sit-and-reach scores are stable from 5 to 8 years after which they decrease to a low point at 11. After this age flexibility increases steadily to age 18. The flexibility scores of girls are stable between 5 and 11 years and then increase dramatically to age 14 after which

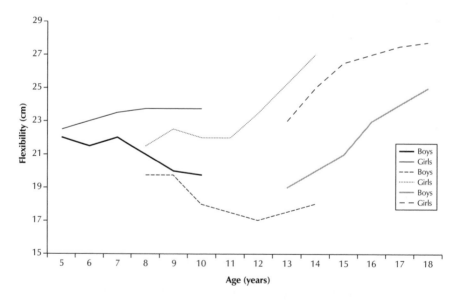

Figure 2.9 Changes in flexibility in 5- to 18-year-old girls and boys
Source: Based on Haubenstricker and Seefeldt, 1986.

values level off. These changes relate to anatomical changes in leg and trunk length through adolescence.

ANAEROBIC FUNCTION, METABOLISM AND POWER OUTPUT

Power output, defined by the product of force and velocity, is a result of body movement generated by muscular contraction. Metabolic factors underpinning the production of power will be considered here. The key principle regarding power output is a balance between energy production and utilisation. This energy supplied in the form of adenosine tri-phosphate (ATP) is defined as anaerobic if it is used to support maximal muscular contraction of short duration and uses mainly creatine phosphate (PCr), glucose or glycogen as its fuel. The phosphagen system consists of PCr and ATP. This system supports maximal muscular contraction for up to 15 seconds. When the phosphagen stores are reduced, ATP is generated via the lactate pathway and this system supports exercise for up to 180 seconds.

The ability to perform anaerobic work varies according to age and sex. Recent data from studies comparing adults with children suggest that during 'supra-maximal' exercise (i.e. power output at exercise intensity higher than that eliciting maximum oxygen consumption) anaerobic capability is lower in children than adults (Zanconato et al., 1993). Children in one study achieved an energy by-product (Pi/PCr) value of 27 per cent of that of adults although resting values of phosphagens are similar. Furthermore, recovery from anaerobic work is also faster in children compared to adults.

Figure 2.10 illustrates sex and age differences in maximal anaerobic power output relative to body weight. Between years 8 and 14 there is a near 50 per cent increase in power output in boys compared to a 20 per cent increase in girls. This difference becomes marked at 11 to 12 years of age. The maximal power output in girls attains a plateau at age 15 whereas that of boys reaches a plateau at 17 to 18 years of age.

The increase in absolute power output in passing from age 10 to 20 years of age is six-fold. When values are corrected for weight in the traditional manner (using a different technique to scale the data for body size produces different results), the rate of increase is just threefold. Adults have a clear and distinct advantage during the first 2–3 seconds of power output. Also, during 20 seconds of all-out exercise adult peak power relative to thigh muscle volume was 40 per cent greater than in children (Sargeant et al., 1984). Girls and boys at 12 years of age show similar time constants for power output to 6-year-olds although girls' values are

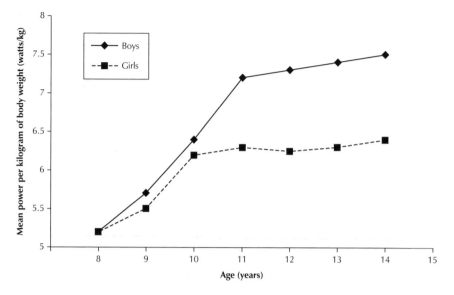

Figure 2.10 The development of anaerobic capacity relative to body weight in 8- to 14-year-old girls and boys

Source: Based on Malina and Bouchard, 1991.

only 75 per cent of those of boys. The absolute power output of 12-year-olds is approximately 3 times greater than that of 7-year-olds.

Differences in anaerobic power output are attributed to muscle size. An ability to express power is essential in youth soccer where sustained short sprints and jumps are commonplace. The ability of children to sprint or jump is significantly affected by growth and development. It also differs between girls and boys according to age.

AEROBIC FUNCTION, METABOLISM AND POWER OUTPUT

Physical activity lasting for several minutes or more is supported by the aerobic production of energy. Aerobic metabolism is also dependent upon a family of interdependent energy systems that work together to sustain muscle contraction. The cardiopulmonary system involving heart, lungs and blood as the central system and the muscle cell at the periphery all operate in concert to support aerobic exercise. A sound knowledge of these factors is important if the football coach is to understand the growth of aerobic fitness.

growth of the physiological systems

First, it is important to note that data representing the development of aerobic fitness can be expressed in a number of forms. The gold standard measure is the $\dot{V}O_{2max}$ test that is reported either relative to weight (note the previous caveat when scaling fitness measures) and time or as an absolute measure (capacity). Furthermore, there is some doubt that the physiological end-points for $\dot{V}O_{2max}$ are consistently attained in children. For this reason, peak $\dot{V}O_2$ ($\dot{V}O_{2peak}$) is used as an alternative expression to $\dot{V}O_{2max}$. In addition, tests for measuring $\dot{V}O_{2peak}$ can be carried out using different ergometers such as treadmills, cycles or rowing machines. Peak $\dot{V}O_2$ results are dependent on the type of ergometer used. Sub-maximal tests of aerobic fitness are also available. The most commonly used test is the PWC_{170} (physical work capacity at a heart rate of 170 beats per minute). This test, undertaken on a cycle ergometer or step bench, predicts work capacity in watts.

There are also various field tests commonly employed to measure endurance performance. These tests include time to exhaustion using a Bruce treadmill run test, time for distance (one mile run time), distance for time (six-minute run) or 20-metre-multistage shuttle run test.

Armstrong and Welsman (1994) documented the growth in aerobic power with age. Their data are similar to those found in other longitudinal studies (Figure 2.11).

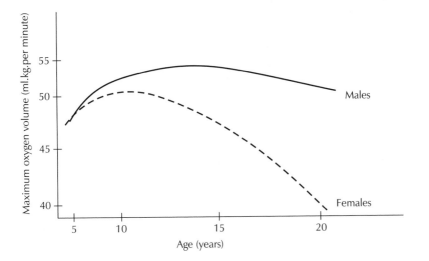

Figure 2.11 Schematic development of aerobic power from childhood to adulthood in females and males

Source: Based on Bar-Or, 1983.

The increase in $\dot{V}O_{2peak}$ closely follows the development of the cardiopulmonary system. Aerobic power in children increases by almost 50 per cent from 1.42 litres·min⁻¹ at age 8 to 2.12 litres·min⁻¹ at age 12. The $\dot{V}O_{2peak}$ in boys increases further to about 3.5 litres·min⁻¹ by age 17. After slightly trailing boys' values, $\dot{V}O_{2peak}$ results for girls during childhood reach a plateau of 2.2 litres·min⁻¹ at age 14–15 and then decrease slowly to early adulthood. When data are reported relative to weight, the $\dot{V}O_{2peak}$ of boys remains remarkably constant between 5 and 18 years of age at about 53 mlO₂ per kilogram per minute. The range is about 8 ml and trained young footballers would be expected to be nearer the top of this range at about 60 mlO₂ kg⁻¹min⁻¹. In a study on child players Bunc and Psotta (2001) reported an average $\dot{V}O_{2max}$ of 56.7 mlO₂ kg⁻¹min⁻¹ in 8–9-year-old boys. Reilly and colleagues (2000) reported a $\dot{V}O_{2max}$ of 59 and 55.5 mlO₂ kg⁻¹min⁻¹ in elite and sub-elite 16–18-year-old soccer players respectively. Furthermore, Baxter-Jones and Helms (1996) reported that elite young soccer players had higher $\dot{V}O_{2max}$ values at all stages of maturation when compared to the untrained population. This finding suggests that increases in $\dot{V}O_{2max}$ are dependent on body size and training stimulus. Females on the other hand experience a weight-related decrease in $\dot{V}O_{2peak}$ from 50 to 45 and 40 mlO₂ kg⁻¹min⁻¹ at 8, 12 and 18 years respectively. Longitudinal studies suggest that $\dot{V}O_{2peak}$ increases by about 200 ml per minute per year prior to puberty at which point it accelerates in males and levels off in females. Differences in body composition, dietary behaviour, levels of physical activity and sport participation may well contribute to sex differences in aerobic power and no data are available comparing elite soccer-playing boys and girls.

Recent methods for scaling $\dot{V}O_{2peak}$ have revealed functional increases between puberty and adulthood with the power exponent having greater influence after, compared to before, puberty. There are still many debates in the paediatric exercise science community about the most effective way to analyse and report physiological data such as aerobic power. One particular approach used to avoid the complexities of size-related scaling of data is the use of 'aerobic scope'. Aerobic scope is the ratio of maximal to resting oxygen uptake. Aerobic scope increases from 6.8 and 6.6 at 4–6 years of age to 13.5 and 12.6 at 16–18 years of age in boys and girls respectively (Rowland, 1996).

Peak $\dot{V}O_2$ velocity

From a growth perspective visual examination of velocity curves is also useful in determining phases when the rate of increase in aerobic power is at its highest. The Saskatchewan longitudinal growth study (see Table 2.2) reported percentile data for 8–16-year-old boys. The growth of $\dot{V}O_{2peak}$ slightly trailed the increases

Table 2.2 Peak $\dot{V}O_{2max}$ velocity between 8 and 16 years of age of boys on the 10th to 90th percentiles

Age (years)	10th percentile	Age (years)	50th percentile	Age (years)	90th percentile
8	−0.15	8	0.1	8	0.42
9	−0.12	9	0.18	9	0.5
10	−0.13	10	0.17	10	0.4
11	−0.05	11	0.19	11	0.45
12	−0.15	12	0.2	12	0.43
13	−0.2	13	0.19	13	0.4
14	0.25	14	0.6	14	1.0
15	−0.4	15	0.1	15	0.5
16	−0.5	16	0.05	16	0.3

Source: Cameron et al., 1980.

in height and was similar to changes in weight. There were slight increases in velocity in mid-childhood and late childhood followed by a rapid acceleration around the adolescent growth spurt, peaking at 14 years. There are no such data available for girls.

ENDURANCE PERFORMANCE: TIME AND DISTANCE

Field tests of fitness such as 1 mile (1.6 km) run times are commonly used to assess endurance performance. Times of children in a one-mile run have been consistently reported for North American children whereas the 20-metre-multistage shuttle run test holds favour in Europe.

From age 5 to 16 years one-mile run time almost halves in boys from 14 to 7 minutes. One-mile run times of girls follow a similar trend but are always better than boys to age 12–13 years. After 12–13 years one-mile run times of girls increase. The AAPHERD results for the nine-minute run indicate average distances for boys at 1160 yards (1070 m), 1690 (1560 m), and 1986 (1833 m) compared to girls' values of 1140 yards (1052 m), 1460 (1348 m) and 1653 (1526 m) for 5, 10 and 15-year-olds respectively.

The 20-metre-multistage shuttle run test

The 20-metre-multistage shuttle run test (20MST) has gained increased popularity as a field test of endurance performance in European studies (Kemper and van

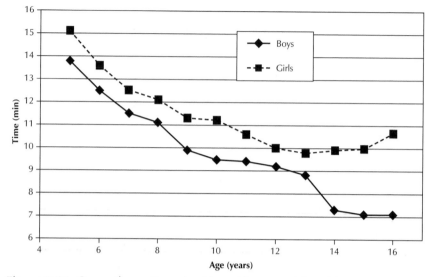

Figure 2.12 One-mile run times in girls and boys aged 5 to 16 years
Source: Based on Rowland, 1990.

Mechelen, 1996; Stratton, 1999). The following cross-sectional data were collected from 1299 9–14-year-old Liverpool school children:

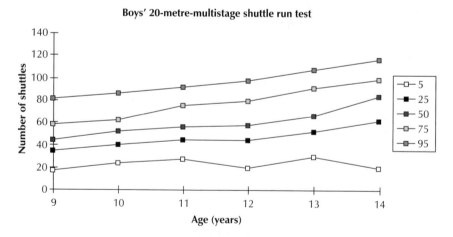

Figure 2.13 Descriptive data for 20-metre-multistage shuttle run, 5th to 95th performance percentiles of Liverpool boys
Source: Stratton, 1998.

growth of the physiological systems

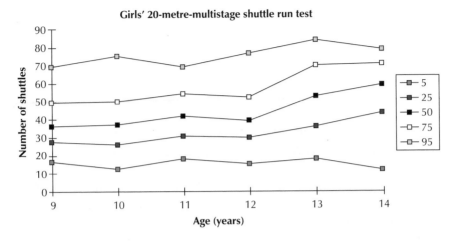

Figure 2.14 Descriptive data for 20-metre-multistage shuttle run, 5th to 95th performance percentiles of Liverpool girls

Source: Stratton, 1998.

The data from the shuttle run tests follow a similar growth pattern to other field tests of performance. The advantage of the Liverpool data is that they are split into 5–95 percentile lines. Elite young soccer players would be expected to record scores on the 75th percentile line or above depending on their stage of maturation. Data were also similar to those produced by Leger *et al.* (1984) on Canadian school children.

Relations between $\dot{V}O_2$ and performance

One of the key problems is interpreting endurance performance and aerobic power together. Endurance performance measured by the 20-metre-multistage shuttle test, time for distance, distance for time and treadmill run times improves with age. Correlation coefficients by single age or stage are mainly positive and significant between $\dot{V}O_{2peak}$ and endurance performance, values usually in the region of around 0.70–0.90. These correlation coefficients do not track with age, thereby making the influence of $\dot{V}O_{2peak}$ on endurance performance extremely difficult to interpret in the average youngster. However, the relationship between $\dot{V}O_{2peak}$ and endurance performance is generally stronger for trained youngsters such as soccer players. The biggest factor affecting the relationship between endurance performance and $\dot{V}O_{2peak}$ is body fat, which can account for half the variance in $\dot{V}O_{2peak}$. Factors such as running efficiency, anaerobic capacity and motivation also contribute to differences in endurance performance. Furthermore, the traditional method of analysing aerobic power may not be best related to endurance performance. New scaling techniques (Armstrong and Welsman, 1994) may result in $\dot{V}O_{2peak}$ that is more closely aligned to endurance performance across the ages.

THE DEVELOPMENT OF SELECTED MOTOR BEHAVIOUR CHARACTERISTICS FROM CHILDHOOD TO ADULTHOOD

Recently grass roots sport has taken note of the limited development of motor skills in children. Whilst a range of skills in ballistic actions, whole-body stability and locomotion exist, this section will focus on the development of movement patterns specific to soccer (for a wider view of fundamental motor skills, see Haywood and Getchell, 2001). Motor skill patterns can be observed from behind, at the side and in front of the performer. Ballistic skills include throwing and kicking. The aim in kicking is to project an object using the foot as opposed to the hand(s). Unskilled kickers tend to use a single rather than a sequence of actions. Single actions do not rotate the trunk and the kicking leg simply pushes forward towards the ball; straightening of the leg rarely occurs after contact. Proficient kicking starts by rotating the trunk back, setting the arms in opposition, and cocking the kicking leg during the run-up to the ball. The combination of the run-up and rotation of the hip prepares for maximum acceleration of the foot towards the ball. If maximal acceleration is achieved and the foot is appropriately shaped and tensed at contact, then maximal force will be applied. The studies that have followed the development of kicking are fewer than those for throwing. In one study, results revealed that one in ten, 8- to 9-year-old North American children demonstrated advanced kicking form. Haywood (2001) speculated that children do not automatically achieve advanced kicking form (see Lees and Nolan, 1998 for a review). Results may be culture specific, as children in North American countries may not have the same soccer participation demographics as other more traditional soccer playing nations. Amongst youngsters from countries where proficiency in kicking may be evident, higher proportions of the age group population are likely to watch the skill of kicking repeatedly through the media as well as in their soccer playing communities.

Unlike some other aspects of child development, there are no longitudinal data available on kicking proficiency. From a coaching perspective, much information can be gleaned by observing individual youngsters' kicking form from various angles. This is especially important when coaching younger children, as

34

accurate feedback at this stage is crucial for improved kicking performance (see Chapter 8).

THE INTERACTION BETWEEN CHRONOLOGICAL AGE, MATURATION AGE AND PERFORMANCE

When a group of 14-year-old male footballers' *biological* ages range from 11–19 years it becomes clear that birth date per se can be detrimental to the early or late maturing player. In a study involving 226 children, Jones *et al.* (2000) revealed how easy it would be to misclassify a player based on his/her age. Furthermore, Richardson and Stratton (1999) have demonstrated that the majority of international and professional footballers were born in the first quarter of their academic year. This bias was mainly found in defenders and goalkeepers. However, only limited information is available on young and elite sports participants by chronological age and stage of maturation. Some investigators have attempted to develop practical solutions to address the problem of playing immature and mature sports people of the same chronological age together. Solutions to these problems are starting to emerge. Anderson and Ward (2002) have suggested that calculating impulse from weight and vertical jump distance can provide a suitable alternative to age-related groupings, particularly when body size and power have a significant bearing on performance. Mirwald and colleagues (2002) were also able to predict maturation age accurately (± 1 year of maturity offset) from a limited number of anthropometric and familial measures. (For a review see Malina and Bouchard, 1991, chapter 18.)

These calculations have provided the football coach with important data when analysing growth development and physical performance in young soccer players. An understanding of important aspects of growth, development and maturation is particularly important as a youngster's soccer performance may depend heavily on gender and biological age and stage. There are few longitudinal data on elite young soccer players of various ages and stages of growth and development. There are some data available from other sports. Data on young swimmers suggest that the differences in adiposity and anaerobic performance between girls and boys are smaller in elite sports children (Taylor, 2003). Cross-sectional data also suggest that elite young soccer players are significantly fitter than their average peers, although this may be due to elite soccer players being more mature. What is very important for the coach is the consideration of the growth of fitness with age and maturation. The increase in quality and quantity of fitness should be evaluated alongside key football skills during the identification and nurturing of talent. For example, a young football academy player, in early puberty but at age 12, may be as technically able as a peer; nevertheless, this player may lack the aerobic power to implement his/her technique to the same degree as an equally skilful but maturer player. Data in this chapter have shown that children who are more advanced in maturation can demonstrate significantly higher amounts of power output than those who are less mature (Jones *et al.*, 2000). Care should therefore be taken in developing soccer skills and identifying talented players alongside changes in maximal power output and associated components of fitness.

OVERVIEW

Growth, development and maturation all have implications for the identification of talent from a young age. Simple and gross measures from a number of countries used to measure fitness barely explain the multiple factors that affect soccer performance. Furthermore, given the global popularity of soccer, it is surprising that there is limited growth-related data in the extant literature. This gap in the literature is particularly evident in girls. If a clear understanding of the growth and development of young male and female soccer players is attained, more effective teaching and coaching structures will almost certainly emerge.

REFERENCES

Al-Hazzaa, H.M., Almuzaini, K.S., Al-Refaee, S.A., Sulaiman, M.A., Dafterdar, M.Y., Al-Ghamedi, A. and Al-Khuraiji, K.N. (2000) Anaerobic performance of adolescents vs adults: effect of age and soccer training. *Medicine and Science in Sports and Exercise*, 32, S1367.

Anderson, G.S. and Ward, R. (2002) Classifying children for sports participation based on anthropometric measurement. *European Journal of Sports Sciences*, 2 (3).

Armstrong, N. and Welsman, J. (1994) Assessment and interpretation of aerobic fitness in children and adolescents. *Exercise and Sports Sciences Reviews*, 22, 435–476.

Bar-Or, O. (1983) *Pediatric Sports Medicine for the Practitioner*. New York: Springer-Verlag.

Baxter-Jones, A. and Helms, P.J. (1996) Effects of training at a young age: a review of the training of young athletes (TOYA) study. *Pediatric Exercise Science*, 8, 310–327.

Berg, K.E., LaVoie, J.C. and Latin, R.W. (1985) Physiological effects of playing youth soccer. *Medicine and Science in Sports and Exercise*, 17, 656–660.

Blimkie, C.J.R (1989) Age- and sex-associated variation in strength during childhood: anthropometric, morphological, neurologic, biomechanical, endocrinologic, genetic and physical activity correlates. In C.V. Gisolfi and D.R. Lamb (eds) *Perspectives in Exercise Science and Sports Medicine. Vol. 2, Youth Exercise and Sport*. Indianapolis: Benchmark Press, 99–164.

Blimkie, C.J.R., Ramsay, D., Sale, D., MacDougall, K., Smith, K. and Garner, S. (1989) Effects of 10 weeks of resistance training on strength development in pubertal boys. In S. Oseid and K. Carlsen (eds) *Children and Exercise XIII*. Champaign, IL: Human Kinetics, 183–197.

Bunc, V. and Psotta, R. (2001) Physiological profile of very young soccer players. *Journal of Sports Medicine and Physical Fitness*, 41, 337–341.

Cameron, N., Mirwald, R.L. and Bailey, D.A. (1980) Standards for the assessment of normal absolute aerobic power. In M. Ostyn, G. Beunen and J. Simons (eds) *Kinanthropometry II*, Baltimore: University Park Press.

Hansen, L., Klausen, K., Bangsbo, J. and Muller, J. (1999) Short longitudinal study of boys playing soccer. Parental height, birth weight and length, anthropometry, and pubertal maturation in elite and non-elite players. *Pediatric Exercise Science*, 11, 199–207.

Haubenstricker, J. and Seefeldt, V. (1986) Acquisition of motor skills during childhood. In V. Seefeldt (ed.) *Physical Activity and Well-being*, Reston, Va.: American Alliance for Health, Physical Education, Recreation and Dance, 41–102.

Haywood, K.M. (2001) *Learning Activities for Life Span Motor Development* (3rd edn). Champaign, IL: Human Kinetics.

Haywood, K.M. and Getchell, N. (2001) *Life Span Motor Development*. Champaign, IL: Human Kinetics.

Janssens, M., Van Renterghem, B. and Vrijens, J. (2002) Anthropometric characteristics of 11–12 year old Flemish soccer players. In W. Spinks, T. Reilly and A. Murphy (eds) *Science and Football IV*. London: Routledge, 258–262.

Jones, M.A., Hitchen, P.J. and Stratton, G. (2000) The importance of considering biological maturity when assessing physical fitness measures in girls and boys aged 10 to 16 years. *Annals of Human Biology*, 27, 57–66.

Kemper, H.C.G. and van Mechelen, W. (1996) Physical fitness testing of children: a European perspective. *Pediatric Exercise Science*, 8, 201–214.

Kids Health Website. *http://kidshealth.org/parent/growth/growth/Charts/BOYS2_20years1.pdf* accessed 1/9/03.

Lees, A. and Nolan, L. (1998) Biomechanics of soccer – a review. *Journal of Sports Sciences*, 16, 211–234.

Leger, L., Lambert, J., Goulet, A., Rowan, C. and Dinelle, Y. (1984) Capacité Áerobie des Québecois de 6 à 17 ans – Test navette de 20 metres avec paliers de 1 minute. *Canadian Journal of Applied Sports Science*, 9, 64–69.

Malina, R.M. (1994) Physical activity and training: effects on height and the adolescent growth spurt. *Medicine and Science in Sports and Exercise*, 26, 759–766.

Malina, R.M. (2003) Growth and maturity status of young soccer players. In T. Reilly and A.M. Williams (eds) *Science and Soccer* (2nd edn). London: Routledge, 287–306.

Malina, R.M. and Bouchard, C. (1991) *Growth, Maturation and Physical Activity*. Champaign, IL: Human Kinetics.

Mero, A., Vuorimaa, T. and Hakkinen, K. (eds) (1990) *Training in Children and Adolescents*. Jyvaskyla, Finland: Gummerus Kirjapaino, Oy.

Mirwald, R.L., Baxter-Jones, A.D.G., Bailey, D.A. and Beunen, G.P. (2002) An assessment of maturity from anthropometric measurements. *Medicine and Science in Sports and Exercise*, 39, 689–694.

Panfil, R., Naglak, Z., Bober, T. and Zaton, E.W.M (1997) Searching and developing talents in soccer; a year of experience. In *The 9th European Congress on Sports Medicine Program*. Conference Proceedings. Porto, Portugal.

Peyna Reyes, M.E., Cardas-Barahona, E. and Malina, R.M. (1994) Growth, physique and skeletal maturation of soccer players 7–17 years of age. *Humanbiologa Budapestinensis*, 5, 453–458.

Reilly, T., Bangsbo, J. and Franks, A. (2000) Anthropometric and physiological predispositions for elite soccer. *Journal of Sports Sciences*, 18, 669–683.

Richardson, D.J. and Stratton, G. (1999) Preliminary investigation into the seasonal birth distribution of England World Cup campaign players (1982–1998). 4th World Congress on Science in Football. Sydney, Australia.

Roche, A.F., Chumlea, W.C. and Thissen, D. (1988) Assessing skeletal maturity of the hand wrist: Fels method. Springfield, IL: Charles C. Thomas.

Rowland, T.W. (1990) *Exercise and Children's Health*. Champaign, IL: Human Kinetics.

Rowland, T.M. (1996) *Developmental Exercise Physiology*. Champaign, IL: Human Kinetics.

Sargeant, A.J., Dolan, P. and Thorne, A. (1984) Isokinetic measurement of maximal leg force and anaerobic power output in children. In J. Ilmarinen and I. Valimaki (eds) *Children and Sport*. Berlin: Springer-Verlag, 93–98.

Scammon, R.E. (1930) The measurement of the body in childhood. In J.A. Harris, C.M. Jackson, D.G. Paterson, R.E. Scammon (eds) *The Measurement of Man*. Minneapolis: University of Minnesota Press.

Stratton, G. (1996) Children's heart rates during physical education lessons: a review. *Pediatric Exercise Science*, 8, 215–233.

Stratton, G. (1998) *The Fitness of Liverpool Schoolchildren*: Sportslink Project, unpublished report. Liverpool John Moores University.

Stratton, G. (1999) *Sportslinx Report*. Liverpool John Moores University.

Tanner, J.M. (1984) *Foetus into Man: Physical Growth from Conception to Maturity* (2nd edn). Ware, Herts, UK: Castlemead Publications.

Tanner, J.M., Hughes, P.C.R. and Whitehouse, R.H. (1981) Radiographically determined widths of bone, muscle and fat in the upper arm and calf from age 3–18 years. *Annals of Human Biology*, 8, 495–517.

Taylor, S.R. (2003) An analysis of anaerobic performance in competitive age group swimmers. Unpublished PhD Thesis. Liverpool John Moores University.

Van Praagh, E. (2000) Development of anaerobic function during childhood and adolescence. *Pediatric Exercise Science*, 12, 150–173.

Wild, M. and Stratton, G. (1992) A multivariate analysis of throwing performance in 12–13 year old girls and boys. *Journal of Sports Sciences*, 13, 246–247.

Zanconato, S., Buchthal, S., Barstow, T.J. and Cooper, D.M. (1993). ^{31}P-magnetic resonance spectroscopy of leg muscle metabolism during exercise in children and adults. *Journal of Applied Physiology*, 74, 2214–2218.

CHAPTER THREE

ENVIRONMENTAL FACTORS IN SOCCER

INTRODUCTION

The environment in which children or youths play soccer may represent a source of stress for them. Environmental factors may cause acute biological responses to facilitate an immediate adaptation and allow the youngster to cope. An adjustment in the performance level may be needed for this coping mechanism to take effect. The youngster may also benefit from repeated exposures by means of physiological adaptations that are known as acclimatisation. Even without these adjustments, learning to cope with unusual environmental stress means that behaviour may be modified in order to tolerate the stress experienced.

The environmental stresses that are considered in this chapter are heat and cold, altitude, air pollution and travel across multiple time-zones. Whilst the majority of studies have been conducted on adults, these nevertheless have implications for the young. Specific concerns for young players are addressed where appropriate. In order to provide a background for heat stress and cold stress, the physiology of thermoregulation is examined first. Later the physiological adjustments to moderate altitude are explained, as far as they might concern young players. Finally, circadian rhythms are covered in order to understand the syndrome known as jet-lag that is associated with long-haul flights.

REGULATION OF BODY TEMPERATURE

The temperature of the human body is regulated about a set point of 37°C. This value refers to temperature within the body's core and is measured usually as rectal temperature, tympanic or oesophageal temperature. Oral temperature tends to be a little lower than these and is less reliable but the temperature within the gut can be reported as a viable alternative to rectal temperature during sport.

For thermoregulatory purposes the body can be considered as consisting of a core and a shell. There is a gradient of about 4°C from core to shell and so mean skin temperature is usually about 33°C. The temperature of the shell is more variable than the core and responsive to changes in environmental temperatures. The usual temperature gradient from skin to the air facilitates loss of heat to the environment.

The human body exchanges heat with the environment in various ways to achieve an equilibrium. The heat balance equation is expressed as:

$$M - S = E \pm C \pm R \pm K$$

where M is metabolic rate, S is heat storage, E is evaporation, C is convection, R is radiation, and K is conduction. Thermal equilibrium is attained by reaching a balance between heat loss and heat gain mechanisms. Heat is produced by metabolic processes, basal metabolic rate being about 1 kcal kg^{-1} h^{-1}. One kilocalorie (4.186 kJ) is the energy required to raise the temperature of 1 kilogram of water through 1°C. Energy expenditure during youth soccer might increase this by a factor of 15, with maybe only 20–25 per cent of the energy expended reflected in power output. (Children are different to adults here: less mechanically efficient, greater oxygen consumption per stride, etc. and therefore lower efficiency.) The rest is dissipated as heat within the active tissues and as a result heat storage in the body increases. In order to avoid overheating, the body is equipped with mechanisms for losing heat. It also has built-in responses to safeguard the thermal state of the body in circumstances where heat might be lost too rapidly to the environment, for example in very cold conditions.

The body temperature is controlled by specialised nerve cells in the hypothalamus deep within the brain. Neurones in the anterior hypothalamus respond to a rise in body temperature whilst a fall is registered by cells in the posterior portion of the hypothalamus. The neurones in the anterior part constitute the heat loss centre since they trigger initiation of heat loss responses. Heat loss processes are affected by a redistribution of blood to the skin where it can be cooled, and stimulation of the sweat glands to secrete a solution on to the skin surface where evaporative cooling can take place. This process is less mature in young people.

Nerve cells within the hypothalamus are sensitive to the temperature of blood that bathes them, thereby controlling thermoregulatory responses. The cells also receive signals from heat and cold receptors located in the skin. In these ways, the heat loss and heat gain centres receive information about both the body's internal thermal state and environmental conditions.

EXERCISE IN A HIGHER TEMPERATURE ENVIRONMENT

When exercise is performed, the temperature within the active muscles is elevated and is soon followed by a rise in core temperature. Exercise carried out in hot conditions causes skin temperature to rise. The hypothalamic response is represented by a diversion of cardiac output to the skin: the body surface can lose heat to the environment (by convection and radiation) due to the warm blood now being shunted through its subcutaneous layers. In strenuous exercise, such as intense competitive soccer, the cardiac output may be maximal or near it and this increased cutaneous blood flow may compromise blood supply to the active muscles. In such instances the soccer player will have to lower the exercise intensity, perhaps by taking longer recovery periods than normal or by less running 'off-the-ball'.

The distribution of blood to the skin is achieved by dilation of the peripheral blood vessels. There is a limit to the extent of vasodilatation that occurs in the regulation of body temperature. This limit is caused by increased vasodilatation which reduces peripheral resistance and so causes a fall in blood pressure. The kidney hormone, renin, stimulates angiotensin which is a powerful vasoconstrictor and this response corrects a drop in blood pressure.

As core temperature rises, the sweat glands are stimulated and loss of heat by evaporation of sweat becomes the major avenue by which heat is lost to the environment during intense exercise. Sweating rate is lower in children than in adults. The glands respond to stimulation by noradrenaline and secrete a dilute solution containing electrolytes and trace elements. Heat is lost only when the fluid is vaporised on the surface of the body, no heat being exchanged if sweat simply drops off or is wiped away. When heat is combined with high humidity, the possibility of losing heat by evaporation is reduced since the air is already highly saturated with water vapour. Consequently, hot humid conditions are detrimental to performance and increase the risk of heat injury.

The exchange of heat with the environment is a function of the body surface area relative to mass. The dimensional exponent for this relation is 0.67. The smaller the individual, the easier it is to exchange heat with the environment. Therefore, children gain and lose heat more quickly than adults, and children are more vulnerable than grown ups in hot conditions. This principle applies to both boys and girls.

A consequence of sweating to avoid overheating is that fluid is lost from body water stores. Therefore hypohydration may compound the effects of rising core temperatures in soccer players. The increase in core temperature at any level of hypohydration is greater in children than in adults (Bar-Or and Unnithan, 1994).

42

Children can maintain normal hydration status during intermittent exercise resembling soccer when made to drink every 15 minutes. An acceptable palatability is likely to affect the amount taken in and so individuals' preferences are important in promoting drinking. Sports drinks that are hypotonic are likely to suit young players, since children's sweat has a lower sodium and chloride content than that of adults (Meyer et al., 1992).

As the player continues to sweat and body water stores decline, the body water present in the cells, in the interstices and in plasma seems to fall in roughly equal proportion. The reduction in plasma volume compromises the supply of blood available to the active muscles and to the skin for cooling. The kidneys and endocrine glands attempt to conserve body water and electrolytes, but the needs of thermoregulation override these mechanisms and the athlete may become dangerously dehydrated through continued sweating. The main hormones involved in attempting to protect against dehydration are vasopressin, produced by the pituitary gland, and aldosterone secreted by the adrenal cortex which stimulates the kidneys to conserve sodium.

Heat injury

Hyperthermia (overheating) and loss of body water (hypohydration) lead to abnormalities that are referred to as heat injury. Progressively they may be manifest as muscle cramps, heat exhaustion and heat stroke. They can occur in soccer matches or training sessions in the heat. A summary of heat-related disorders is provided in Table 3.1.

Muscle cramps are associated with loss of body fluid, particularly in games players competing in intense heat. The body loses electrolytes in sweat, but such losses cannot adequately account for the occurrence of cramps. These seem to coincide with low energy stores as well as reduced body water levels. Schwellnus et al. (1997) provided evidence that abnormal spinal reflex activity, secondary to local muscle fatigue, supplied the best explanation of muscle cramps occurring during exercise. Generally the muscles employed in the exercise are affected, but most vulnerable are the leg (upper or lower) and abdominal muscles. The cramp can usually be stopped by stretching the involved muscle which invokes the reverse stretch reflexes, and sometimes massage is effective.

A core temperature of about 40°C is characteristic of heat exhaustion. Associated with this state is a feeling of extreme tiredness, dizziness, breathlessness and tachycardia (increased heart rate). The symptoms may coincide with a reduced sweat loss but usually arise because the skin blood vessels are so dilated that blood flow to vital organs is reduced.

Table 3.1   Heat disorders

1   Heat cramps
    Muscle spasms
    (usually in the unacclimatised)

2   Heat syncope:
    General weakness and fatigue; brief loss of consciousness

3   Heat exhaustion:
    Dizzy, tired, breathless; reduced sweat loss
    Reduced blood flow to vital organs
    Loss of coordination
    Rise in heart rate, vasodilatation

4   Heat stroke:
    Confused and irrational
    Skin and core temperature high; dry skin
    Pale blue colour
    May hallucinate
    May stop sweating
    Medical emergency

Source: Reilly, 2000.

Heat stroke is a true emergency, especially in children. It is characterised by core temperatures of 41°C or higher. Hypohydration – due to loss of body water in sweat and associated with a high core temperature – can be driven so far as to threaten life. Heat stroke is characterised by cessation of sweating, total confusion or loss of consciousness. In such cases treatment is urgently needed to reduce body temperature. There may also be circulatory instability and loss of vasomotor tone as the regulation of blood pressure begins to fail.

Heat acclimatisation

The body adapts to repeated exposures to hot environments and to living in warm climates. The adaptations to cope with the natural climate are referred to as acclimatisation. Acclimation refers to physiological changes occurring in response to experimentally induced changes in one particular climatic factor, such as an exposure to laboratory-based environmental chambers.

Youth teams may experience unaccustomed hot conditions when playing overseas in international or friendly tournaments. They may also have opportunities for warm-weather training, when the climate at home is not conducive to training hard outdoors. Besides the physiological adjustments that are acquired when playing in hot conditions, young players also gain experience in how to pace themselves appropriately for the heat.

The main features of heat acclimatisation are an earlier onset of sweating (sweating produced at a lower rise in body temperature) and a more dilute solution from the sweat glands. The heat-acclimatised individual sweats more than an unacclimatised counterpart at a given exercise intensity. There is also a better distribution of blood to the skin for more effective cooling after a period of acclimatisation, although the acclimatised player depends more on evaporative sweat loss than on distribution of blood flow (see Figure 3.1).

Heat acclimatisation occurs relatively quickly and a good degree of adaptation takes place within 10–14 days of the initial exposure. Further adaptations will enhance the player's capability to perform in heat stress conditions. Ideally, therefore, the team should be exposed to the climate of the host country for at least ten days before the event. An alternative strategy is to have an acclimatisation period of two weeks or so well before the event with subsequent shorter exposures nearer the contest. If these are not practicable in young players, attempts should be made at some degree of heat acclimatisation before the athletes leave for the host country. This may be achieved by means of pre-acclimatisation for which the following activities are suggested.

1   Physiological adaptations occur on exposure to hot and humid environments, the players seeking out the hottest time of day to train at home.
2   If the conditions at home are too cool, players may seek access to an environmental chamber individually for periodic bouts of heat exposure. It

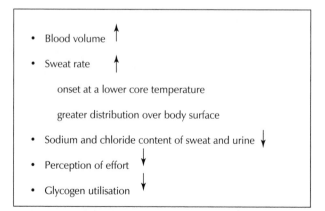

Figure 3.1 Main effects of heat acclimatisation

is important that players exercise rather than rest under such conditions. Repeated exposure to a sauna or Turkish bath is only partially effective. About 3 hours per week exercising in an environmental chamber should provide a good degree of acclimatisation.

3   The microclimate next to the skin may be kept hot by wearing heavy sweat suits or windbreakers. This will add to the heat load imposed under cool environmental conditions and induce a degree of adaptation to thermal strain.

On first exposure to a hot climate players should be encouraged to drink copiously to maintain a pale straw-coloured rather than dark urine. They should drink much more fluid than they think they need since thirst is often a very poor indicator of real need. When they arrive in the hot country the players should be discouraged strongly from sunbathing as this itself does not help acclimatisation except by the development of a suntan which will eventually protect the skin from damage via solar radiation. This is a long-term process and is not beneficial in the short term, but negative effects of sunburn can cause severe discomfort and a decline in performance. Players should therefore be protected with an adequate sunscreen if they are likely to be exposed to sunburn.

Training should initially be undertaken in the cooler parts of the day so that an adequate exercise intensity can be achieved and adequate fluid must be taken regularly. Arrangements should be made to sleep in an air-conditioned environment but to achieve adequate acclimatisation, some part of the day should be spent exposed to the ambient temperature other than in air-conditioned rooms.

COMPETING IN A COLDER ENVIRONMENT

Soccer in many countries is often played in near-freezing conditions. Core temperature and muscle temperature may fall and exercise performance will be increasingly affected. A fall in core temperature to hypothermic levels is life-threatening and the body's heat gain mechanisms are designed to arrest the decline.

The physiological responses to cold initiated by the posterior hypothalamus include a generalised vasoconstriction of the cutaneous circulation. This mechanism is mediated by the sympathetic nervous system. Blood is displaced centrally away from the peripheral circulation and this redistribution causes the temperature gradient between core and shell to increase. The fall in skin temperature in turn decreases the gradient between the skin and the environment which protects against a large loss of heat from the body. Blood returning from the limbs via superficial veins is diverted from them to the venae comitantes that lie adjacent to the main arteries. In this way the arterial blood is cooled by the venous return almost immediately it enters the limb by means of counter-current heat exchange.

The fall in limb temperature leads to a deterioration in performance. In addition to a drop in muscular strength and power output as the temperature in the muscles falls, conduction velocity of nerve impulses to the muscles is impaired. The sensitivity of muscle spindles is also impaired and there is a loss of manual dexterity. For these reasons it is important to preserve limb temperatures in soccer players during competition. The goalkeeper in particular must maintain manual dexterity for handling the ball and so choice of clothing including gloves is important.

Shivering is a response of the body's automatic nervous system to the fall in core temperature. It constitutes involuntary activity of skeletal muscles in order to generate metabolic heat. Shivering tends to be intermittent and may persist during exercise if the intensity is insufficient to maintain core temperature. It may be evident during stoppages in play, especially when cold conditions are compounded by sleet.

Warning symptoms of hypothermia include shivering, fatigue, loss of strength and coordination and an inability to sustain work-rate. Once fatigue develops, shivering may decrease and the condition worsens. Later symptoms include collapse, stupor and loss of consciousness. This risk applies to young recreational players who might not be able to sustain a work-rate to keep themselves warm in extreme cold. In such an event the referee would be expected to abandon play before conditions became critical.

Cold is less of a problem than heat in that the body can be protected against exposure to the ambient environmental conditions. The important factor is the microclimate next to the skin and this may be maintained by appropriate choice of clothing. Players may respond to cold conditions by maintaining a high work-rate. Alternatively, they may be spared exposure to the cold by conducting training sessions in indoor facilities where these are available.

Natural fibre (cotton or wool) is preferable to synthetic material in clothing for cold and cold-wet conditions. The clothing should allow sweat produced during exercise in these conditions to flow through the garment. The best material will allow sweat to flow out through the cells of the garment whilst preventing water droplets from penetrating the clothing from the outside. Once the fabric becomes saturated with water or sweat, it loses its insulation and in cold-wet conditions the body temperature may quickly drop.

The trunk area of the body should be well insulated when training in the cold. Warm undergarments beneath a full tracksuit may be needed. Dressing in layers is well advised: the outer layers can be discarded as body temperature rises and if ambient temperature gets warmer.

When layers of clothing are worn the outer layer should be capable of resisting both wind and rain. The inner layer should provide insulation and should also wick moisture from the skin to promote heat loss by evaporation. Polypropylene and cotton fishnet thermal underwear have good insulation and wicking properties and so are suitable to wear next to the skin.

Prior to competing in the cold, young players should stay as warm as possible. A thorough warm-up regime (performed indoors if possible) is recommended. It is thought that cold conditions increase the risk of muscle injury in sports involving intense anaerobic efforts; warm-up exercises may afford some protection in this respect. Competitors may need to wear more clothing than they normally do during matches and give priority to safety over considerations of fashion.

Aerobic fitness is not in itself a protection against cold, although it will enable games players to keep more active when not directly involved in play. Outfield players with a high level of aerobic fitness will also be able to maintain activity at a satisfactory level to achieve heat balance. On the other hand the individual with poor endurance may be at risk of hypothermia if the pace of activity falls dramatically. So too may the unskilful player who stays on the margin of the activity. Shivering during exercise signals the onset of real danger.

ALTITUDE

Young players unaccustomed to altitude will experience discomfort if competing or training there. The problem is presented by hypoxia caused by the fall in ambient pressure of the air. Whilst the proportion of oxygen in the air is similar to that at sea level, the reduced partial pressure means the air is less dense than normal. Less oxygen is inspired for a given volume of inspired air, leading to a decrease in the amount of oxygen delivered to the active tissues.

The body compensates for the reduction in alveolar oxygen tension by an increase in ventilation. This increase is achieved by a greater frequency of breathing and an increased tidal volume. The elevation in minute ventilation (volume of air breathed per minute) during exercise leads to elimination of CO_2 in the breath, leaving the blood more alkaline. This change is known as respiratory alkalosis.

The main problem for the oxygen transport system is the reduction in the O_2 carried in the red blood cells bound to haemoglobin. Normally the red blood cells are 97 per cent saturated with O_2 but this figure drops when PO_2 levels decline at a point corresponding to this altitude (1200 m). The O_2–Hb curve is little affected for the first 1000–1500 m of altitude because of the flatness at its top. As the pressure drops further to reach the steep part of the curve, the supply of oxygen to the body's tissues is increasingly impaired.

At an altitude of 2.2 km the average decline in $\dot{V}O_{2max}$ is 15 per cent, although this figure varies among individuals. Some may experience desaturation at a lower altitude and will have more difficulty in sustaining their normal level of performance for a full game. Corresponding to the decline in aerobic power there is a greater reliance on anaerobic metabolism. Blood lactate is higher for a given exercise intensity than it is at sea level, the elevation in lactate depending on the decrease in $\dot{V}O_{2max}$.

The thinner air at altitude means that all-out sprint performance can be improved due to the decreased air resistance. Although sprinting is easier at altitude, the recovery between bouts of intense activity is more difficult, being reliant on oxygen transport. There is therefore a need to pace efforts appropriately when playing or competing at altitude.

For young soccer players going to experience training at altitude under camp conditions, it is important to avoid hard training for a few days. The tempo of play can also be adjusted so that players do not get into breathing difficulties. Players suffering from asthma may be particularly vulnerable, and should therefore be careful with their medication.

The short-term adjustments which help the body adapt to altitude can have transient adverse side-effects. The most common problem is referred to as acute mountain sickness. This condition is characterised by headaches, nausea, vomiting, loss of appetite, sleep disturbance and irritability; these problems can be encountered at altitudes above 2000–2500 m. The syndrome develops progressively, reaching a peak within about 48 hours of initial exposure, and then disappears with adaptation. The problems are related to changes in the pH of the cerebrospinal fluid consequent to respiratory alkalosis and also increases in cerebral blood flow stimulated by hypoxia. Onset of acute mountain sickness may be sudden when ascent is rapid and exercise may increase the likelihood of its development.

Individuals with low body stores of iron may have trouble at altitude once red blood cell production is stimulated by erythropoietin. This problem can be accentuated if appetite is affected by acute mountain sickness. Careful attention to diet is needed when going to altitude and during the immediate period of adaptation. Young female soccer players who experience large losses of blood in menstruation may be vulnerable and a check of their serum ferritin concentration prior to departure is advised.

Adequate hydration is also a concern. The air at altitude tends to be drier than at sea level. More body fluid is lost by means of evaporation from the moist mucous membrane of the respiratory tract. This loss is accentuated by the hyperventilatory response to hypoxia. The nose and throat get dry and irritable which can cause discomfort. It is important to drink more than normal to counteract the fluid loss.

One advantage of a sojourn at altitude for young players is the learning experience it provides for them. Apart from the physiological adjustments, they learn about the necessity to utilise rhythmic aspects of the game, especially the processes of recovery during it. Ball flight characteristics are altered at altitude, and players acquire an understanding of how to deal with playing in the altitude environment.

Where young players are concerned, exposure to altitude is encountered in the course of their competitive schedule or employed as an opportunity for training. There are physiological adjustments to altitude associated with prolonged stays there, reflecting the body's ability to acclimatise to hypoxia. The adaptations are mainly in the oxygen transport system, especially the improved oxygen carrying capacity of the blood, although some adaptations occur in the muscles later. Nevertheless, acclimatisation is at best partial so that the physiological capabilities of sea-level dwellers are not fully restored at altitude. The adaptations that are realised have been exploited by athletes using altitude training camps for improving performance at sea-level. This strategy has little place in the preparation of young soccer players, where emphasis should be placed on their holistic development.

AIR POLLUTION

The quality of the air breathed in has relevance for both the health and performance of young soccer players. The purity of air is affected by pollutants; the major sources are either primary or secondary, depending on whether they retain the form in which they were emitted from source when their effects are manifested, or if they are formed through chemical reaction between source and target. Sulphur dioxide (SO_2), carbon monoxide (CO), nitrogen dioxide (NO_2), benzene and particulate matter like dust and smoke constitute primary pollutants. The secondary pollutants ozone (O_3) and peroxyacetyl nitrate are formed by means of ultraviolet radiation affecting the primary pollutants NO_2 and hydrocarbons. Ozone is formed by a reaction cycle involving nitrogen monoxide (NO), NO_2, O_2, hydrocarbons and energy from ultraviolet radiation. Photo-chemical smog refers to the pollutant mixture generated in this process and typified by the pollution of the Los Angeles Basin. Acid fog refers to the formation of sulphuric acid in dilute solution when SO_2 is present along with a high moisture content in the air.

Sulphur dioxide and ozone are both airway irritants with potential harmful effects on the epithelial cells lining the airways and alveoli. The effects depend on the dose delivered and the ventilation rate. They are reflected in increases in inflammatory neutrophils in the broncho-alveolar fluid and a decrease in lung function. Both pollutants are rarely at high levels simultaneously since O_3 is formed from the reactive cycles that incorporate SO_2 produced as a result of burning impure carbon fuels.

The World Health Organisation has established standards for health-based air quality for pollutants such as ozone and their concentrations are regularly monitored in the major cities worldwide. Where standards have not been provided, for example for PM–10s, separate national standards have been provided. The standard in the United Kingdom for PM–10s is 50 μg.m^3, measured as a 24-hour running average. Particulates less than 10 μm in diameter are referred to by the abbreviation PM–10 and the raised levels are evident at busy roadsides. A main adverse effect of these particulates is an exacerbation of asthmatic symptoms, attributable to oxidative stress-mediated inflammation (MacNee and Donaldson, 1999).

During exercise intensities commensurate with soccer, players tend to breathe through the mouth, as compared to ventilation at rest which is predominantly through the nose. The result is that the filtering of impurities by means of the nasal passages is bypassed during exercise. Therefore a greater dosage is delivered to the lungs at the higher exercise intensities and adverse reactions, not evoked at rest, become evident during match-play.

Ragweed and grass pollen act as antigens which stimulate the production of antibodies after penetrating the mucous epithelium of the respiratory tract. Some individuals are allergic to antigens, the antibody classically associated with allergy being immunoglobulin E. Allergic reactions of the airways begin in the nose where allergens such as pollen are first filtered out. The resultant inflammatory reaction blocks the nose, promoting oral breathing and giving allergens direct access to the lower respiratory tract. Here the same inflammatory response gives rise to asthma instead (Harries, 1998).

Young soccer players should be extra careful when playing in pitches close to sources of air pollution such as roadside traffic, local smoke stacks and industrial processes utilising polluting forms of energy. Special precautions should be taken in foggy conditions when it is advisable to abandon training. Referees usually do not allow matches to proceed in fog, for reasons of visibility as well as health.

Young players liable to asthma need to be especially alert to potential adverse reactions to their condition when pollution levels are high.

TRAVEL STRESS AND THE BODY CLOCK

Many physiological functions follow a 24-hour cycle that is termed circadian rhythm. The rhythm reflects the alternations between external light and darkness and corresponding wakefulness–sleep cycles. The rhythms are controlled by the suprachismatic cells of the hypothalamus and entrained by the environmental changes in daylight and darkness.

The most commonly used marker of circadian rhythm is that of core body temperature. Various human performance measures follow closely the circadian curve in body temperature. An example is the freely chosen work-rate which, similarly to the change in rectal temperature, shows a diurnal peak at about 17:00 hours. These observations indicate that individuals spontaneously operate at a higher tempo when pre-exercise body temperature is at its circadian high-point.

The circadian rhythms may be disturbed in young players when sleep is disrupted or after travelling across multiple time zones. Adolescents do seem to sleep longer than adults, although the influence of habit in this difference is unknown. Adequate sleep is thought to be important in growing individuals, due to links between sleep and the consolidation of neural processes linked with learning. It is thought also to have a role in the integrity of the immune system (Reilly et al., 1997).

The major disruption to circadian rhythms occurs after long-haul flights across multiple time zones. During the period when the body is out of harmony with the local time in the new time zone, the body's rhythms are desynchronised. The result is a general malaise known as jet-lag. Symptoms include a feeling of fatigue, inability to sleep at the right time, difficulty in concentrating and effects on appetite.

It is thought that young people are less affected than adults by jet-lag but observations do not bear this out. Experienced travellers seem to benefit from previous trips and acquire good practices that seem to work for them as individuals (Waterhouse et al., 2002). Fitness helps in alleviating symptoms and continuing light training in the new time zone can help accelerate the adjustment of the body clock that is required. Symptoms disappear once the circadian rhythms have re-adjusted to synchronise once again with the time of day in the new environment.

In general, guidelines available to adults for easing travel stress are applicable to young soccer players. Their mentors should ensure that they arrive early enough in the new time zone for the body clock to adjust before any serious competitive engagement. Coping strategies should incorporate the direction of flight and the number of time zones crossed. A behavioural approach is recommended, including what to do during the journey itself, as any benefit of a pharmacological treatment cannot be guaranteed (Reilly *et al.*, 1997).

REFERENCES

Bar-Or, O. and Unnithan, V.B. (1994) Nutritional requirements of young soccer players. *Journal of Sports Sciences*, 12, Special Issue, S39–S42.

Harries, M. (1998) The lung in sport. In M. Harries, C. Williams, W.D. Stanish and L.J. Micheli (eds) *Oxford Textbook of Sports Medicine*. Oxford: Oxford University Press, 321–326.

MacNee, W. and Donaldson, K. (1999) Particulate air pollution: imperious and protective mechanism in the lungs. In T. Holgate, J. Serret, H. Koren and R. Maynard (eds) *Air Pollution and Health*. London: Academic Press, 653–672.

Meyer, F., Bar-Or, O., MacDougall, D. and Hegenhauser, G.J.F. (1992) Sweat electrolyte loss during exercise in the heat: effects of gender and maturation. *Medicine and Science in Sports and Exercise*, 24, 776–781.

Reilly, T. (2000) Temperature and performance: heat. In M. Harries, C. McLatchie, C. Williams and J. King (eds) *ABC of Sports Medicine*. London: BMJ Books, 68–71.

Reilly, T., Atkinson, G. and Budgett, R. (2001) Effect of low-dose temazepam on physiological variables and performance tests following a weekly flight across five time zones. *International Journal of Sports Medicine*, 22, 166–174.

Reilly, T., Atkinson, G. and Waterhouse, J. (1997) *Biological Rhythms and Exercise*. Oxford: Oxford University Press.

Schwellnus, M.P., Derman, E.W. and Noakes, T.D. (1997) Aetiology of skeletal muscle 'cramps' during exercise. A novel hypothesis. *Journal of Sports Sciences*, 15, 277–285.

Waterhouse, J., Edwards, B., Nevill, A., Carvalho, S., Atkinson, G., Buckley, P., Reilly, T., Godfrey, R. and Ramsay, R. (2002) Identifying some determinants of 'jet-lag' and its symptoms: a study of athletes and other travellers. *British Journal of Sports Medicine*, 36, 54–60.

CHAPTER FOUR

INJURY PREVENTION

INTRODUCTION

Children who play football may incur injury as a result. The damage can be due directly to physical contact during play or may be attributable to training. Differences between children and adults in physical and physiological characteristics explain why children may be the more vulnerable to injury. The factors that contribute to this greater risk in children include a larger surface area relative to mass, growing cartilage which can be easily stressed, and the fact that children have not yet gained the complex motor skills or experience associated with injury avoidance (Adirim and Cheng, 2003).

In theory, pre-pubescent players are less likely to suffer traumatic injury from physical contact as their relatively modest running velocities do not generate high collision forces at impact. This is not the case with the adolescent player whose circulating androgen concentrations, increased muscle mass and higher running velocities lead to greater forces at impact than occur when adolescents play. Furthermore, the adolescent playing with abandon is likely to engage in contests for possession quite vigorously whatever the risk involved. The ability to read the game, anticipate the actions of others around the playing area and avoid danger develops with experience.

Just as with adults, there are injuries to children that can be prevented. Some of these may be due to environmental factors, poor organisation of practices or playing in unsafe conditions. Others may be due to dangerous play, inappropriate rules in the control of training, use of faulty equipment or being pitted against bigger and stronger opponents. In some instances, individual players may be predisposed to injury due to congenital physical factors, deficient fitness levels or a tendency towards reckless behaviour. In others, injury may develop insidiously arising from over-training or playing too much for their growing biological tissues

54

to tolerate. In general, the greater the frequency of participation, the higher is the risk of injury (Hyndman, 1998).

Any consideration of injuries in young soccer players must take into account that the individual is still growing. Biological growth refers to all of the body's tissues and the process is especially evident in the development of the skeleton (see Chapter 2). Longitudinal growth continues until the epiphyseal growth plates close. The state of maturation varies among individuals and according to sex and ethnic background. The late developer is at a disadvantage compared to the early developer in the components of the game that entail physical contests and contact between individuals. Gross differences in body size should be avoided as far as possible by coaches when setting up opposing groups for training practices.

There are skeletal injuries associated with the growth process that are triggered by physical training. Whilst growing bones are more easily fractured than in the mature skeleton, the junction between bone and the tendonous insertion is vulnerable during periods of rapid growth. The more common of these apophyseal injuries are described in the next section.

OVERUSE APOPHYSEAL INJURIES

The insertion of the patella tendon on the tibial tubercle is a common site of miniature avulsions due to overuse. Sometimes this type of injury occurs as a result of rapid growth even when exercise levels are within accepted norms. Apophysitis at this point is known as Osgood-Schlatter's disease. The knee joint is not involved and there are no serious long-term consequences of this complaint. The condition can last for some months with tenderness lingering over the tibial tubercle. The tubercle can swell and become permanent. Treatment includes rest, ice and analgesic or anti-inflammatory agents whilst stretching the quadriceps generally can alleviate the discomfort. Flexibility exercises for the knee extensors may help prevent further occurrence (Adirim and Cheng, 2003). This problem occurs most typically between 11 and 15 years and although multiple factors contribute to this condition, the main ones are rate of growth and overuse.

Another vulnerable apophyseal site is at the insertion of the Achilles tendon and plantar fascia on the calcaneus. This condition is known as Sever's disease and typically manifests between 7 and 10 years of age. This means the patient is younger than the typical individual with Osgood-Schlatter's disease, reflecting the earlier growth spurt in the foot compared to the leg (Hyndman, 1998). Proportionally short calf muscles combined with heavy exercise can precipitate the complaint. The range of motion in dorisflexion is reduced and tenderness is felt at the back of the heel. Whilst rest will alleviate the pain, stretching the gastrocnemius and soleus muscle complex is recommended. Lifting the heel by means of a padded insert in the shoe may also be helpful.

JOINT INJURIES

Young football players incur injury mainly to the lower limbs. In the main, injury patterns resemble those observed among adults. Ankle sprains can be caused by playing on poor quality pitches or on hard surfaces. They may also occur on losing balance whilst running for the ball. Lateral sprains occur when the foot is plantar-flexed and inverted. Referral for x-ray is recommended when swelling is observed along with tenderness over the lateral malleolus. This precaution is advocated in case a fracture has occurred. Early treatment of ankle sprains should entail rest combined with ice, compression and protection by taping.

Knee pain focused on the patella can indicate 'patellar femoral pain syndrome'. Pain is experienced as a chronic, dull ache, especially when climbing stairs or sitting for long periods. The onset of pain is insidious and may not necessarily be related to game activities. The syndrome may be due to any of a number of biomechanical problems. These include poor tracking of the patella over the joint, malalignment of the lower limbs, muscle weaknesses or tightness, flat feet (pes planus) or high arches (pes cavus).

Irrespective of age, damage to the cruciate ligaments within the knee joint is a risk factor in playing football. Injury to the anterior cruciate ligament can be caused by 'cutting movements' that incorporate changing the direction of a run or decelerating abruptly. It seems that injuries to the anterior cruciate ligament are more commonly experienced in girls than in boys; reasons proposed for this greater frequency of occurrence have included differences between girls and boys in anatomical factors, conditioning and locomotion (or landing) techniques. A complete rupture of the ligament is a serious injury in a young player, probably requiring surgery.

Whilst the majority of injuries incurred in soccer are to the lower limbs, the upper body may also be prone to injury. Dislocations of the shoulder can result from falling on an outstretched arm. Damage to soft tissue around the joint may be experienced, rendering it unstable. Participation in training and matches may be prohibited since an intact upper body is needed for the balance and coordination required for soccer activities. Young players are also liable to incur a range of minor contact injuries including bruised ribs, facial abrasions or hand injuries from being hit with the ball.

EPIDEMIOLOGY AND INTERVENTIONS

A majority of the injuries occurring in soccer are due to incidents in competitive games. The most common sources of events leading to an injury are tackles, charging an opponent to contest possession, and aggressive play (Rahnama et al., 2002). Nevertheless, injuries do arise as a result of poor conditioning, deficiencies in specific aspects of physical fitness and the onset of fatigue. It is therefore a sensible practice to reduce the time of matches in under-age groups relative to the duration of 90 min that normally applies to adults. The size of pitch, the ball and the dimensions of the goal should all be reduced relative to the sizes used by mature players.

The adoption of resistance training to improve the fitness of adolescent players has proved to be effective in reducing the number and severity of injuries over a competitive season (Cahill and Griffith, 1978). The period of recovery from injury was shortened as a result of the use of structured resistance training by male and female subjects in a study by Hejna et al. (1982). The conditioning of skeletal muscles, especially those of the lower limbs, which are most vulnerable to injury in soccer, does seem to be beneficial in coping with the loads experienced in match situations.

A strategy to reduce the injury incidence in players in the major leagues in Sweden was found to be effective. Ekstrand et al. (1983) conducted a classical study utilising a randomised trial among 12 teams. The programme included not only exercises for muscle strength and flexibility but also education about disciplined behaviour in matches and training camps. The intervention was successful over the season in reducing hamstring and adductor muscle injuries. Whilst the project was conducted on mature soccer players, its principles can be applied equally to under-age participants.

In a broadly similar study of 300 female high school players, Heidt et al. (2000) implemented a targeted training programme for seven weeks. The exercises included soccer-specific aerobic fitness work, strength training, plyometrics, flexibility and 'speed cord drills' for speed and agility. Those girls who engaged in the pre-season training sustained fewer injuries (14 per cent) over the following season than did the control group (38 per cent).

Junge and co-workers (2002) concentrated on male youth amateur players in their prospective intervention study. Seven teams took part over two seasons in Switzerland, the intervention group completing a systematic injury prevention programme whereas the control group trained and played soccer as usual. The intervention programme was unique in that emphasis was placed on improving the structure and content of training by educating and supervising the coaches and players. The intervention regime incorporated an improved warm-up, a regular cool-down, taping unstable ankles and promoting a sense of fair play. The amount and quality of training were tailored to the teams and their individual players. The exercises consisted of 10 sets designed to improve the stability of the ankle and the knee, flexibility and strength of trunk, hip and leg muscles and also endurance, coordination and reaction time. There were 21 per cent fewer injuries in the intervention group compared to the controls. The most pronounced successes were observed for mild injuries, overuse injuries and those incurred in training. The players of low skill benefited more from the prevention programme than did those of a higher skill level. The latter experienced a reduction of injuries in competition more so than in training.

EXERCISE-INDUCED ASTHMA

Children may be vulnerable to disturbances of the respiratory system, quite apart from the muscle skeletal damage already described. Asthma is the most common chronic respiratory disorder in children and its existence among the young soccer-playing population should be considered. In the United States asthma affects 7 per cent of youths, but its prevalence is higher in boys than in girls (7.8 vs 5.5 per cent), blacks versus whites (9.4 vs 6.2 per cent) and in children who live in urban in contrast to rural areas (7.1 vs 5.7 per cent) (Gergen et al., 1988). Asthma is a blanket term but the condition is characterised by increased responsiveness of the trachea and bronchial airways to various stimuli, causing a narrowing of their airways. The effects are manifest in wheezing, shortness of breath and sometimes a cough that may restrict activities, affect attendance at school or necessitate chronic use of medication. The symptoms can be reversed or at least reduced by use of appropriate medical therapy.

Hyper-reactivity of the airways is a feature of the reversible airway obstruction associated with asthma. There are recognised stimuli that may trigger an asthma attack. Factors that provoke an attack in children and adolescents include viral infections in the upper respiratory tract, allergies such as cat and dog dander, irritants such as cigarette smoke or air pollution, cold air and exercise.

Asthmatic symptoms may be related solely to exercise in some individuals. In others symptoms of asthma may be experienced daily and be worsened by physical activity. Exercise-induced asthma is normally self-limiting, in comparison to chronic asthma. Nevertheless exercise-induced asthma may restrict a child's engagement in physical activities, although its likelihood of occurrence is lower in soccer than in continuous running due to the intermittent activity that constitutes the game (Godfrey, 1984). The young soccer player may be especially vulnerable in spontaneously arranged activity, as short intense periods of exercise (up to 10 min) are the most likely to induce asthmatic symptoms (Anderson et al., 1989).

After exercise, about 50 per cent of individuals prone to exercise-induced asthma are less responsive to identical exercise performed within 2 hours. This phenomenon is referred to as the 'refractory state' and may reflect depletion of mediator release from pulmonary mast cells which leads to bronchospasm or elevations in circulatory catecholamines. The existence of a refractory period suggests the value of a warm-up prior to exercise, although the dimensions of an optimal warm-up have not been subject to a rigorous determination.

Whilst exercise in warm moist air performed after an adequate warm-up is less likely to provoke exercise-induced asthma, children with chronic asthma will exacerbate their symptoms during exercise. Other children may suffer asthmatic symptoms following exercise. Both groups of children should get used to pre-medicating 10–15 minutes before the start of exercise either with beta agonists or chromolyn sodium. Beta agonists can be used both for prevention and treatment and are usually prescribed first in case the child neglects to use the prescribed medication pre-exercise. Nebulized agents or metered doses with spacing devices are employed usually with children under 5–7 years of age. In view of the excellent treatment available, children liable to exercise-induced asthma can be encouraged to engage in soccer training and games rather than have their participation restricted.

INJURY PREVENTION

Any strategy to reduce injury risk in under-age football should take into consideration the likely mechanisms. These factors can be separated into extrinsic and intrinsic aspects, even though the causes may be complex in nature.

Individual factors are intrinsic in nature but may be modified by training and football practice. They include lack of fitness, muscle tightness, joint instability and inadequate rehabilitation from a previous injury. Young players can incorporate poor balance and coordination, awkwardness and poor ability in education programmes about injury avoidance.

Extrinsic factors accommodate an inadequate playing environment. Safety features should be considered by the coach or physical education teacher so that there are no obvious environmental hazards. For football games in a physical education context, it would be useful for the teacher to conduct a risk assessment first. This process would also ensure that any equipment used is safe. Attention should be directed also to shoes and shin guards and, depending on weather conditions, to clothing worn.

It is important that the size of the ball is suitable for the age group concerned. A young player may be momentarily stunned if hit in the face by a ball in flight. The possibility of damage from heading the ball has been addressed by various researchers and reviewed by Lees and Lake (2003). Skilled players can stiffen the head and neck region when making contact with the ball, thereby reducing the effective forces at impact. It is important that this skill is taught properly and carefully to children and a reduced ball mass used.

An important external factor concerns the manner in which rules of play are implemented by the official in charge. The referee has to be especially vigilant in incidents where contact is likely, in challenges for possession in congested areas and in circumstances where vigorous tackles are executed. It is imperative that the authority of the official in charge is not undermined and that infringement of the rules is dealt with appropriately. Parents may tend to become emotionally involved when their children are playing and have a responsibility not to condone or support any foul play.

Whilst competing too frequently may be a factor in overuse injuries, training for too long in one session may also be linked with injury. Fatigue can occur in prolonged activities due to a depletion of energy stores, a gradual dehydration or a loss of concentration due to time on the task. It is therefore important that practices are structured with specific learning outcomes in mind for participants.

In the USA the rules of youth soccer have been outlined with safety in mind. Age-group games for under-8s are divided into four 12-minute quarters, with 5-minute breaks between quarters and an intermission of 10 minutes at half-time. Each half lasts 25 minutes at under-10 level. The duration of each half increases from 30 minutes at under-12 to 45 minutes by under-18 years of age. Games at both under-8 and under-10 levels are formed of seven players on each side. From under-11 upwards, games are played on the regulation full-sized pitch with 11 players on each side. There is no limit to the number of substitutes permitted although, at the national championship level, two substitutes per side are used for the under-16 age group and upwards. These regulations are intended to reduce the overall energy expenditure of young players, and hence the physiological demands (Bar-Or and Unnithan, 1994).

Kohno and colleagues (1997) provided broad guidelines to protect young soccer players from injury at various ages (see Table 4.1). This plan placed emphasis on enjoyment and safety. The recommendations were based on observations of injuries and physical fitness in young Japanese players aged from 12 to 19 years. As knee extension strength increases generally between the ages of 12 and

Table 4.1 Recommendations for training in young soccer players

Age (years)	Activity
12–13	Focus on mini-games, short passing and dribbling, avoid overloading joints
14–15	Muscle training may start, sprint training can be performed. Use appropriate loads
16–17	Aerobic training introduced

Source: Kohno *et al*., 1997.

13 years, they recommended the avoidance of kicking exercises which place strain on the knee joint. Muscle strength training was deemed appropriate between 14 and 17 years of age as strength increases greatly within this time. Sprint training may also be performed safely at this time. Endurance training can be emphasised at age 16 as the maximum oxygen uptake approaches values expected of adult players.

AN ERGONOMICS MODEL

It is clear that injuries are not highly predictable. Injury risk may be increased as a result of the prevailing competitive or training environment. In such cases a check-list approach towards eliminating risks should help to promote safety. A risk assessment is therefore an important part of an approach towards injury reduction. Weather conditions can also pose an immediate threat to the safety of young soccer participants. Wet weather can change good playing pitches into treacherous surfaces where slips and falls can cause casualties. Likewise players on hot days can encounter problems of heat injury since the body temperature of children can rise more quickly than is the case with adults. Education about rehydration strategies and the importance of replacing fluids lost can enhance safety in these circumstances.

During play or training, an injury may be the end result of a chain of events in which the outcome was unintentional. The sequence may start with an error which in turn causes an accident in which one or more players are injured. Not all errors lead to accidents, and in some accidents the players involved may emerge unscathed. Nevertheless, a focus on reducing errors, whether by means of tactics or improvement in technique, is likely to benefit both performance and safety (Figure 4.1).

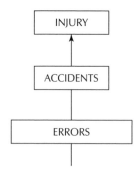

Figure 4.1 The causal chain whereby a critical event can precipitate an injury
Source: Based on approach of Rahnama *et al.*, 2002.

A fundamental principle in ergonomics is that the capacities of individuals enable them to meet the demands of the tasks in hand. In preparing young players to meet the demands of games, training programmes should be designed to minimise risk. For this purpose game drill may be modified to reduce contact, emphasise care in tackling and so on. These alterations should be done without compromising behaviour in actual games. They can also be helpful in promoting a sense of the ethics of the game in which the activity is vigorous but fair.

Training for performance can entail exercise regimens that are not necessarily soccer-specific. Resistance training can be used to improve musculoskeletal factors, the resultant enhancement of strength and power having an indirect impact on performance in the game. Special attention to lifting techniques should be given to young players using weight training for their programmes. Injuries in weight training are mainly a result of using loads that are too heavy for the individual concerned or operating with faulty techniques. Guidelines are now available for the safe conduct of resistance exercise in young athletes.

There are a few important considerations for the coach or trainer to bear in mind prior to training or matches. It is important that any predispositions to injury are identified and existing injuries are not exacerbated. No risks should be taken if rehabilitation from a previous injury is incomplete. The warm-up should contain flexibility exercises, be intensive enough to elevate muscle temperature and include game-specific actions. The coach should also be aware of individual personalities so that any anxieties and fears can be allayed as much as possible.

injury prevention

OVERVIEW

An overriding consideration in under-age soccer is that the young player is still growing. It is important therefore that undue strains are not placed on the musculoskeletal system, especially on the long bones where the growth plates are still open. Games can be modified to suit the sex and age group concerned. Early emphasis should be placed on enjoyment and on the development of games skills. As biological growth stages vary among individuals, the coach should safeguard against imperfect matching of young players in practice sessions. The coach should also be on guard in the case of individuals with particular susceptibilities, such as asthma. It is also important that those with a duty of care for the young player should place individual health and well-being above the performance of the young player.

REFERENCES

Adirim, T.A. and Cheng, T.L. (2003) Overview of injuries in the young athlete. *Sports Medicine*, 33, 75–81.

Anderson, S., Seale, J.P., Ferriss, L., Schoefler, R. and Lindsay, D.A. (1989) An evaluation of exercise induced asthma. *Journal of Allergy and Clinical Immunology*, 64, 612–624.

Bar-Or, O. and Unnithan, V.B. (1994) Nutritional requirements of young soccer players. *Journal of Sports Sciences*, 12, S39–S42.

Cahill, B.R. and Griffith, E.H. (1978) Effect of pre-season conditioning on the incidence and severity of high school football knee injuries. *American Journal of Sports Medicine*, 6, 180–184.

Ekstrand, J., Gillqvist, J., Moller, M. *et al.* (1983) Incidence of soccer injuries and their relation to training and team success. *American Journal of Sports Medicine*, 11, 63–67.

Gergen, P.J., Mullally, D.I. and Evans, R. (1988) National survey of prevalence of asthma among children in the United States, 1977–80. *Pediatrics*, 81, 1–7.

Godfrey, S. (1984) Symposium on special problems and management of allergic athletes. *Journal of Allergy and Clinical Immunology*, 73, 630–633.

Heidt, R.S. Jr., Sweeterman, L.M, Carlonas, R.L. *et al.* (2000) Avoidance of soccer injuries with preseason conditioning. *American Journal of Sports Medicine*, 28, 659–662.

Hejna, W.F., Rosenberg, A., Buturusis, A.J. and Krieger, A. (1982) The prevention of sports injuries in high school students through strength training. *National Strength and Conditioning Association Journal*, 4, 28–31.

Hyndman, J.L. (1998) The growing athlete. In M. Harries, C. Williams, W.D. Stanish and L.J. Micheli (eds) *Oxford Textbook of Sports Medicine*. Oxford: Oxford University Press, 727–741.

Junge, A., Rosch, D., Peterson, L., Graf-Baumann, T. and Drorak, J. (2002) Prevention of soccer injuries: a prospective study in youth amateur players. *American Journal of Sports Medicine*, 30, 652–659.

Kohno, T., O'Hata, N., Ohara, M., Shirahata, T., Endo, Y., Satoh, M., Kimura, Y. and Nakasima, Y. (1997) Sports injuries and physical fitness in adolescent soccer players. In T. Reilly, J. Bangsbo and M. Hughes (eds) *Science and Football III*. London: E. and F. N. Spon, 185–189.

Lees, A. and Lake, M. (2003) The biomechanics of soccer surfaces and equipment. In T. Reilly and A.M. Williams (eds) *Science and Soccer*. London: Routledge, 120–135.

Rahnama, N., Reilly, T. and Lees, A. (2002) Injury risk associated with playing actions during competitive soccer. *British Journal of Sports Medicine*, 36, 354–359.

CHAPTER FIVE

THE YOUNG FEMALE SOCCER PLAYER

INTRODUCTION

Soccer play has grown in popularity among young females since the First World Cup for women's teams was held in China in 1991. It has proved to be an attractive recreational activity and competitive sport in many developed countries. There has been a step-wise increase in women's clubs over the last quarter of a century in the majority of European countries and a similar growth in participation has occurred in American and Asian countries. Nevertheless the sport is still hardly played at all by girls in many countries worldwide where it is restricted by cultural, domestic and economic considerations.

In this chapter, special attention is given to the young female footballer. The growth and physical development of girls are compared with the same phenomena in boys. The reproductive cycle in females is described and changes during each cycle that impact on soccer play are highlighted. The consequences for physiological responses to exercise are considered. The impact of strenuous exercise and regular competitive stress on the normal menstrual cycle has relevance for young female soccer players. One possibility is that hard training in very young girls may delay the first appearance of the menstrual cycle. There is potential also for the menstrual cycle to be disturbed by strenuous training, leading to irregular, or complete absence of, cycles. There are links between nutrition, eumenorrhoea and bone health, which in extreme cases are referred to as the 'female athlete triad'. The relevance of these phenomena for soccer players is addressed before the question of whether participation in soccer by young girls subsequently affects reproductive health.

THE NORMAL MENSTRUAL CYCLE

Menarche

The first appearance of the menstrual (ovulatory) cycle in girls is known as menarche. It is recognised as menstrual bleeding and reflects the maturation of the reproductive system. Once menarche is evident, the girl is nubile and capable of child-bearing.

The age of menarche varies among individuals, reflecting other growth phenomena, and biological age is often dissociated from chronological age. There has been a secular trend of earlier menarche, attributed to improved material well-being, better nutrition and life-style factors. The variation between races and ethnic groups has also been linked with climatic factors, although these do not provide a consistent explanation of differences among countries with similar environmental temperatures.

At the start of the twenty-first century, the average age at menarche in the United Kingdom is 11 years. A range of 9 to 14 years is common. Menarche signals the start of potential fertility which terminates in the disappearance of the regular menstrual cycle at the menopause. This period of fertility lasts almost four decades, the menopause usually occurring at about the age of 50 years.

The physiology of the menstrual cycle

The menstrual cycle incorporates cyclical changes in both the ovaries and the uterus with the production of ova as part of the reproductive process. A normal ovulatory cycle has a length of 28 days on average, and hence is referred to as a circamensal biological rhythm. The length may vary between 23 and 33 days, and may be especially variable in young girls during the early years when its regulatory system is still maturing.

The menstrual cycle is regulated by a complex system incorporating the hypothalamus (producing gonadotrophin-releasing hormone or GnRH), the anterior pituitary gland with its output of follicle stimulating hormone (FSH) and luteinising hormone (LH), the ovaries, follicles and the corpus luteum (producing oestrogens, progesterone and inhibin). The feedback loops to the pituitary and hypothalamus (Figure 5.1) illustrate why the system is referred to as the hypothalamic-pituitary-ovarian axis (Reilly, 2000).

The menstrual cycle starts with menses (menstruation), a phase which lasts 4–5 days during which about 40 ml of blood is discharged along with the surface part

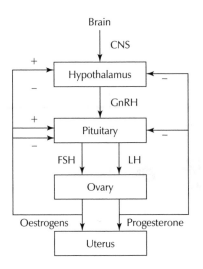

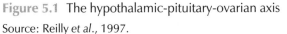

Figure 5.1 The hypothalamic-pituitary-ovarian axis

Source: Reilly *et al.*, 1997.

Notes: CNS – central nervous system; GnRH – gonadotrophin-releasing hormone; FSH – follicle stimulating hormone; LH – luteinising hormone.

of the endometrial wall. Blood losses may vary from 25 to 65 ml, but can in some instances exceed 200 ml. Consistent heavy losses of blood with menstruation can lead to anaemia and a decrease in oxygen-carrying capacity in the circulatory system, which may adversely affect endurance athletes. Once menses cease, renewal of the endometrial lining is promoted by oestrogens (mainly oestradiol), whilst FSH stimulates the maturation of the ovum into a graafian follicle. This part of the cycle constitutes the follicular phase. The maturing follicle ovulates about mid-cycle (Day 14), ovulation being triggered by a sharp rise in LH and signified by an elevation of about 0.5°C in body temperature. For conception to occur, the liberated ovum has to be fertilized within 24 hours. The cycle now enters the luteal phase characterised by the collapse of the ruptured follicle from which the ovum has burst to form the corpus luteum which produces increased amounts of progesterone. If implantation of a fertilised egg has not occurred, the corpus luteum usually regresses by Day 21. The main function of progesterone is to prepare the uterine wall for implantation of the fertilized ovum, and so progesterone falls to a low level pre-menses if this event has not occurred. Consequently the endometrium regresses and about two-thirds of its lining is shed in menstruation as the next cycle starts.

The hormonal changes affecting the uterus are closely integrated with ovarian functions within the overall regulation of the menstrual cycle (Figure 5.2). The

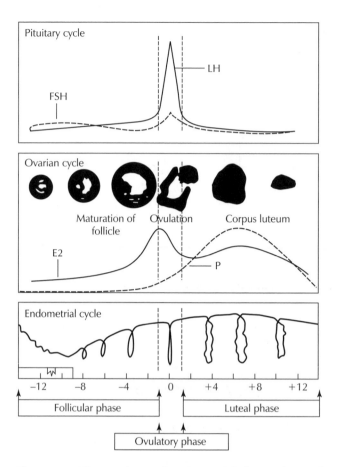

Figure 5.2 The ovarian and endometrial phases during the normal circamensal (menstrual) cycle

Source: Reilly et al., 1997.

Notes: Progesterone is indicated by P, oestradiol by E2.

proliferative phase of the endometrium following menses is stimulated by oestradiol and progesterone which are steroid hormones. Output of oestradiol enhances development of the endometrial surface and the spiral arteries. At ovulation progesterone causes the endometrium to develop mucous-secreting glands and endometrial cells to accumulate glycogen in anticipation of receiving a fertilised ovum. Once the ovum reaches the uterus, the follicular cells now form the corpus luteum which, as explained above, secretes large amounts of oestrogen (oestradiol) and progesterone. Negative feedback of the concentrations of these hormones acts to suppress the release of GnRH, FSH and LH. When the fertilised ovum is implanted in the uterus, progesterone protects the integrity of the endometrium and inhibits uterine contractions during pregnancy.

Biological events in the ovarian phases are harmonised with the thickening and subsequent shedding of the endometrial lining in a complete menstrual cycle. During the follicular phase of the ovarian cycle that follows menstrual bleeding, both FSH and LH levels remain fairly constant until a peak in oestradiol secretion occurs on the day before ovulation. Oestradiol acts by means of positive feedback to induce a rise in LH and GnRH which then stimulates the output of both FSH and LH. The outcome is a pronounced surge in LH and a lesser rise in FSH.

At onset of the luteal phase post-ovulation, progesterone levels increase further, linked to the secretory phase of the endometrial cycle. In the absence of implantation, oestrogen and progesterone drop towards their lowest level as the corpus luteum regresses and GnRH, FSH and LH are no longer subject to negative feedback. The loss of endometrial lining is a result of the large drop in progesterone secretion which causes blood vessel spasms, ischaemia and death of the surface cells of the endometrium. As menstruation begins, FSH promotes follicle development and the cycle gets under way again.

A gain in body weight represents another change that is evident pre-menses. The extra weight is due to storage of water and is associated with altered potassium: sodium ratios. This fluid retention is due to a rise in secretion of aldosterone (normally blocked by the elevated progesterone level) which stimulates the renin-angiotensin system and causes an increase in anti-diuretic hormone. The extra weight could be a disadvantage in sports events such as jumping or hurdle races where body mass has to be lifted repeatedly against gravity.

Mood changes

The appearance of menarche may itself present emotional problems for a young girl. The extent of any emotional trauma may depend on her specific education. Along with these new emotions, the cyclical hormonal milieu may give rise to mood changes to which she has not been accustomed. There may also be pain or discomfort associated with menstruation.

An appreciable proportion of women experience dysmenorrhoea or painful menses and are unlikely to be able to concentrate on maximal exercise in such circumstances. Regular exercise training appears to ameliorate the problem of abdominal cramps, probably due to lowering the levels of prostaglandins. Premenstrual tension (PMT) is a syndrome which is linked with increased prostaglandin production and may be relieved by administration of prostaglandin inhibitors. In its extreme form PMT is characterised by irritability, aggression, confusion and sometimes abnormal behaviour. In less extreme forms subjects may feel anxious, tired and unable to relax. A diurnal variation in bouts of irritation has been linked with fluctuations in blood glucose, irritation peaking late in the morning when breakfast is missed. Alternative mechanisms linked with PMT have implicated a range of neurotransmitters including monoamine oxidase and serotonin (5HT), the latter leading to the use of 5HT-reuptake inhibitors in treatment.

The mental predisposition for participating in sport and in soccer training is influenced by psychological entities such as attitude, motivation and a readiness for strenuous effort. In normal eumenorrhoeic women in their twenties, mood factors have been found to change consistently with menstrual cycle phase (O'Reilly and Reilly, 1990). Positive moods were pronounced in the follicular and post-ovulatory (early luteal) phases whereas more negative moods were evident preceding and during menses (Table 5.1). Although moods are essentially labile, these variations should nevertheless be taken into account by mentors and coaches of young female players engaged in physical training programmes and weekly matches.

SEX DIFFERENCES

A comparison of growth rates between the sexes is covered in detail in Chapter 2. In this section, the main factors that have a direct impact on performance are emphasised.

Table 5.1 Profile of mood states at the four phases of the menstrual cycle, means and standard deviations

	Menses	Follicular	Ovulatory	Luteal
Tension-anxiety	13.2 ± 3.4	8.2 ± 1.9	6.9 ± 2.5	14.4 ± 3.5
Depression	16.1 ± 6.7	8.1 ± 4.2	8.3 ± 5.1	17.4 ± 6.2
Anger-hostility	3.9 ± 10.0	4.4 ± 2.3	4.7 ± 3.4	7.4 ± 3.0
Vigour-activity	9.0 ± 2.4	16.2 ± 1.9	22.7 ± 1.3	12.2 ± 2.3
Fatigue-inertia	11.2 ± 2.8	5.5 ± 0.7	1.5 ± 0.7	10.4 ± 1.8
Confusion	9.1 ± 1.4	4.8 ± 1.0	2.8 ± 1.4	8.2 ± 2.0

Source: O'Reilly and Reilly, 1990.

Note: A higher score means a greater tendency towards each mood description.

Up to the onset of puberty boys slightly outperform girls in the majority of gross motor skills. These differences are exacerbated during adolescence, when boys at a similar stage of maturation generally outperform girls in running, jumping and throwing activities (Reilly and Stratton, 1995). With the exception of flexibility, there are similar sex differences in health-related fitness measures of strength, local muscular endurance and cardiorespiratory endurance. During puberty, females' greater relative increase in adiposity compared to males clearly disadvantages them in any task that involves the translocation of body mass. As females start puberty an average of 2 years before males, at this stage females have advantages in stature, body mass, absolute strength and flexibility over males. With the exception of flexibility, these advantages disappear when males pass through puberty approximately 2 years later.

Research suggests that the bases of sex differences in performance are not necessarily biological. Differences in opportunity to participate in sport, conflict between sport and femininity, and clear differences in rearing styles suggest that wider biosocial factors may influence differences in performance. This may imply that sex differences in soccer participation and performance will continue to exist if sex stereotyping of children's play remains entrenched in society.

Any attempt to match girls according to the demands of soccer competition is fraught with practical difficulty. Chronological age is not a perfect marker of biological maturity as growth rates differ among individual children. Consequently, the timing of the stage of peak growth may provide advantages for participation in certain sports. In general, early maturing males have an advantage over females because of their significant increase in muscle mass during peak growth. Females may also be at a disadvantage because the relative increase in adiposity has a negative effect on their performance. Late maturing girls tend to be better at motor tasks than early maturing girls, whereas early maturing girls are at an advantage in circumstances where absolute strength and size are important. Overall, the stage of maturation has a far greater influence over motor performance in boys than in girls, where circumpubertal differences are not quite as marked. Whereas some boys may be disadvantaged in age-group competitions by virtue of having a birth date late in the year, the extent of this bias in young female soccer players is unknown. If the same phenomenon exists it may be related to the high level of females dropping out in teenage years. Alternatively, early maturing girls are at a physiological disadvantage compared to their prepubertal peers. Performance is negatively affected by change in body shape and an oestrogenic increase in fat mass. In contact sports where strength and size are important, such a bias may increase the risk of injury.

There is some evidence that women are more vulnerable to error during pre-menses and this has been reflected in the incidence of injuries incurred by

Swedish soccer players (Moller-Nielsen and Hammar, 1989). Oral contraceptives are used to regulate the cycle by some sportswomen and the Swedish researchers found fewer traumatic injuries in those players using contraceptive pills to reduce premenstrual and menstrual symptoms of discomfort.

Women soccer players are more vulnerable to serious knee-joint injuries than are male players. Injuries to the anterior cruciate ligament (ACL) are a particular concern, being many times more likely to occur in a game than in training. The higher incidence of ACL injuries in female players has been attributed to their smaller intercondylar notches, although other factors are likely to be implicated. These include poor techniques on landing when off-balance, fitness, lack of quality coaching and poor decision-making (see Reilly, 2000 for review). These factors apply to girls as well as to adult female players.

Soccer performance is not necessarily impaired during any particular stage of the menstrual cycle. In contemporary society female participation in sport is widely accepted as is the principle that menses are no bar to training or competing. Nevertheless, the experience of young women participating in sport is variable and it is relevant to consider how the alterations during menstrual cycle phases might affect physiological responses to exercise, and hence soccer performance. An associated issue is the extent to which strenuous training effects changes in the normal menstrual cycle, thus offsetting potential impairment and enabling the young female player to adapt to the training level.

PHYSIOLOGICAL RESPONSES TO EXERCISE

The changes in steroid hormones during the normal menstrual cycle can influence physiological responses to exercise. Whilst the majority of studies have been conducted on mature female athletes, the same mechanisms are likely to occur in teenage females after menarche.

Progesterone has a thermogenic effect and its activity is linked with a rise in core temperature after ovulation. It also elevates minute ventilation ($\dot{V}E$) and is responsible for an increased $\dot{V}E$ in response to continuous exercise during the luteal phase. The rise in $\dot{V}E$ would cause an increased output of CO_2, without affecting oxygen consumption ($\dot{V}O_2$). The consequence of a rise in $\dot{V}E$ is an increased respiratory alkalosis, which has been linked with a higher rating of subjective exertion in the early luteal phase of the menstrual cycle (O'Reilly and Reilly, 1990).

In the mid-luteal phase of the menstrual cycle it seems that the elevated levels of oestrogen and progesterone diminish the utilisation of glycogen as a substitute for oxidative metabolism. Circulating levels of free fatty acids rise, confirming the switch to fat as a preferred source of energy during the luteal phase. The sparing of muscle glycogen is likely to have a beneficial effect towards the end of a competitive match or long training session. At the same time, lower blood lactate concentrations are observed in response to a set exercise load.

The mechanism for altering fuel utilisation is likely to be a hormone-sensitive lipase which promotes lipolysis and is activated by the hormonal changes in the luteal phase. The time-span over which performance might be enhanced is likely to be only a matter of 3–4 days, before progesterone falls pre-menses. This possible enhancement may be counteracted in a competitive context at other phases of the menstrual cycle when catecholamine secretion, which leads to similar effects, is increased in the course of competitive stress (see Table 5.2).

It has been suggested that low oestrogen levels may have an adverse influence on human strength. An ergogenic effect of oestrogen has been demonstrated in post-menopausal women when the adductor pollicis muscle (which draws the thumb in over the palm of the hand) was isolated for measurement of isometric force under experimental conditions (Phillips et al., 1993). The active stretch force – the tension within the muscle in response to its being stretched – is not impaired and the weakness can be offset by hormone-replacement therapy. This loss of strength in the muscles of ageing females may accentuate the loss in bone strength due to demineralisation. It should also be emphasised that gross muscular strength is influenced by a host of factors other than circulating hormone levels and an alteration in muscle strength has not been shown in young females.

The menstrual cycle phase can also be relevant in training contexts when physiological responses to physical exercise are being interpreted. In 16 eumen-orrhoeic subjects studied by Birch and Reilly (1997), the heart rate response to a standard 10-minute lifting task was elevated by 10 beats per minute in the post-ovulation phase of the cycle. Although the impact of the menstrual cycle on lifting

Table 5.2 Summary of comparisons in physiological responses to exercise during mid-follicular and mid-luteal phases of the menstrual cycle

Mid-follicular	Mid-luteal
RER ↑	RER ↓
Glycogen utilisation ↑	Glycogen sparing
Blood lactate ↑	Blood lactate ↓
FFA ↓	FFA ↑

Notes: RER = Respiratory exchange ratio; FFA = Free fatty acids.

performance was minimal, the recommendation was that the changes in heart rate should be taken into account when considering such data. The conclusion was that in studies employing heart rate as a variable for examining fatigue, training intensity, risk of injury during repetitive lifting or predicting maximal oxygen consumption, allowance must be made for the menstrual cycle phase.

INFLUENCE OF EXERCISE ON THE MENSTRUAL CYCLE

Delayed menarche has been linked with the more advanced competitive levels in girls' running, but also with low body mass and low percentage body fat. Menarche is markedly late in girls who start systematic training at an early age and whose training regimens entail very high overall energy expenditure. These females include ballet dancers and gymnasts, average age of menarche in these groups being 15.4 and 15.0 years, respectively. There is no evidence of any influence of playing soccer on the timing of menarche. The delay in menarche observed in some athletic girls, potentially caused by strenuous training, has no subsequent adverse effect on female reproductive processes. Females engaged in strenuous athletic training programmes are known to experience disruption of the normal menstrual cycle. One irregularity is a shortened luteal phase. Secondary amenorrhoea, or absence of menses for a prolonged period, is also regularly reported. So-called 'athletic amenorrhoea' is linked with low levels of body fat, low body weight, energy imbalance and high training loads, while psychological stress is also implicated.

Secondary amenorrhoea is associated with low values of body fat, though the mechanism responsible for a link between them has not been clearly established. Endurance training lowers body fat which in turn leads to a reduced peripheral production of oestrogens through aromatisation of androgens, catalysed by aromatase in fat cells. The peripheral production of oestrogens is thought to be important in stimulating the hypothalamic-pituitary-ovarian axis. Hard exercise or intentional weight reduction will lower pituitary FSH secretion, prevent follicular development and ovarian oestrogen secretion, and decrease secretion of progesterone.

Exercise-induced amenorrhoea occurs in 20 per cent of female athletes, compared to a prevalence of 5 per cent in the general population. In runners, the prevalence increases linearly with training volume. This linear increase is not found in swimmers and cyclists as these athletes do not have to support their body weight during exercise and their bones are not subject to the same repetitive loads as in runners. Stress may also be implicated in the occurrence of amenorrhoea or oligomenorrhoea (irregular menstrual cycles). Amenorrhoeic athletes tend to be younger and lighter, have less body fat, experience more life stress, have a higher training load and train harder than those with normal cycles. A high frequency of competition is a powerful discriminator of amenorrhoeic individuals from other groups. It is possible that increased outputs of catecholamine, cortisol and endorphins interfere with the normal menstrual cycle by down-regulating the hypothalamic-pituitary-ovarian axis. Training-induced amenorrhoea does not necessarily mean the athlete is infertile. Ovulation can occur spontaneously and fertility can be restored after a long absence of menses. Exercise-related menstrual disturbances are quickly reversed with a reduction of high training loads (by about 10 per cent), and a marginal increase in body fat (up to 2 kg in weight).

Whilst secondary amenorrhoea is experienced by young females whose training load is associated with very high levels of energy expenditure, it does not seem to be above average in young soccer players. The reasons for this are likely to be complex, including social as well as nutritional factors. Young soccer players tend to be moderate in life-style with no tradition of 'body image' requirements or inordinate training stress.

THE 'FEMALE ATHLETE TRIAD'

The 'female athlete triad' is a syndrome occurring in physically active girls and women and is a contemporary concern to sports medicine practitioners. The triad refers to the links between amenorrhoea, disordered eating and bone mineral loss. Demineralisation of bone is a result of prolonged low levels of circulating oestrogen which upset the balance between bone resorption and bone formation. The result is a reduction in bone density akin to the rapid bone loss which occurs post-menopause. Although a moderate level of exercise stimulates bone growth, decreased bone density and occurrence of stress fractures reflect overtraining, particularly in younger athletes. Reducing the training load and decreasing the frequency of competing help to restore the normal menstrual cycle. It may also be restored by increasing daily energy intake. However, the interactions between training parameters and liability to bone demineralisation have yet to be explored in young girls engaged in habitual strenuous exercise.

Disordered eating refers to a variety of harmful and frequently ineffective eating behaviours adopted to lose weight or produce a lean look. These behaviours vary from restricting intake of food, to bingeing and purging. There is evidence that disordered eating behaviours can lead to short-term and long-term morbidity, decreased physical performance, amenorrhoea and even more extreme conditions. The latter include anorexia nervosa and bulimia nervosa, which can affect 1 per cent and 1–4 per cent of young women, respectively (Otis et al., 1997).

75

The reduction in body fat resulting from disordered eating is one of many factors linked with secondary amenorrhoea. Exercise stress can disrupt the pulse generated by the gonadotrophin-releasing hormone (GnRH) which regulates the hypothalamic-pituitary-ovarian axis. There have been suggestions that a failure to compensate for energy expenditure with an adequate energy intake, rather than a direct effect of exercise per se, is a cause of amenorrhoea. The mechanism proposed is a reduction in the frequency of pulses in luteinising hormone which results in a failure of ovulation.

Low concentrations of ovarian hormones in amenorrhoeic and oligomenorrhoeic young athletes are linked with reduced bone mass and increases in bone loss. The bone loss is more marked in trabecular bone than in cortical bone. This loss may be accentuated by disordered eating practices and low calcium intake combined with menstrual dysfunction. The extent of bone loss will depend on the duration of hypoestrogenia and the severity of menstrual irregularity, as well as the type of skeletal loading in training, nutritional factors and genetics.

The density of the skeleton is relevant in those displaying the 'female athlete triad'. Dual energy x-ray absorptiometry (DEXA) provides a laboratory-based means of analysing the density and composition of various regions of the body. Bone mineral density and percentage of body fat can be computed for the body as a whole. The technology was originally developed for diagnosis of osteoporosis but is used also in sports science laboratories for assessment of body composition in footballers (see Figure 5.3).

All physically active girls could be at risk of developing one or more components of the 'female athlete triad'. Precipitating factors can include peer pressure and a preoccupation with body image which mean that adolescence is a vulnerable time for girls (Otis et al., 1997). Soccer does not predispose towards risk since low body weight is not a special consideration and clothing does not necessarily reveal body contours.

OVERVIEW

The rise in the number of young girls participating in soccer has outstripped the growth rates in traditional girls' sports. Coaches and mentors responsible for the training of young female players should recognise that they are not miniature women and that their maturation does not exactly parallel that of boys.

Physiological events during the normal menstrual cycle are determined by feedback loops within the hypothalamic-pituitary-ovarian axis.

76

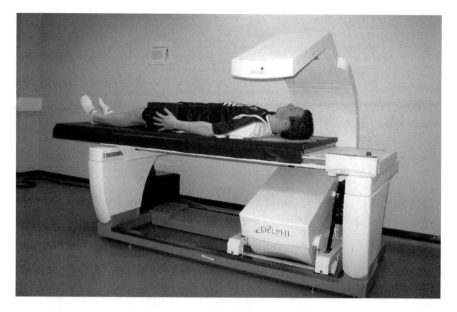

Figure 5.3a Dual energy x-ray absorptiometry (DEXA) analysis

Source and notes: A young female soccer player is analysed by means of DEXA at the Research Institute for Sport and Exercise Sciences at Liverpool John Moores University. The results are displayed on a computer print-out (Figure 5.3b).

Hormonal changes within the menstrual cycle have potential impact on human performance. Relevant stages to consider are pre-menses and menses, the follicular and luteal phases separated by an abrupt elevation in luteinising hormone and characterised by a sharp rise in body temperature coinciding with ovulation. Strenuous training may affect the normal menstrual cycle. Such disruptions include delayed menarche, shortened luteal phase and secondary amenorrhoea associated with high training loads and competitive stress. The so-called 'female athlete triad' embraces secondary amenorrhoea, abnormal eating behaviour and osteoporosis (attributed to chronic hypoestrogenia). Disordered eating is a particular concern among adolescent girls due to perceived peer pressure and a preoccupation with body image. Although delayed menarche, secondary amenorrhoea and low bone mineral density have been linked with sports where low body mass, a lean physique and low adiposity are emphasised, there is no evidence that young soccer players are more at risk than girls in the general population.

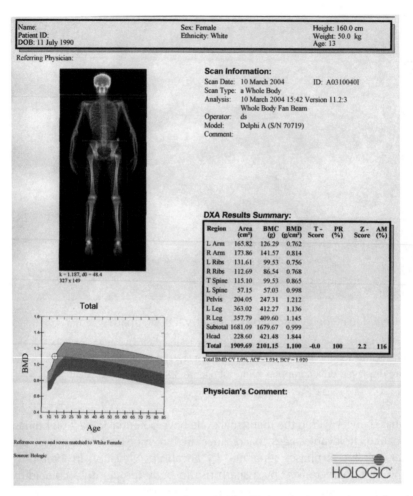

Figure 5.3b A DEXA print-out: the individual's data for bone mineral density are compared to reference values in the graph at bottom left

REFERENCES

Birch, K. and Reilly, T. (1997) The effect of eumenorrheic menstrual cycle phase on physiological responses to a repeated lifting task. *Canadian Journal of Applied Physiology*, 22, 148–160.

Moller-Nielsen, I. and Hammar, M. (1989) Women's soccer injuries in relation to the menstrual cycle phase and contraceptive use. *Medicine and Science in Sports and Exercise*, 21, 126–129.

O'Reilly, A. and Reilly, T. (1990) Effects of the menstrual cycle and responses to exercise. In E.J. Lovesey (ed.) *Contemporary Ergonomics*. London: Taylor & Francis, 149–153.

Otis, C.L., Drinkwater, B., Johnson, M., Loucks, A. and Wilmore, J. (1997) The female athlete triad: American College of Sports Medicine Position Stand. *Medicine and Science in Sports and Exercise*, 29, i–ix.

Phillips, S.K., Rook, K.M., Siddle, N.C., Bruce, S.A. and Woledge, R.C. (1993) Muscle weakness in women occurs at an earlier age than men, but strength is preserved by hormonal replacement therapy. *Clinical Science*, 84, 95–98.

Reilly, T. (2000) The menstrual cycle and human performance: an overview. *Biological Rhythm Research*, 31, 29–40.

Reilly, T. (2001) Physiology and the female footballer. *Insight: The F.A. Coaches Association Journal*, 4 (3), 26–29.

Reilly, T. and Stratton, G. (1995) Children and adolescents in sport: physiological considerations. *Sports Exercise and Injury*, 1, 207–213.

Reilly, T., Atkinson, G. and Waterhouse, J. (1997) *Biological Rhythms and Exercise*. Oxford: Oxford University Press.

CHAPTER SIX

DEVELOPING FITNESS IN THE YOUNG SOCCER PLAYER

INTRODUCTION

In Chapter 2 the effects of growth, development and maturation on biological characteristics of young soccer players were considered. It was clear that during growth and development, soccer performance improved as players grew stronger, faster and had more endurance. Furthermore, their skills and game understanding became more sophisticated. Nevertheless, scientists are unsure of the precise effects that growth and development have on performance and whether it is influenced by sustained periods of sport-specific training. Intuitively, a combination of growth and training would be expected to optimise performance but there are limited data on this aspect of youth soccer.

In this chapter, data from youth soccer and training studies in athletic and average groups of children and adolescents are considered. From these studies key principles and concepts in the development of cardiorespiratory and anaerobic fitness, speed, strength and power are highlighted. Initially, the chapter aims to outline the basic components of fitness as well as the demands of the game played by youngsters. Models of fitness training are then considered in the context of ages and stages of development. Finally, the effects of training on components of fitness are outlined.

COMPONENTS OF FITNESS

Fitness is multidimensional and involves several sub-components. Whilst the layperson may recognise the fitness terms of speed, strength, skill, stamina and suppleness, factor analysis of fitness measures reveals 11 components of fitness; five of these are health-related and six are skill-related. Both skill- and health-related measures of fitness are relevant to successful soccer performance. The distinction between skill- and health-related fitness is that health-related measures are thought to be most important for general health, whereas skill-related components provide the added qualities required for participation in sport. Every individual possesses a certain standard in each of the 11 components of fitness. It is the quality and quantity of these components that determine overall fitness. Specialisation in these components enables players to demonstrate their advanced competence in sport-related contexts such as soccer. Deficiencies in fitness will affect the ability of a player to express technical and tactical abilities during game play. The following describes the sub-components of skill- and health-related fitness.

Health-related fitness (HRF)

Cardiovascular fitness refers to the ability of the body to engage in whole-body exercise that lasts for several minutes or more. The main form of cardiovascular exercise in soccer is running. *Strength* is defined as the maximal amount of force that the skeletal muscles can exert. Strength is required in various aspects of soccer but particularly when in contact for the ball with an opponent. Strength is also a significant sub-component of power. *Local muscular endurance* is the ability to use the muscles repeatedly without undue fatigue or stress. Local muscular endurance may be observed during repeated short sprints over a phase of play. *Flexibility* can be described as the range of movement around a joint or series of joints. This component of fitness is thought to be crucial in applying skill and reducing the risk of injury. *Body composition* represents the relative contributions of major tissues of the body that are conveniently split into two compartments: lean body mass and fat mass.

Skill-related fitness (SRF)

Agility is the ability to change the position and control the movement of the body quickly and efficiently. Agility is central to successful soccer performance because of the requirements to twist, turn, jump and sprint. *Balance* is also a key component of fitness for soccer players. The ability to control posture while stationary or in motion is essential for ball control and the application of skill to the game situation. *Coordination* requires an efficient integration of the nervous system that controls movement of body parts in relation to each other. *Power* refers to the ability to exert large amounts of force over short periods of time. Strength and speed are key components of power which can be defined as mechanical work done per unit of time. *Reaction time* is the amount of time it takes to react to an external stimulus and finally *speed* is the ability to perform a movement or cover ground quickly. The ability to react rapidly and powerfully is clearly a prerequisite for the developing young soccer player.

The components of fitness are reasonably straightforward to understand and interpret when considered in isolation. However, match play involves interplay of all the components of fitness. To understand the demands of match play young players' physiological responses and movement behaviour need to be analysed. The demands of youth soccer have been studied using various notational and physiological measurement techniques. An analysis of youth soccer game play and the integration of fitness requirements for performance are considered next.

THE DEMANDS OF THE GAME

In Chapter 10 various game playing and game training situations are described for different ages and stages of development. The main principle adhered to in most football nations is that the number of players and the size of the pitch increase with age and stage of development. In the USA matches for under 8s are split into quarters of 12 minutes; this schedule progresses to two 25-minute halves by under 10, 30-minute halves by under 12, progressing to 45-minute halves by under 19.

The demands of soccer depend on a number of factors, such as the environmental conditions, level of performance, positional role and tactics, strategies and playing style used by the team. Youth soccer games involve multiple short sprints, slow jogging, walking, jumping, tackling, kicking and changing direction. Rapid recovery from efforts to maintain or regain possession of the ball is essential if high exercise intensities during match play and practice are to be maintained. These efforts place significant demands on the energy systems of young players.

One of the few studies on the demands of pre-pubertal football used heart rate monitoring to estimate physiological stress during game play. Drust and Reilly (1997) monitored the heart rates of 11 boys and 7 girls at the mean age of 10 years. These players had between 4 and 5 years' playing experience. Mean heart rates were 170 ± 18 beats per minute and 167 ± 20 for boys and girls respectively after playing a 10-minute game and were similar to heart rates of 160–180 beats per minute in soccer matches involving German 11- and 12-year-old players (Klimt *et al.*, 1992). Heart rates increased by a further 10 beats after a second playing period of 10 minutes, in an eight-a-side game on a pitch 60 × 40 metres. These data show that youth football is a highly stressful game. Furthermore, heart rate ranges of 35 beats per minute also indicate the intermittent nature of the activity. Drust and Reilly's findings revealed a high cardiopulmonary strain during age-group football.

Klimt and colleagues (1992) also measured the anaerobic demands of the game and found mean blood lactates of 3–4 millimoles per litre during game play, supporting the theory that children have a limited anaerobic capacity. Furthermore, Felci and colleagues (1995) revealed that metabolic demand during child soccer was below the 'anaerobic threshold' although this depends on the threshold being used. In essence both studies demonstrated the highly aerobic nature of youth soccer. In adult soccer the demands of the game also vary by position. Felci and colleagues (1995) also found that heart rate and $\dot{V}O_2$ varied according to position. Furthermore, heart rates were more closely related to $\dot{V}O_2$ in midfielders than in forwards and defenders because of the more continuous nature of their running during match play. For most players divergence of heart rate and $\dot{V}O_2$ is a result of the intermittent nature of soccer play and highlights one of the main limitations in using heart rate in intermittent activities. Elite adult soccer has players running between 8 and 13 km at about 70–80 per cent of $\dot{V}O_{2max}$, the exercise varying from walking, sprinting, jogging, cruising, jumping, passing, tackling, heading and shooting. Each player is in contact with the ball for almost 3 minutes producing some 400 or more turns during the game.

There are limited parallel data available on age-group match play. An analysis of competitive matches of 12 junior teams showed that players made an average of 29 passes each (50 per cent successful), they received 34 passes (69 per cent successful), dribbled five times (38 per cent success rate), made two shots on goal (technical success 66 per cent, scoring success 8 per cent) and attempted 20 interceptions (59 per cent successful). Losers were less successful than winners in all movements, with particularly large differences for dribbling and shots on goal (Luhtanen, 1994).

Luhtanen and colleagues (2002) reported data on 106 16–18-year-old players from 6 first division clubs. Playing time ranged from 57 to 74 minutes. Boys and girls engaged in 31–37 and 32–34 offensive manoeuvres respectively. Boys also engaged in 20–22 defensive manoeuvres compared to 24–25 in girls. Boys' understanding of games was better than that of girls although movement in match play was similar.

Small-sided games may promote fitness more effectively than large-sided games. In a study comparing the demands of three-a-side and five-a-side junior soccer, Platt and colleagues (2001) found that three-a-side resulted in more high intensity activity, more overall distance covered, less jogging, less walking and higher heart rates than five-a-side. The research group concluded that three-a-side also provided a better learning experience for youngsters.

In summary, data on youth soccer game play reveal demands similar to those reported for adults. However, in competitive match play, adolescent footballers representing their academies spent 63 and 37 per cent of the match in anaerobic and aerobic zones respectively (Billows et al., 2003). These data are different to responses in adult matches where players spend 66 and 34 per cent of the time in aerobic and anaerobic zones respectively. Grant and colleagues (1999) also discovered that players in eight-a-side youth soccer matches spent less time standing still, covered more distance, made more passes and provided more activity near goal than eleven-a-side soccer. The effects of reduced pitch dimensions, game duration and number of players per team need more detailed investigation as does the scientific study of female soccer players. The following section on principles of training for age-group soccer is therefore constructed on expert opinion and child training theories rather than on direct evidence from youth soccer game play.

PRINCIPLES OF TRAINING

Training should attempt to match the functional movements and precise demands of game play as closely as possible. The major aim of training for soccer should be to improve performance in game-related tasks. The sports scientist should have knowledge of the effects of training on specific biological systems before attempting to identify those that contribute most to elite performance. Training should be designed with safety and injury avoidance as priorities. If soccer players are to reap the benefits of investing time and energy in training, then programmes should be designed to provide optimal effects. This aim requires adherence to carefully planned and executed activities. Moreover, the principles of training are broadly the same for elite athletes maximising performance, and individuals training to promote their health. During the early years of sports participation players should not be expected to specialise but should participate in a range of activities that promote sound movement fundamentals; later specialisation allows greater focus on specialist football skills.

For the purposes of this section, five principles of training are identified and coaches of young footballers should consider these. They are: specificity, progression, overload, reversibility and type. In addition, training is quantified by frequency, intensity and time (duration). The acronym for these terms grouped together is SPORTFIT.

Specificity

Exercises should be specific to the activity that is to be undertaken. Demands of the game should be used to develop programmes of training and exercise. Genetic, maturational, age and psychological factors contribute to individual differences in training responses. Young players arrive at training with varying levels of fitness. The effects of training are maximised when coaches are able to develop programmes that are specific to the individual capacities of the young players.

Progression

After soccer fundamentals have been developed, training volume should be increased progressively. Coaches should ensure that the physiological system being trained is loaded to full capacity to allow training adaptations to take place. Progression needs to take account of growth periods and incorporate gradual increases in a safe and effective manner. Coaches should plan training stages in a graded manner by adjusting the duration, intensity and/or frequency of training according to individual needs.

Overload

To bring about improvement, a physiological system should be loaded to full capacity. By exercising above a normal level, a variety of training adaptations (such as an increase in muscle size and coordination, improvements in cardiopulmonary function) enable the body to function more efficiently. Growth velocity increases during puberty causing young male players to lose flexibility as bone grows more quickly than other tissues. The flexibility of girls increases at this stage due to hormonal changes and structural alterations to the pelvis.

The appropriate overload for each individual can be achieved by manipulating combinations of training duration, intensity, frequency and mode. Coaches should avoid 'overtraining' young players, otherwise burnout and/or injury may occur (see Chapter 4). Particular care should be taken during periods of rapid growth, especially during puberty.

Reversibility

Training must be maintained if performance level is to be sustained. Detraining occurs rapidly when an adult stops exercising, although decrements in fitness of youngsters may not be so apparent because of growth. In studies of adults undergoing 7 to 30 days' complete bed rest, $\dot{V}O_{2max}$ decreased by between 5 and 28 per cent. Limited data are available on children and none has been reported on elite, young soccer players. Rowland (1994) serially measured the $\dot{V}O_{2max}$ of five, 7- to 11-year-old children who had been in a non-weight bearing condition for over 10 weeks due to femoral fractures. He reported that $\dot{V}O_{2max}$ increased by 13.3 per cent from 37.2 to 42.9 ml·kg^{-1}·min^{-1} by the third month of recovery. On average a 5 per cent increase in $\dot{V}O_{2max}$ would be expected (Payne and Morrow, 1993) thus suggesting that $\dot{V}O_2$ had decreased to a point where large and rapid increases would be expected after bed rest. This study on the effect of detraining in growing children revealed results similar to those in adults. Decreases in more highly trained youngsters such as elite young soccer players would probably be greater than their sub-elite counterparts.

Type

Different types of training should be utilised and matched to the demands of the game. Variety is important and training activities should be interesting and educational. Greater focus on soccer-specific training occurs with increase in age. During childhood to early teens, it is essential that coaches encourage participation in a range of activities. This may involve participation in other sports and activities that develop key fundamental skills and fitness components. Activities may involve game play, athletics, gymnastics and resistance exercises using body weight. Fixed apparatus may also be used where appropriate.

Frequency

Training frequency refers to the number of times an individual trains in a given period of time. A youngster may train three times a week including physical education lessons in order to improve health and fitness levels whereas an elite young swimmer may train 12 times a week. Frequency of training in youngsters depends on their stage of training, stage of maturation, level of performance and type of sport in which they participate. Early specialisation sports such as gymnastics and swimming require high frequency of training before the teen years. Sports such as soccer do not require specialisation at this early stage.

Intensity

Training-induced adaptations are closely related to the magnitude of overload. Exercise intensity reflects both the calorific cost of the work and the specific energy systems activated. Relative intensity can be measured as a percentage of maximum function, e.g. maximum heart rate, weight lifted, exercises completed. Intensity of exercise should not decrease motivation or risk injury in the growing athlete. Care should be taken during periods of rapid growth to monitor closely how players respond to the intensity of training. Coaches should be aware of typical injuries that can occur around the growth spurt during monitoring (see Chapter 4).

Time (duration)

Training duration refers to the length of time that is spent in a training session. Duration of training will vary among elite, sub-elite and recreational players and will also be affected by age and stage of maturation. Training sessions of young soccer players should include elements of game play and should last no longer than an hour. As training becomes more specific, the time spent training and playing can be gradually increased to adult levels.

The principles of SPORTFIT should assist coaches in developing training programmes. The contextual background for these training programmes will vary according to ability level, age and stage of maturation and development of the players. A combination of the long-term athlete development model (LTADM) (see Balyi and Hamilton, 1999), the identification of sensitive periods for training certain components of fitness by Mero and colleagues (1990), and the structuring of training for potentially elite athletes (Arbeit, 1998) should help soccer coaches identify priorities for training at each age and stage of development. These three reports are discussed in the sections that follow.

THE LONG-TERM ATHLETE DEVELOPMENT MODEL (LTADM)

Each stage of this model is discussed from an educational perspective in Chapter 10. The LTADM concept is discussed in two chapters in this text. Each stage of the model is described in this chapter from an exercise training perspective, whereas Chapter 10 concentrates on educational goals. The LTADM of Balyi and Hamilton (1999) provides clear aims for each stage of athlete development. This model is suitable for all sports including activities such as gymnastics and

Table 6.1 Major principles for training using the long-term athlete development model

	Fundamentals 5–11 years	Training to train 11–14 years	Training to compete 14–16 years	Training to win 16–18 years
Guidelines for training programmes	• Basic skills • Short duration activities • Endurance developed through game play • Body awareness activities • Strength developed through hopping and skipping and other body weight exercises	• Players 'learn how to train' during this phase. • Monitor and individualise training • Chronological age may not be the best way to categorise players • Limb growth may require refinement of skill and technique • More structured aerobic training • Short duration anaerobic work • Develop speed and neurological capacity in the warm-up	• Largest changes occur during this phase • Aerobic and anaerobic systems trained for maximum output • Strength training maximised • Gradual progression in training overload • Learning how to compete – technical, tactical, etc.	• Specialist support used when required including sport science and medicine professionals • Advanced physical training techniques utilised • Close monitoring to avoid overtraining

Source: Adapted from Balyi and Hamilton, 1999.

developing fitness in young soccer players

swimming where early specialisation is imperative. As soccer is not a sport characterised by early specialisation the four stages of the LTADM – fundamentals, training to train, training to compete and training to win – cater for 5–11, 11–14, 14–16 and 16–18-year-olds respectively. Each stage provides flexible, generic guidelines for training youngsters.

Coaches should use these guidelines when developing programmes for each stage of the model. Even though this model is not 'perfect in all respects', it is well thought out and clearly developed. However, this is not a complete model as one of the problems with the LTADM is that while maturation is mentioned no practical methods of adapting training during pubertal stages are suggested. Coaches should refer to Chapter 2 in this text for information on maturation and stages of development. Soccer training intensity can be gradually increased through the growth cycle. Coaches would also benefit from direction and guidance on 'sensitive periods' during growth and development. The LTADM has four stages, each stage having clear goals. These goals become more specific starting from a generic fun approach in the 'fundamentals' stage through to a highly scientific, medically and professionally supported programme in the 'training to win' stage. Mero and colleagues (1990) have proposed a complementary training model to the LTADM for youngsters. This model focuses specifically on components of fitness. The model of Mero and colleagues is useful in that it highlights 'sensitive periods' for training aspects of fitness by age.

Figure 6.1 illustrates sensitive development periods for the progression of stride rate, flexibility and fundamental skills from ages 5 to 15 years followed by strength, stride length, aerobic and anaerobic endurance around the adolescent growth spurt. The parallel model for maturation age is not available in the literature. Such a model would account for the intensity of exercise and practice in training plans during the adolescent growth spurt. Arbeit (1998) further developed the content of training for pubescent to adult stages of development in potentially elite youth athletes. Arbeit suggested that the importance of speed in training programmes gains significance for invasive games such as soccer. In this approach training is subdivided into four distinct and progressive phases – basic, build-up, connecting, and high performance and these are described below.

Basic training

Basic training involves a range of sports where emphasis is placed on developing techniques and fitness individually and in groups. Basic training takes place in 90-minute blocks, 4 times per week for 45 weeks per year. This would occur during early to late puberty phases in boys and girls. The ability of youngsters to cope with the psychological and physiological demands of training is also assessed.

89

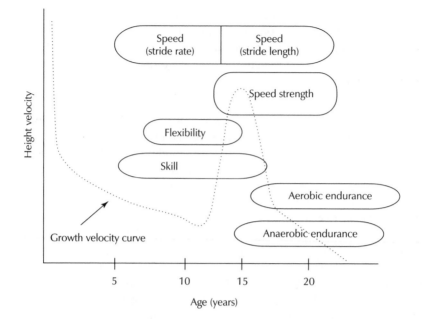

Figure 6.1 The importance of training components of fitness according to chronological age and height velocity

Source: Adapted from Mero et al., 1990.

Build-up training

This form of training should be delivered through specialist sports involving 12–18 hours per week and two 14–18 day training camps annually. During this stage, coaches decide whether athletes can tolerate and adapt to the loads. The development of coordination and speed also occupies a significant part of the training programme during this phase. Furthermore, loads should not increase by more than 25 per cent over the period (1st–2nd phase of puberty). Resistance exercise using body weight is prioritised over more specialised forms of weight training. Fitness is monitored twice a year.

Connecting phase of training

The connecting phase of training progresses the build-up phase. In this phase individually tailored training plans are the norm. Loads are increased progressively on an annual basis by 15–20 per cent and time spent training is increased by 5–10 per cent. Fitness is monitored up to four times per year.

High performance training

High performance training includes all the aspects of the previous phases whilst specialist training for strength, speed, endurance and flexibility is added. Fitness is monitored at least four times per year depending on the structure of the training programme and competitive season.

Arbeit's training programme is similar in emphasis and progression to the 'training to train', 'training to compete' and 'training to win' phases of the LTADM. The difference is that his programme emphasises maturation as opposed to chronological age. This training programme suggests that 6–8 years are required before an athlete is psychologically and physically shaped and ready for competitive performance at a high level. Furthermore, regular monitoring of fitness during training is recommended for this programme. Fitness testing is therefore central to conducting effective training programmes.

FITNESS TESTING

If young soccer players are going to invest time in physical training, an effective monitoring and evaluation programme needs to be used to assess progress. Fitness testing enables soccer coaches to judge whether a player has particular strengths and weaknesses, whether training has been effective in improving fitness and performance, or to help decide when a player should best return from injury. Monitoring should enable coaches to create individual training pathways using the LTADM and Mero's and Arbeit's approaches for guidance. When it forms part of a planned programme, fitness assessment serves as a vehicle to promote excellence in young players. There are many reasons for implementing fitness testing programmes and coaches should understand the broad-reaching aims that fitness testing can meet in young soccer players.

Aims of fitness testing

1   To develop youngsters' understanding of fitness and how it is related to performance (training to train).
2   To provide measures of fitness for girls and boys of different ages and stages of development.
3   To track changes in fitness related to growth.
4   To assist in identifying talented soccer players.
5   To enable children to recognise their strengths and weaknesses.

6 To check fitness levels before returning from injury.
7 To help children develop strategies to cope with success and failure.
8 To develop cooperation and support in a competitive situation.
9 To compare players' fitness against that of others in similar age groups.

There are two main categories of fitness testing – field and laboratory tests. The number of fitness tests available is almost infinite and it is beyond the scope of this chapter to describe individual fitness tests. The Eurofit test battery (Adam and Filliard, 1985) will be described later (for a review of fitness tests for soccer see Reilly and Doran, 2003; for paediatric fitness testing see Docherty, 1996). 'Field tests' are particularly suitable for large population groups; they require limited equipment and expertise to implement and are portable for field contexts. 'Laboratory tests' on the other hand require specialist equipment used by personnel who have expertise in advanced measurement systems and are able to interpret scientific test data. Laboratory tests provide sensitive measures of physiological systems compared to field tests that provide measures of gross motor performance.

In both field and laboratory, the single most important aim is quality control in the conduct of the tests. It is then possible to have confidence in the results. To achieve this confidence, tests must be administered consistently and accurately. All fitness tests must be *valid*, *reliable* and *objective*. Valid fitness tests are those that measure the component of fitness that they purport to measure. For example, if a test of cardiorespiratory fitness is required then the exercise should last for at least 6 minutes; if a test of maximal strength is required then one maximal effort of no more than 3 seconds is required. Players must also have tests clearly and consistently described to them in a positive motivational climate that emphasises personal achievement above (but not excluding) competition.

When implementing field tests (known as a battery), grouping players of similar fitness level should assist in this process. Finally when youngsters understand 'why' they are doing the test they will comply with test conditions and achieve good results. Fitness testing should be well planned, with all resources and facilities checked for availability, safety and suitability. Back-up replacements of certain pieces of equipment that may fail or break down is essential and contingency plans for poor weather, different numbers and ages of players, illness of testers and injury to participants should be allowed for.

Prior to conducting any tests a formal risk assessment should be completed. The risk assessment should outline the relative risks of the tests and the steps taken to minimise and control them. In addition the project leader should gain signed and informed consent from parents/guardians and assent from players (under the age of 18). To achieve this, a letter must be sent to parents/guardians outlining the aims of the battery and the nature of the tests to be undertaken. Appended to the information letter should be two forms to be signed, one by the parent/guardian and one by the child. Both forms should include a clause that allows the child to withdraw from any part of the testing at any time. All testers and coaches who work with children must also seek clearance from child protection and criminal register bureaux. Where testing is part of a research project ethical clearance should be sought.

Much of the data presented in Chapter 2 from the Liverpool children's fitness project used the Eurofit motor fitness test battery (Adam and Filliard, 1985) as well as measures of height, weight and skin fold thickness. The test battery is outlined in Table 2 and each test subsequently described.

Eurofit test battery

To support the principles of reliability and validity of fitness tests, each item of testing should be placed in the most effective order. The 'battery' of tests proposed by the Eurofit programme was carried out in the order outlined in Table 6.2.

Table 6.2 The Eurofit fitness test battery

Dimensions	Factor	Eurofit test	Other tests	Order of test
Balance	Total body balance	Flamingo balance	None	1
Speed	Limb speed	Plate tapping	None	2
Flexibility	Flexibility	Sit and reach	None	3
Power	Explosive strength	Standing broad jump	Vertical jump	4
Strength	Static strength	Hand grip	None	5
Muscular endurance	Trunk strength	Sit ups	None	6
Muscular endurance	Functional strength	Bent arm hang	Modified pull up	7
Speed	Running speed agility	Shuttle run 10 × 5m	30 m sprint	8
Cardiorespiratory fitness	Cardiorespiratory fitness	Endurance shuttle run	None	9

Source: Adam and Filliard, 1985.

Flamingo balance

Total-body balance is measured using a metal beam 50 cm long, 5 cm high and 3 cm wide. The beam is stabilised by two supports at each end. Each child is requested to stand on the beam barefoot (preferred foot). The free leg is flexed at the knee with the foot held close to the buttocks. The child moves into balance by holding the instructor's hand. On leaving go of the instructor's hand the stopwatch is started. Each time the child loses balance (by leaving go of the foot being held or falling off the beam) the clock is stopped. The child may then get back on to the beam and repeat the process. The number of losses of balance over 60 seconds is recorded. A child losing balance more than 15 times in the first 30 seconds scores zero.

Speed

Upper limb speed is measured using a plate-tapping test. Two yellow discs 20 cm in diameter are placed with centres 60 cm apart on a table. A rectangle (30 × 20 cm) is placed equidistant between both discs. With the non-preferred hand on the triangle the child moves the preferred hand back and forth between the discs as quickly as possible. This action is repeated and the time taken to complete 25 cycles is recorded.

Sit-and-reach test

The sit-and-reach test is primarily a measure of lower back and hip flexibility. The subject sits down with bare feet against a purpose-designed sit-and-reach box. The child is asked to reach with the fingertips as far forward as possible while keeping the legs straight. A score of 15 cm indicates that the subject has touched his/her toes. A score greater than 15 indicates a reach past the toes.

Power

Although power output is not measured or calculated, the standing broad jump is used as an indirect index of leg power. A graduated mat is used to record distances. Subjects are required to jump with a two-footed take-off from the scratch line. The furthest distance achieved in three trials is recorded.

Hand grip strength

Hand grip strength is measured using a grip dynamometer. The grip size is adjusted individually. Avoiding contact with the body, the dynamometer is

94

squeezed as hard as possible for 3 seconds. The best score from two trials is recorded.

Abdominal curl (sit up) test

This test varied from the one described in the Eurofit manual. Children were far better at pacing their sit ups if given audio cues. The National Coaching Foundation's (NCF) abdominal curls test is a multistage sit-up test in which the children sit up in time with beeps that become progressively faster at the end of each minute of the test. Children have good compliance to this test and complete full sit ups correctly.

Modified pull ups

The modified 'pull up' is a measure of local muscular endurance and functional strength of the upper body. This test represents another deviation from the standard Eurofit test. This YMCA youth fitness test (Franks, 1989) is more suitable for children because of their difficulty in completing one single orthodox pull up. The modified pull up allows children to hang from a bar supine, body straight, heels on floor and arms at full length in the start position. The chin is then raised above the bar. The maximum number of pull ups completed in 30 seconds is recorded.

The 10 × 5 metre shuttle run

The 10 × 5 m shuttle run is designed to measure running speed and agility. The test assesses the time it takes for a child to complete 10 runs of 5 m. At the end of each 5-m length both feet should cross the line indicating the 5-m mark. The time taken to complete 50 m is recorded.

The 20-metre-multistage shuttle run test

This test requires children to run shuttles of 20 m in time to bleeps recorded on an audiotape. Every minute the space between the beeps is reduced and therefore the children have to run faster to keep up with the beeps. Children continue with the test until they are exhausted and can no longer keep up with the beeps. The number of 20-m shuttles completed is recorded. The $\dot{V}O_{2max}$ can also be estimated from the results of the 20-m-multistage shuttle run test.

The Eurofit test battery is one field method of assessing the fitness of youth soccer players. There are other batteries such as the Fitnessgram and the AAPHERD Physical Best. For a critical review of fitness test batteries, see Docherty (1996).

Monitoring fitness is central to any fitness programme. Training programmes to improve cardiorespiratory and anaerobic fitness as well as strength, speed and power in children and adolescents will be discussed next.

CARDIORESPIRATORY FITNESS

In young soccer players, cardiorespiratory fitness can increase because of the combined or separate effects of growth and training. Training has a number of positive effects on the player's physiological systems within skeletal muscle. Mitochondria have a greatly increased capacity to generate ATP and increase in size and number with training in adults. Children would normally be expected to have a greater mitochondrial density than adults although this comparison has not been extensively studied. Training increases the body's ability to mobilise and metabolise fat and trained muscle has an increased capacity to oxidise carbohydrate. Furthermore, the activity of aerobic enzymes decreases from childhood to adulthood. In addition, positive structural changes result from endurance training. Increase in heart contractility, left ventricular volume and wall thickness, decreased peripheral resistance, increased stroke volume and cardiac output occur in children but not to the same extent as in adults. In children blood volume tends to remain stable after training compared to adults who experience training-induced increases in plasma and haemoglobin concentrations. Likewise, children do not experience the same increases in capillary density after training as adults do. Resting and sub-maximal heart rate decreases but maximal heart rate remains unchanged in both children and adults. Overall, children and adults do not necessarily adapt to training modes in the same way. This difference tends to disappear after puberty when training adaptations in adolescents are similar to adults.

Testing cardiorespiratory endurance

There are a number of maximal and sub-maximal tests for laboratory and field use with children. These have been comprehensively reviewed by Leger (1996) and the main ones are dealt with here in outline only.

Laboratory testing

Maximal oxygen uptake can be tested in the laboratory using an ergometer and indirect calorimetry system. Values depend on the ergometer used, treadmill protocols yielding the highest values. Oxygen kinetics ($\dot{V}O_2$ 'on response') are twice as fast in children as in adults and subsequently physiological steady state during exercise is reached earlier in youngsters. Because steady state is reached earlier, incremental increases in workload of 2–3 per cent can be applied every 2 minutes. Tests should last between 6 and 12 minutes ideally. A similar approach is applied when using cycle ergometers where loads are increased every 2 minutes by 0.35 and 0.30 $W \cdot kg^{-1}$ for boys and girls respectively. To ensure that children have worked to maximum during the exercise test, criterion end points for exercise are used. Age-predicted maximal heart rate (up to 200 beats per minute max), respiratory exchange ratio ($\dot{V}CO_2/\dot{V}O_2$) of 1.05 for the treadmill and 1.10 for the cycle ergometer are commonly used physiological end points. In addition to physiological end points, other parameters such as signs of extreme exhaustion, ataxic gait or dyspnoea should also be used. True maximal aerobic power is rarely achieved in children so the criteria for maximal end points should be applied before the test is deemed valid. Where sub-maximal tests are used, raw results should be reported rather than using adult prediction equations to predict child results. Sub-maximal tests are most commonly implemented by measuring heart rate and relating values to exercise intensity (treadmill) or load (cycle ergometer). There is a linear relationship between heart rate and $\dot{V}O_2$ within the heart rate range of 120 and 170 beats per minute although this has not been proven in children. There are two commonly used sub-maximal tests, the Astrand-Rhyming test and the PWC_{170} test, with the former predicting $\dot{V}O_{2max}$ and the latter the work rate (watts) that can be achieved when heart rate is at 170 $beats \cdot min^{-1}$. Since resting and sub-maximal heart rates reduce from childhood to adulthood, sub-maximal tests such as these should be used with caution in children. Time to reach $\dot{V}O_{2max}$ is a simple, repeatable and acceptable test of performance but does not help to explain mechanisms that cause changes in fitness. There are similar issues with the 20-metre-multistage shuttle run test and other field tests of endurance such as the 6 and 9 minute or 1 and 1.5 mile (1.6 and 2.4 km) runs. Details of exercise protocols can be found elsewhere in the literature (Leger, 1996; Armstrong and van Mechelen, 2000).

In adults, appropriate volumes of aerobic training will increase cardiorespiratory fitness by up to 15–20 per cent. As $\dot{V}O_{2max}$ is significantly correlated to distance covered during the adult game, developing this aspect of fitness in the long term is important. A review of training studies on pre-pubertal children reported that cardiorespiratory fitness only increased if exercise was undertaken three times per week for 20 minutes at an intensity equivalent to 75 per cent of maximum heart rate. Even when these criteria were met, there was only a 5 per cent increase in $\dot{V}O_{2max}$ suggesting a difference in training adaptation between children and adults. To compare soccer players' cardiorespiratory fitness to the general untrained population the mean results for girls and boys of 5–18 years of age are required. The mean $\dot{V}O_{2peak}$ in girls decreases from 50 to about

predictor of future endurance performance (Jankovic et al., 1997). It is also worth noting that even though the maximal aerobic power of young soccer players is high, it does not reach the levels reported for young elite swimmers and runners (Rowland, 1996).

TRAINING TO INCREASE MAXIMAL AEROBIC POWER

Training studies involving youngsters have demonstrated that training can increase aerobic power although results are equivocal. Physical education programmes designed to maintain high activity levels (165–172 beats per minute) similar to those reported for child soccer play (Drust and Reilly, 1997) did not significantly increase $\dot{V}O_{2max}$. In contrast, rigorous training programmes of long duration can increase maximal aerobic power in children by up to 10 per cent. In youngsters, training programmes that involve continuous running and intermittent exercise (games, interval running) also tend to be more successful in increasing weight-related aerobic power and running time in 8–13-year-olds. In adolescents over the age of 13, changes in body composition, cardiac structure and haematological parameters should result in greater changes at this age. Katch (1983) has described adolescence as a more effective period to induce training effects (the 'trigger hypothesis'). But the literature suggests that increases in aerobic power in children before and during puberty are similar. It appears that adolescence is a better time to promote aerobic fitness training than before puberty (Rowland, 1996). Both Arbeit's and Balyi and Hamilton's LTADM training stages also indirectly acknowledge Katch's view. Soccer coaches should note that 'interval' as well as continuous running can increase aerobic power in youngsters. As intermittent running is typical of soccer, then appropriate game play activities that focus on fitness as well as skill should promote cardiorespiratory endurance in young soccer players particularly before puberty.

One of the problems with comparing elite athletes to the normal population is the fact that athletes may respond differently to training. On the basis that soccer players tend to be fitter than the average population, studies that attempt to improve the aerobic power of children with high aerobic power would be of interest to soccer coaches. Pate and Ward (1990) failed to find a relationship between pre-training aerobic power and increases after training. Therefore, changes in $\dot{V}O_2$ were not dependent on whether the initial state of training was high or low. The majority of evidence also suggests that increases are smaller for weight-related $\dot{V}O_{2max}$ compared to absolute values. This suggests that changes in body mass (growth) contribute significantly to changes in $\dot{V}O_{2max}$ during growth. The increases in maximal aerobic power resulting from a variety of exercise training modalities support the hypothesis that children and adolescents are 'metabolic non-specialists'. Therefore, there is scientific evidence to support training plans that include a varied diet of game playing, fun and exercise type activities whilst avoiding over-specialised training during childhood.

Changes in sub-maximal responses to exercise are commonly reported to result from training. In a classical study Massicote and McNab (1974) matched training frequency and duration but varied intensity by using training heart rates of 130–140, 150–160 and 170–180 beats per minute in three groups of boys. All groups increased their physical work capacity but only the group training at the highest intensity significantly increased their $\dot{V}O_{2max}$. The increase in work capacity is most likely to be a result of an increased stroke volume. Another measure of sub-maximal change is ventilatory anaerobic threshold (T_{vent}) which occurs when ventilation increases out of proportion to $\dot{V}O_2$ during incremental exercise. Twenty to 30 per cent increases in T_{vent} can occur after training. Paterson and colleagues (1987) measured T_{vent} annually on a group of active boys involved in a variety of sports training. The ventilatory threshold increased from 56 per cent at 11 to 61.6 per cent of $\dot{V}O_{2max}$ at 15 years of age. Ventilatory threshold is more sensitive to training than is $\dot{V}O_{2max}$ and changes in this physiological parameter are usually greater. Blood lactate also reflects the load placed on the anaerobic system and the onset of blood lactate accumulation (OBLA) has been used to detect sub-maximal adaptations in much the same way as ventilatory threshold.

Blood lactate accumulates when the aerobic system is unable to meet the energy demands of the working muscle. This excess demand is met by the anaerobic system resulting in increased lactate production. The net OBLA is a result of lactate production by the working muscle and hepatic clearance. Effective training programmes result in increased running velocity for the same fixed blood lactate concentration. Figure 6.2 illustrates how the lactate curve 'shifts to the right' after training in young populations.

Children produce smaller concentrations of lactate than adults during exercise because of lower concentrations of anaerobic enzymes and higher concentrations of aerobic enzymes such as citrate synthase and succinate dehydrogenase. Little work has been done concerning OBLA in elite child athletes and many methodological considerations with respect to lactate concentrations corresponding to set exercise interventions need to be considered with youngsters. Mahon (2000) has suggested that the increase in running velocity after training on OBLA is likely to be a result of improved clearance of lactate by the heart and liver. As distance run is an important aspect of soccer performance the ability to maintain high work rates before blood lactate accumulates is advantageous for the young soccer player.

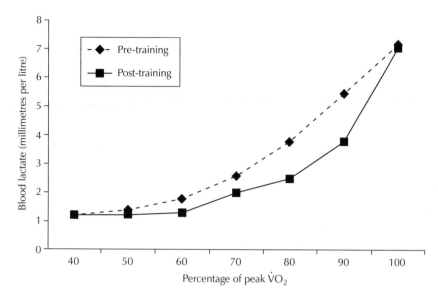

Figure 6.2 Changes in blood lactate before and after training

Source: Redrawn from Armstrong and Van Mechelen, 2000.

Field tests of aerobic performance such as the 20-metre-multistage shuttle run test (20MST), 1 mile run, 6 or 9 minute run have all been used as indirect measures of aerobic fitness. These tests are really measures of 'endurance performance' which is constituted of running economy, $\dot{V}O_{2max}$ and maximal speed at $\dot{V}O_{2max}$. Endurance performance may also be affected by psychological factors such as motivation. Nevertheless, Berthoin (1994) suggested that endurance time at any percentage of $\dot{V}O_{2max}$ remains stable throughout childhood and adolescence. Therefore, field measures of endurance performance such as the 20MST are useful tools of measurement for coaches who do not have easy access to laboratory instruments. Whatever mode of measurement is used to detect training effects, increases in aerobic performance are normally greater in adults than children. As soccer players develop from childhood to adulthood, qualitative (skill, running economy, decision-making) and quantitative (size, speed, power, distance) changes combine to increase sensitivity to training. Coaches should consider these issues carefully before making training programmes too specific too early.

ANAEROBIC FITNESS

During high intensity, short-term exercise lasting from 1–2 seconds to 2 minutes, the rate of energy production required is high. This energy demand is met largely through anaerobic sources. Soccer game play is made up of many short bursts of high intensity exercise and therefore the development of this aspect of fitness is crucial for optimal game performance. Perhaps the first aspect to consider is the relative difference in anaerobic power output between adults and children. A schematic representation of power output by time for an adult and a 13-year-old male reveals children's disadvantage in both alactic and lactic anaerobic components of fitness (Figure 6.3).

Children are described as metabolic non-specialists and have a relatively inefficient anaerobic metabolism compared to adults. When training youngsters, high intensity activity that lasts for up to 15 seconds or lower intensity aerobic type activity is preferable prior to puberty.

As with aerobic power, maximal anaerobic power seems to be greater in elite athletes than their average counterparts. In a typical anaerobic sport such as wrestling, Sady and co-workers (1984) found significantly greater peak and mean power than in child wrestlers compared to untrained children. There are also limited anaerobic power data on young soccer players. In a study that used the

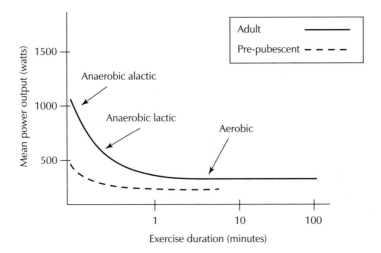

Figure 6.3 Maximal power output for a child and adult male in relation to the duration of exercise

Source: Adapted from Van Praagh, 1998.

Wingate anaerobic test (WanT) Walden and Yates (2000) reported mean and peak power values for 18–22-year-old and 14–18-year-old female soccer players of 363 ($\pm$51) and 415 ($\pm$60) and 340 ($\pm$43) and 391 ($\pm$47) watts respectively. These were lower than those reported for elite players. Engels and Wirth (2000) revealed mean and peak power output of 374.3 ($\pm$57) and 503 ($\pm$85.3) watts respectively, and a relative peak power output of 10.1W·kg^{-1} for 13–14-year-old elite female players. Al Hazzaa and colleagues (2000) also found significant differences in mean power between 13- and 14-year-old untrained boys and their soccer-playing peers.

Few authors have investigated the effects of training on anaerobic performance. In a context similar to football training, Grodjinovsky and Bar-Or (1984) examined the effects of a 7-month training programme on mean and peak anaerobic power. The exercise programme consisted of six physical education classes per week and three days' training in European handball after school. The experimental group significantly increased their mean and peak anaerobic power after the programme in comparison to the control group. Mosher and co-workers (1985) trained 10–11-year-old elite soccer players for 12 weeks. Training involved high-speed interval runs for 15–20 minutes, three times per week. A 7 mph (11.2 km·h^{-1}) treadmill run at an 18 per cent gradient and a 40-yard sprint time were used to assess anaerobic fitness. Trained children's treadmill endurance increased by 20 per cent from 51.5 to 62.3 seconds and differences were significantly larger than those found in the control group. When analysing training modalities, McManus and colleagues (1997) reported a 20 per cent increase in peak power in pre-pubertal girls following an 8-week endurance-training programme. The gains in the endurance-trained group were twice those achieved in a sprint-trained group. On the other hand Docherty and co-workers (1987) found no significant increases in peak power after a 4-week resistance exercise programme. Their training programme was probably too short in duration to stimulate significant changes.

In summary the effects of exercise training result in increased mean and peak power output and anaerobic performance. Furthermore, young male and female soccer players are reported to have higher anaerobic power output than average children. This characteristic is either inherited, and thus one of the reasons why they are successful at soccer, or is a result of the stimulus of playing soccer or more likely a combination of both. As with cardiorespiratory fitness, increases in anaerobic power may be best stimulated during adolescence as changes may be mediated by increases in muscle mass although more allometrically scaled data need to be reported before this issue is fully elucidated.

STRENGTH, POWER AND SPEED

Strength, power and speed are inextricably linked to successful soccer performance. Coaches and physical educators are aware that training can increase speed, strength and power during childhood and adolescence. The factors contributing to strength, speed and power development are illustrated in Figure 6.4.

Figure 6.4 primarily outlines the key mechanisms contributing to change in strength towards adult strength potential. It is clear that both neural development and muscle fibre distribution mature rapidly after birth whereas testosterone plays a role at puberty and thereafter. Furthermore, strength through childhood to early puberty largely relies on motor patterning, whereas the consolidation of strength factors, including the effects of testosterone, occur after puberty through to adulthood where strength potential is reputed to be optimal. As in adults, the ability to exert force rapidly relies on muscle fibre distribution. It has been thought that young children have a greater proportion of fast twitch fibres than adults because they participate in short bursts of high intensity exercise on a frequent

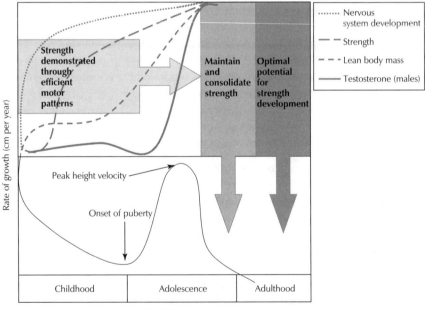

Figure 6.4 Factors affecting muscle strength during growth and maturation
Source: Adapted from Kraemer et al., 1989.

developing fitness in young soccer players

basis. It seems that the percentages of fast and slow twitch fibres for athletic boys and girls are similar to those found in adults. Mero and co-workers (1990) reported that youngsters who participated in sports that required speed and power had over 50 per cent fast twitch fibres whereas children who participated in aerobic activities possessed about 40 per cent fast twitch fibres. Muscle biopsies on 37 14–16-year-old Spanish amateur soccer players revealed that 51–54 per cent of fibres were fast twitch (Amigo et al., 1998). These percentages are similar for athletes specialising in speed and power events (Mero et al., 1990). Furthermore, the percentage of fast twitch muscle increased from 51 per cent at 14 to 54 per cent at 16 years of age showing a slight increase in fast twitch fibres with age. However, the subjects were amateur players and, as in other sports, differences in fibre composition vary between elite and sub-elite participants.

Regular participation in high intensity soccer should result in higher than average strength, power and speed in young players. In a rare study on females Walden and Yates (2000) reported 40-metre sprint times of 6.1 (±0.3) and 6.0 (±0.3) seconds in 14–18- and 18–22-year-old players respectively. Sprint times were slower than the 6.2 seconds reported for young adult females. When analysed by position, there were no significant differences in anaerobic power, speed, push-ups or vertical jumps by position. Franks and colleagues (2002) took various measurements on 64 international 14–16-year-old English soccer players and reported that players had high anaerobic power results measured through 15 and 40 metre sprints.

Training studies that aim to increase speed, power and strength have demonstrated greater relative changes than training programmes aimed at increasing cardiorespiratory fitness. On average, increases in performance have been impressive. Falk and Tenenbaum (1996) concluded from their meta-analysis that a child with an average score before a resistance exercise programme was 72 per cent stronger than a non-participating child after the programme. Increases in strength are also stimulated by interesting and varied exercise modalities, as long as the exercise is of very high intensity and sufficient duration. Diallo and colleagues (2000) implemented a plyometric training programme that involved hurling, skipping and jumping exercises three times per week for 10 weeks. This programme was followed by an 8-week period of detraining. Compared to the control group the 'jump' group demonstrated significantly greater increases in the squat jump, standing long jump, repeated rebound jump for 15 seconds and the counter-movement jump.

Further to these increases in performance using established field tests, laboratory studies also suggest that resistance exercise programmes have significant and positive effects on strength before puberty. Capranica and colleagues (1992) found no difference in isokinetic power between preferred and non-preferred legs

105

of young soccer players but revealed that players produced greater force output and power than non-athletes. This observation suggests that either soccer training promotes strength or that youngsters who inherit higher than average strength are more likely to be successful at soccer. Sadres and co-workers (2001) found significant differences in knee-extensor torque between control and experimental groups of pre-pubertal boys who trained twice a week for nine months for two consecutive school years. The programme involved two sessions per week, each session was made up of 3–6 exercises, 1–4 sets of 5–30 repetitions using loads equivalent to 30–70 per cent of repetition maximum. Similar results were found in Sadres' and Capranica's investigations, suggesting that soccer training may have a similar effect to a specific strength-training programme. These findings are useful as quadriceps strength and ball kicking velocity are related in adults (Lees and Davids, 2002).

Although resistance exercise can improve strength and power in youngsters, coaches would benefit from advice on the types of programme that would be most effective. Faigenbaum and co-workers (2001) compared different resistance training protocols on upper body strength and endurance development in pre-pubertal children. Four experimental and one control group were included in the twice weekly, 8-week exercise programme. Group G1 completed 6–8 repetitions on chest press; G2 6–8 reps and 6–8 passes of medicine ball weighing 1 or 2 kg. G3 completed 13–15 chest press repetitions; G4 13–15 medicine ball passes. The programme resulted in a 16 per cent increase in strength in groups G2 and G3 (p <0.05), 5 and 7 per cent increases in groups G1 and G4. Even though this programme was of short duration and had relatively small numbers of youngsters it demonstrates the differential effects of various training programmes on strength. The most successful resistance exercise programmes are those that include high loads and are carried out for significant periods.

Strength, power and speed development are stimulated by circulating androgens that increase at the onset of puberty in boys. Increases in muscle volume are a result of increasing levels of androgens and scientists therefore assume that increases in strength may be greatest after puberty. Conversely, Tsolakis and colleagues (2000) found that the effect of resistance exercise training in the strength of 11–13-year-old boys (124 per cent increase) was four times greater than 14–16-year-old boys (32 per cent). Hansen and colleagues (1999) in a short longitudinal study revealed that elite 11–12-year-old soccer players had significantly higher circulating testosterone and testicular volume than their non-elite counterparts. Baxter-Jones and Helms (1996) also found higher muscular strength scores in elite 10–18-year-old soccer players compared to the average population. Increases in strength, power and speed may result from a combination of factors. First, high intensity exercise stimulates increases in the release of androgens into the circulation. Second, continuous participation in soccer practice of high intensity improves muscle fibre coordination with subsequent increases in strength, speed and power output.

In summary, some of the largest increases in fitness have been the result of youngsters' participation in resistance exercise programmes of high intensity. These programmes involved a variety of exercise programmes and were developmentally appropriate.

OVERVIEW

Key aspects of fitness and training in young soccer players have been considered. The principles of training applied to children and adults are similar with the exception of reversibility. Reversibility is affected by growth; that is, if a child soccer player stops training his/her fitness may still increase. The progress will not be at the same rate as a similar youngster who continues training. Another key principle for coaches of young soccer players to understand is that children are not mini-adults. Children are described as metabolic non-specialists reflecting the positive effects of varied training programmes on their physical fitness performance. Young players should therefore not be pressed into specialising in soccer activity at too early an age.

The key principle outlined in the training models is that the initial phases of training should be based on the development of fundamentals with increasing specialisation with age (Mero et al., 1990; Balyi and Hamilton, 1999) and maturation stage (Arbeit, 1998). These models clearly state how and when to target specific aspects of fitness within a broad and motivating training programme. Furthermore, participation in regular and varied training 'can make a difference' to fitness performance in this age group. Gains in explosive aspects of fitness are greater than cardiorespiratory fitness.

When considering the demands of game play in youth soccer, it is clear that appropriate training can improve performance in this age group. However, one of the limitations in research studies is that much of the data are reported in relation to body size. This approach advantages smaller individuals and disadvantages larger ones. Scaling and allometric approaches should be adopted when accounting for differences in body size.

Coaches may need to consider that there may be sensitive periods for fitness promotion, particularly around adolescence. Katch's trigger hypothesis (1983) proposes that increases in circulating androgens cause increases in lean body tissue. In females little is known about training at this stage other than that puberty tends to promote an accumulation of adipose tissue that has negative effects on performance. What is surprising given the global popularity of the game is the lack of good empirical scientific data on the fitness and training of young soccer players and this deficit needs to be addressed.

Finally the data available suggest that elite young soccer players are fitter than their average counterparts in the population. It is not clear to what extent young players develop fitness through soccer playing and training or play soccer because they have inherited high levels of fitness.

REFERENCES

Adam, C. and Filliard, J.R. (1985) Eurofit: une batterie européenne pour évaluer l'aptitude physique *EPS–éducation-physique-et-sport*, 192, 48–49.

Al Hazzaa, H.M., Al-Refaee, S.A., Almuzaini, K.S., Sulaiman, L.A. and Dafterdar, M.Y. (2000) Anaerobic performance of adolescents versus adults: effect of age and soccer training. *Medicine and Science in Sports and Exercise*, 32, S1367.

American Alliance for Health, Physical Education, Recreation and Dance (1988) Physical Best: The American Alliance Physical Fitness Education and Assessment Program. Reston, VA.

Amigo, N., Cadefau, J.A., Ferrer, I., Tarrados, N. and Cusso, R. (1998) Effect of summer intermission on skeletal muscle of adolescent soccer players. *Journal of Sports Medicine and Physical Fitness*, 38, 298–304.

Arbeit, E. (1998) Practical training emphases in the first and second decades of development. *New Studies in Athletics*, 13, 13–20.

Armstrong, N. and van Mechelen, W. (2000) *Paediatric Exercise Science and Medicine*. Oxford: Oxford University Press.

Balyi, I. and Hamilton, A.E. (1999) Planning of training and performance. *British Columbia's Coaching Perspective*, 3, 6–11.

Baxter-Jones, A. and Helms, P.J. (1996) Effects of training at a young age: a review of the training of young athletes (TOYA) study. *Pediatric Exercise Science*, 8, 310–327.

Berg, K.E., LaVoie, J.C. and Latin, R.W. (1985) Physiological training effects of playing youth soccer. *Medicine and Science in Sports and Exercise*, 17, 656–660.

Berthoin, S. (1994) Evaluation des aptitudes aerobics à l'école: leur évolutions avec l'age, le sex et l'entraînement. Unpublished doctoral dissertation, Université de Lille II.

Billows, D., Reilly, T. and George, K. (2003) Physiological demands of matchplay in elite adolescent footballers. In *Science and Soccer V: Fifth World Congress Book of Abstracts*. Lisbon, Portugal.

Bunc, V. and Psotta, R. (2001) Physiological profile of very young soccer players. *Journal of Sports Medicine and Physical Fitness*, 41, 337–341.

Capranica, L., Cama, G., Fanton, F., Tessitore, A. and Figura, F. (1992) Force and power of preferred and non-preferred legs in young soccer players. *Journal of Sports Medicine and Physical Fitness*, 32, 358–363.

Chin, M.K., So, R., Yuan,Y., Li, R. and Wong, A. (1994) Cardiorespiratory fitness and isokinetic muscle strength of elite Asian junior soccer players. *Journal of Sports Medicine and Physical Fitness*, 34, 250–257.

Diallo, O., Dore, R. and Van Praagh, E. (2000) Effects of jump training and detraining on athletic performance in pre-pubertal boys. *Medicine and Science in Sports and Exercise*, 32, S1365.

Docherty, D. (1996) *Measurement in Pediatric Exercise Science*, Champaign, IL.: Human Kinetics.

Docherty, D., Wenger, H.A. and Collis, M.L. (1987) The effects of resistance exercise training on aerobic and anaerobic power in young boys. *Medicine and Science in Sports and Exercise*, 19, 318–322.

Drust, B. and Reilly, T. (1997) Heart rate responses of children during soccer play. In T. Reilly, J. Bangsbo and M. Hughes (eds) *Science and Football III*. London: E. & F.N. Spon, 196–200.

Engels, H.J. and Wirth, J.C. (2000) Anaerobic leg power of elite female youth soccer players: a playing field position-specific analysis. *Medicine and Science in Sports and Exercise*, 32, S358.

Faigenbaum, A.D., LaRosa-Loud, R., O'Connell, J., Glover, S., O'Connell, J. and Westcott, W.L. (2001) Effects of different resistance training protocols on upper-body strength and endurance development in children. *Journal of Strength and Conditioning Research*, 15, 459–465.

Falk, B. and Tenenbaum, G. (1996) The effectiveness of resistance training in children. *Sports Medicine*, 3, 176–186.

Felci, U., De Vito, G., Macaluso, A., Marchettoni, P. and Sproviero, E. (1995) Functional evaluation of soccer players during childhood. *Medicina Dello Sport*, 48, 221–225.

Franks, B.D. (1989) *YMCA Youth Fitness Test Manual*. Champaign, IL: Human Kinetics.

Franks, A.M., Williams, A.M., Reilly, T. and Nevill, A.M. (2002) Talent identification in elite young soccer players: physical and physiological characteristics. In W. Spinks, T. Reilly and A. Murphy (eds) *Science and Football IV*. London: Routledge.

Grant, A., Williams, M., Dodd, R. and Johnson, S. (1999) Physiological and technical analysis of 11 v 11 and 8 v 8 youth football matches. *Insight – The F.A. Coaches Association Journal*, 2, 29–30.

Grodjinovsky, A. and Bar-Or, O. (1984) Influence of added physical education hours upon anaerobic capacity, adiposity, and grip strength in 12–13 year-old children enrolled in a sports class. In J. Ilmarinen and I. Vaelimaeki (eds) *Children and Sport: Paediatric Work Physiology*, Berlin: Springer-Verlag, 162–169.

Hansen, L., Bangsbo, J., Twisk, J. and Klausen, K. (1999) Development of muscle strength in relation to training level and testosterone in young male soccer players. *Journal of Applied Physiology*, 87, 1141–1147.

Jankovic, S., Matkovic, B.R. and Matkovic, B. (1997) Functional abilities and process of selection in soccer. In 9th European Congress on Sports Medicine, 23/26 September 1997: Program and Abstract Book. Porto, Portugal, European Congress on Sports Medicine, p. 1.

Katch, V.L. (1983) Physical conditioning of children. *Journal of Adolescent Health Care*, 3, 241–246.

Klimt, F., Betz, M. and Seitz, V. (1992) Metabolism and circulation of children playing soccer. In J. Coudert and E. Van Praagh (eds) *Children and Exercise XVI: Paediatric Work Physiology*. Paris: Masson, 127–129.

Kraemer, W.J., Fry, A.C., Frykman, P.N., Conroy, B. and Hoffman, J. (1989) Resistance training and youth. *Pediatric Exercise Science*, 1, 336–350.

Lees, A. and Davids, K. (2002) Co-ordination and control of kicking in soccer. In K. Davids (ed.) *Interceptive Actions in Sport: Information and Movement*. New York: Routledge, 273–287.

Leger, L. (1996) Aerobic performance. In D. Docherty (ed.) *Measurement in Pediatric Exercise Science*. Champaign, IL.: Human Kinetics, 183–223.

Luhtanen, P. (1994) Biomechanical aspects in football. In B. Ekblom (ed.) *Football (Soccer)*, Oxford: Blackwell Scientific, 59–77.

Luhtanen, P., Vantinnen, T., Hayrinen, M. and Brown, E.W. (2002) Game performance analysis by age and gender in national level Finnish youth soccer players. In W. Spinks, T. Reilly and A. Murphy, *Science and Football IV*, London: Routledge, 275–279.

McManus, A., Armstrong, N. and Williams, C.A. (1997) Effect of training on the aerobic and anaerobic performance of pre-pubertal girls. *Acta Paediatrica*, 86, 456–459.

Mahon, A.D. (2000) Exercise training. In N. Armstrong and W. van Mechelen (eds) *Paediatric Exercise and Medicine*, Oxford: Oxford University Press, 201–222.

Massicote, D.R. and McNab, R.B.J. (1974) Cardiorespiratory adaptations to training at specific intensities in children. *Medicine and Science in Sports and Exercise*, 6, 242–246.

Mero A., Vuorimaa, T. and Hakkinen, K. (eds) (1990) *Training in Children and Adolescents*. Jyvaskyla, Finland: Gummerus, Kirjapaino, Oy.

Mosher, R.E., Rhodes, E.C., Wenger, H.A. and Filsinger, B. (1985) Interval training: the effects of a 12 week programme on elite pre-pubertal soccer players. *Journal of Sports Medicine and Physical Fitness*, 25, 5–9.

Pate, R.R. and Ward, D.S. (1990) Endurance exercise trainability in children and youth. In W.A. Grana (ed.) *Advances in Sport Medicine and Fitness*, Vol. 3. Chicago: Yearbook Medical Publishers, 37–58.

Paterson, D.H., McLellan, T.M., Stella, R.S. and Cunningham, D.A. (1987) Longitudinal study of ventilation threshold and maximal oxygen uptake in athletic boys. *Journal of Applied Physiology*, 62, 2051–2057.

Payne, V.G. and Morrow, J.R. (1993) Exercise and $\dot{V}O_{2max}$ in children: a meta-analysis. *Research Quarterly for Exercise and Sport*, 64, 305–313.

Platt, D., Maxwell, A., Horn, R., Williams, M. and Reilly, T. (2001) Physiological and technical analysis of 3 v 3 and 5 v 5 youth football matches. *Insight – The F.A. Coaches Association Journal*, 4, 23–24.

Reilly, T. and Doran, D. (2003) Fitness Assessment. In T. Reilly and A.M. Williams (eds) *Science and Soccer* (2nd edn). London: Routledge, 21–46.

Rowland, T.W. (1994) Effects of prolonged inactivity on aerobic fitness of children. *Journal of Sports Medicine and Physical Fitness*, 34, 147–155.

Rowland, T.W. (1996) *Developmental Exercise Physiology*. Champaign, IL: Human Kinetics.

Sadres, E., Eliakim, A. Constantini, N., Lidor, R. and Falk, B. (2001) The effect of long-term resistance training on anthropometric measures, muscle strength, and self concept in pre-pubertal boys. *Pediatric Exercise Science*, 13, 357–372.

Sady, S. (1984) Physiological characteristics of high-ability pre-pubescent wrestlers. *Medicine and Science in Sports and Exercise*, 16, 72–76.

Tsolakis, C., Messinis, D., Stergioulas, A. and Dessypris, A. (2000) Hormonal responses after strength training and detraining in prepubertal and pubertal boys. *Journal of Strength and Conditioning Research*, 14, 399–404.

Van Praagh, E. (1998) *Pediatric Anaerobic Performance*. Champaign, IL: Human Kinetics.

Walden, S.I. and Yates, J.W. (2000) Physical and performance traits of female soccer players of different competitive levels. *Medicine and Science in Sports and Exercise*, 32, S1823.

Williford, H.N., Scharff-Olson, M., Duey, W.J., Pugh, S. and Barksdale, J.M. (1999) Physiological status and prediction of cardiovascular fitness in highly trained youth soccer athletes. *Journal of Strength and Conditioning Research*, 13, 10–15.

CHAPTER SEVEN

NUTRITION FOR YOUNG SOCCER PLAYERS

INTRODUCTION

Nutrition refers to the study of how food nourishes the body. People tend to be fascinated by the topic of food, whether they are concerned about eating well or interested in cooking. There is rarely any escape from thoughts of food since everybody feels hunger several times each day and then plans for the next snack or meal are made. Food selection depends on personal tastes and so the choice of meal may be individually determined. When presented with the restaurant menu on an evening out, the choice of meal is rarely made immediately and individuals may be quickly swayed by the choices of their companions.

The range of meals offered to the restaurant customer may contrast to the restricted choice available to young people in many domestic circumstances. Low family income dictates that food items are purchased with an eye to their cost. In such circumstances meals may become repetitive, lack variety and may not be wholesome. Young family members may then depend on parental education about diet and its impact on health and development. Since attitudes towards eating properly are embedded in childhood, educating youngsters about eating well can instil good eating habits which will benefit them later in their adult life.

For the young soccer player a thoughtful attention to diet is important. Youngsters need to eat a range of foods that will promote health and they must drink sufficiently to maintain their hydration status. Food supplies energy and nutrients: extra energy is needed to provide the fuel utilised in training and playing football. The main nutrients that provide energy are carbohydrates and lipids, whilst protein can also contribute in a minor way to yielding energy for exercise. Extra protein is required by growing tissues; protein deficiency in malnourished children leads to the condition known as kwashiorkor. Alcohol yields energy too but it is not a nutrient. The other classes of nutrients essential for life are water (which is constantly being lost from the body and must be replaced on a regular basis), vitamins and minerals. Vitamins and minerals do not furnish energy for the body but serve as regulators for a legion of physiological processes necessary to maintain life.

Faced with the harsh commercialisation of the food industry, eating nutritiously may well become a difficult task for the young soccer player. Barriers to education about nutrition include the low cost of widely available junk food, convenience 'fast food' and the promotion of packaged snacks. There is also a lack of 'role models' for many young players to follow. Besides, they can easily be misled by the array of food supplements advertised in sports and other periodicals.

In this chapter the contributions of the macronutrients to the young athlete's diet are considered. Special attention is given to energy balance and lifestyle factors influencing dietary habits. The other components of a balanced diet are outlined before focusing on the needs of young players engaged in strenuous training.

THE ENERGY BALANCE EQUATION

The body needs energy from food to support its metabolic processes. Basal metabolism represents the sum total of all the involuntary activities needed to sustain life. These physiological activities include respiration, circulation, synthesis of new tissue and so on. In addition, energy is needed to support digestive processes and voluntary activities. The latter include habitual activities such as walking, sitting and locomotion as well as exercise and sports participation. These activities comprise the largest component of the average young person's daily energy requirements.

When energy intake and energy expenditure are equal, body weight remains unchanged. The growing child needs a net gain of body mass and so must take in more energy in food than is expended on a daily basis. There is an additional requirement among young athletes to compensate for energy costs incurred in training and match-play. Without an adequate supply of appropriate energy sources in the diet, performance in training and competitive contexts may be impaired.

The major macronutrient contents of the diet are in the form of lipids, carbohydrates and protein. Lipids are stored in abundance in the body as fat within adipose cells, each gram of fat contains 9 kcal.g^{-1} (37.7 kJ.g^{-1}). The stores of carbohydrate in liver and muscle are much less and energy density is lower than for fat, amounting to 4 kcal.g^{-1} (16.7 kJ.g^{-1}). Protein in the form of branched-chain amino acids is used as fuel for exercise but its contribution is small: its energy density is 4 kcal.g^{-1} (16.7 kJ.g^{-1}). Alcohol has an energy density of 7 kcal.g^{-1} (29.3 kJ.g^{-1}) but is not available for skeletal muscle to use during exercise. As alcohol is a drug as well as a food, it is prohibited for under-18-year-olds and has no real place in the diet of young footballers.

Young players experiencing a negative energy balance are poorly prepared for supplying fuel for strenuous exercise. In training camps over 1–2 weeks, a negative balance is associated with over-training and fatigue (Ekblom, 2002). In normal circumstances a low dietary intake in young female players can lead to inadequate zinc, magnesium and calcium status (Fogelholm, 1994). It would be prudent to assess the iron status of young female soccer players, including serum ferritin measurements, at least once a year. A low intake of calcium can lead to its loss from the skeleton. Bone mineral density is not so easily determined but may be assessed by means of dual energy x-ray absorptiometry (see Figure 5.3). Sources of dietary calcium include milk, cheese, nuts and green vegetables.

A major concern among the population at large is the incidence of obesity among children. Whilst the root causes of obesity are complex, incorporating genetic and environmental factors, solutions entail incurring a negative calorie balance until weight-control is achieved. A sedentary lifestyle among contemporary children and a tendency to consume food in excess of requirements are to blame for the so-called obesity epidemic. Participation in recreational games of soccer can increase habitual energy expenditure and, combined with a planned diet, becomes an effective means of regulating body weight. Even though fat is a preferred source of fuel in children during exercise, there is no evidence that the percentage of fat in the diet should be greater than for adults.

The recommendation for young soccer players is that the fat content should not exceed 30 per cent of the total energy and the calories in the form of saturated fats should be less than 10 per cent of the total energy intake (Bar-Or and Unnithan, 1994). The carbohydrate content should be about 55 per cent of the total energy with the remaining 15 per cent derived from protein. Positive changes in macronutrient composition such as a reduction in fat intake, together with an increased intake of complex carbohydrates, will at the same time lead to an increase in the intake of micronutrients.

HEALTHY EATING

Poor dietary practices have been linked with major diseases of the cardiovascular system, diabetes and high blood pressure. Such habits may have been acquired in childhood. Poor practices include a high proportion of saturated fat in the diet, overuse of sugar and salt, lack of fibre in the diet, and inadequate amounts of fruit and vegetables. The major food groups can be classed into five main types including bread and cereals (whole grain or enriched), vegetables, fruits, meat

114

Table 7.1 Function and food sources of a selection of essential nutrients

Mineral	Role/function	Food source
Calcium	Bone and tooth structures, nerve conduction, muscle contraction, blood clotting	Milk, cheese, nuts, green vegetables, bread
Phosphorus	Bone and tooth structures, energy metabolism	Milk, cereals, meat, green vegetables
Magnesium	Nerve–muscle transmission, energy metabolism	Dairy products, cereals, meat, green vegetables
Sodium	Nerve–muscle conduction, fluid balance, acid-base balance	Salt, cheese, meat
Potassium	Nerve–muscle conduction, fluid balance, acid-base balance	Meat, milk, cereals, nuts, vegetables
Chloride	Major extracellular and intracellular ion	Variety of foods
Iron	Oxygen transport via haemoglobin and myoglobin	Meat, liver, eggs, nuts, green vegetables
Zinc	Essential component of key metabolic enzymes	Meat, seafood, green vegetables, nuts, dairy products
Copper	Component of key enzymes involved in aerobic metabolism	Shellfish, liver, nuts, legumes, bananas, bran cereals
Selenium	Component of key antioxidant enzyme	Seafood, liver, kidney, grains
Iodine	Thyroid function	Seafoods, eggs, dairy products

Source: Compiled from information in Sizer and Whitney, 1994, and other sources.

and meat alternatives, milk and milk products. Essential nutrients are outlined in Table 7.1. An appropriate emphasis on each of these groups is provided in recommendations for servings per day for children and teenagers in nutrition texts (e.g. Sizer and Whitney, 1994).

A healthy diet should also contain the appropriate mixture of micronutrients, specifically vitamins, minerals and trace elements. These substances are generally found in sufficient quantities in the food consumed in a well-balanced diet. They play important roles in facilitating energy transfer within the cells of the body.

Recommended daily intakes have been established for 13 different vitamins, classified either as fat-soluble or water-soluble. The fat-soluble group includes vitamins A, D, E and K and are usually obtained in dietary fat. Supplementation of these vitamins in excess can lead to harmful toxic effects. The water-soluble group includes vitamin B-complex and vitamin C. They act as co-enzymes, combining with a larger protein molecule to form an active enzyme. Due to their solubility in water these vitamins are carried in body fluids and in excess are eliminated from the body in the urine. Since they are not stored in the body to any great extent they are ingested in the normal diet on a daily basis. Vitamins can be used repeatedly in metabolic reactions, and so the recommended daily allowances for non-athletic children are likely to suffice for young soccer players. Whilst vitamin deficiencies can have serious adverse effects on bodily functions, such deficiencies are rare in young players in developed countries.

About 4 per cent of body mass is composed of 22 mostly metallic elements, collectively known as minerals (McArdle et al., 1991). Major minerals are present in large quantities and have known biological functions. Trace elements are present in minute amounts totalling less than 0.05 per cent of body mass. Most of the major and trace minerals are found in nature, either in the earth's waters, roots of plants or trees or in animals that consume plants and water containing these minerals. Recommended daily allowances for the important minerals in the body, dietary sources and the effects of deficiencies and excesses are published in the literature (National Academy of Sciences, 1989). Recommended allowances for young females are higher than for males in order to account for losses during menses. Calcium is one of the most frequently lacking nutrients in the diet and adolescents and youths need about 50 per cent more of this mineral in their daily dietary intake than do adults (McArdle et al., 1991). This recommendation would apply to young female soccer players in particular, in order to optimise bone mass. Sodium, potassium and chlorine are referred to as electrolytes due to the fact that these minerals are dissolved in the body as electrically charged particles called ions. Sodium is distributed widely in foods and supplementation is not usually necessary. Excessive salt intake has been linked with elevated blood pressure and cardiovascular risk whilst in the case of shortage the kidney acts to conserve the sodium by means of the hormone aldosterone.

Good dietary habits entail much more than attention to the type and composition of meals: the timing of food intake is also important. Children who miss breakfast lose concentration in the schoolroom and experience distracting hunger before they have an opportunity to eat lunch. Performance at games is also likely to suffer due to reduced glycogen stores in the liver and falling blood glucose concentrations. If breakfast is avoided on a habitual basis, meals later in the day may not provide all the nutrients needed for an adequate and balanced diet. Children may also not like the choice provided in their school cafeteria for lunch so there should be a compromise between what children would like to eat and what will nourish them. Those youngsters participating in specialist soccer training in the evening should have a light meal or snack in good time (at least 2 hours) before their practice commences.

NUTRITIONAL ERGOGENIC AIDS FOR YOUNG PLAYERS

The degree to which ergogenic aids should be administered to young soccer players has not been agreed in any consensus. Adolescents and youths may need a higher level of protein in their diets during any periods of intense training. A protein intake of 1 g.kg^{-1} body mass would satisfy requirements of 11–14-year-olds and should be available in the normal diet. A higher allowance should be made for youngsters below 10 years of age (see Table 7.2), and an intake of up to 1.4 g.kg^{-1} might be prudent when teenage players are engaged in hard training (Lemon, 1994). This amount would render any supplementation of protein compounds superfluous.

Carbohydrate loading is an effective means of increasing performance capability for mature players, especially towards the end of the game. The strategy of boosting glycogen stores prior to competition has not been investigated in as comprehensive a manner among young players. Nevertheless, it would be prudent for youngsters to avoid hard training in the days immediately before full competitive games, and to bias the diet towards carbohydrates in the 48 hours prior to matches. They should not need to empty glycogen stores by means of exhausting exercise 2–3 days before the initial part of the classical 'super-compensation' regimen used by adult athletes.

In adult athletes it has been established that performance in repeated bouts of short sprints can be enhanced by employing a regimen of creatine loading. It is questionable whether the benefits transfer to performance within a game context, although creatine loading is likely to have been used in a number of youth soccer teams. The most plausible benefits are likely to accrue from the training stimulus

Table 7.2 Recommended dietary intake of protein for young people

Age (years)	Protein intake (grams per kilogram)
7–10	1.2
11–14	1.0
15–18	0.8

Source: Based on Bar-Or and Unnithan, 1994.

Notes: The values compare with 0.8 grams per kilogram for adults, and apply to both girls and boys.

provided by an increased power output during repeated sprints. There should be more long-term benefits from executing well-designed training programmes rather than relying on creatine-mediated training stimuli. Vegetarian athletes are the exception in that being non-meat eaters they lack the major source of creatine intake in their diets. In studies of creatine loading among adults, vegetarian subjects derive most benefit from additional intake of creatine in the form of creatine monohydrate.

Some young female athletes may benefit from supplemental iron intake, especially those complementing their soccer play with endurance training (Snyder et al., 1989). Iron deficiency anaemia can impair athletic performance due to the reduced oxygen carrying capacity in the blood. Dietary iron is needed as a component of the proteins haemoglobin in red blood cells and myoglobin in muscle cells. Haemoglobin carries oxygen from the lungs to the body's tissue whereas myoglobin carries and stores a limited amount of oxygen for the muscles. Iron deficiency is the most common nutrient deficiency worldwide, with the highest prevalence in developing countries (Gable, 1992). Heavy menstrual losses constitute the most likely cause of borderline anaemia in young female soccer players, iron losses in sweat, possible destruction of red blood cells on ground contact (the so-called 'foot-strike haemolysis') being less important. Meat, poultry and fish provide the heme form of iron in the diet, whilst non-heme iron is contained in plants as well as meat.

During the course of intense training and high consumption of oxygen, the body produces so-called oxygen-free radicals. The body has its own scavenging system (e.g. superoxide dismutase) to prevent a build up of free radicals and resulting damage to internal tissues. In such cases it is suggested that supplementation with antioxidants would be of benefit. Ekblom (2002) studied young players throughout a one-week training period at a camp. Despite supervision of their diet, the players incurred a negative energy balance, reduced appetite and reduced stamina over the duration of the training period at camp. In a related study, antioxidant supplementation for 22 days with ubiquinone (Q_{10}) failed to offset the adverse effects on muscle soreness and muscle performance incurred during the intensive training.

WATER INTAKE

The body water pools are regulated so that functions essential to life can be maintained. Without access to water, death from dehydration would occur within days. Its main functions are to transport nutrients throughout the body (as well as wastes) and to serve as a solvent for minerals, vitamins, glucose, amino acids and various small molecules.

Water makes up about 60 per cent of the total mass in adolescents, almost two thirds being located inside the body's cells whereas the extracellular compartments contain the remainder. Extracellular fluid includes blood plasma and lymph, saliva, fluid in the eyes, spinal nerves, synovia in joints and that secreted by the intestines and glands. About 72 per cent of skeletal muscle is comprised of water. There is little variation between adults and children but boys have larger water pools than girls due to their larger muscle mass, lower adiposity and lower blood volume. Water is also bound to glycogen stored in the liver and skeletal muscle, is held within protein molecules and participates actively in many basic chemical reactions.

Thirst is the most obvious physiological indicator of hydration status. During football matches or training practices young players may lose sweat at a rate in excess of one litre per hour. It is important to restore fluid lost during exercise and thirst is not a perfect indicator of whether body water stores have been completely restored. It is good practice to advise young players to drink until their thirst is sated, and then imbibe a little bit more. Urine osmolality is a better index of hydration status than is thirst, especially when young players are in a training camp environment or after exposure to hot conditions. Urine colour can provide a crude indication of hydration status, a pale straw-colour being associated with euhydration. Education about the need for rehydration can be provided by encouraging players to develop good habits. These practices should include carrying their own water bottles or sports drinks and keeping them readily available on the sidelines, where possible.

Bar-Or et al. (1992) reported that children can maintain hydration status during prolonged intermittent exercise when they are made to drink every 15–20 minutes. Such drinking can be more easily encouraged if the fluid is palatable. A grape flavour proved the most palatable in a study of boys and girls aged 9–13 years, and induced the greatest amount of rehydration following mild dehydration (Meyer et al., 1994). Nevertheless, some of the children preferred orange or apple flavours, so allowing the individual a choice of drinks would be prudent. Fluid absorption is facilitated by including electrolytes in the drink, even though children lose less Na^+ and Cl^- in sweat than do adults (Meyer et al., 1992).

A considerable amount of water is also contained in foodstuffs. Many fruits and vegetables contain large quantities of water, whilst meats and cheeses do so to a lesser extent. Broccoli and lettuce provide a plentiful source of water. Water is also released during metabolic reactions; when glycogen is broken down as an energy substrate, for each gram of glycogen there is a net 2.7 g of water made available to the body's water pools. When the daily fluid balance is achieved, the water lost from the body corresponds to that gained. Water is lost not just in sweat but also in insensible perspiration through the skin, in expired air and in faeces.

119

The latter could be an important factor in debilitation of young players suffering stomach upsets or cases of diarrhoea. In such events a systematic rehydration strategy must be executed for euhydration to be restored.

OVERVIEW

Nutrition is a very important consideration in young people, and especially those participating in systematic training for soccer. The recommended daily allowances for adults may be inadequate for application to young athletes in the case of many nutrients. Special attention is directed towards dietary calcium so that the achievement of peak bone density during growth is not compromised. Young females need to have adequate sources of iron in their diet to ensure that internal stores are sufficient for supporting haemoglobin in new red blood cells. Children differ from adults in another respect: their protein needs are relatively greater than those of adults during their growing years, although the differences are reduced during the late teenage years.

Children rely more than adults on fat as an energy source during exercise such as playing football, but there is no evidence that they require a corresponding difference in intake of dietary fat. Indeed there is a pronounced secular trend towards an increased percentage of overweight youngsters in the population and a worrying rise of obesity in children. These developments have been linked with a sedentary lifestyle – expressed in hours watching television and playing computer games – and to the availability of large portions in 'fast food' outlets. The roots of life-long habits in both diet and exercise are laid down during the years of growth. As the world's most popular sport, it would seem plausible that regular recreational soccer combined with dietary interventions could have a role to play in health promotion and reversing the rise of the overweight epidemic among young people.

REFERENCES

Bar-Or, O. and Unnithan, V.B. (1994) Nutritional requirements of young soccer players. *Journal of Sports Sciences*, 12, 539–542.
Bar-Or, O., Blimkie, C.J.R., Hay, J.A., MacDougall, J.D., Ward, D.S. and Wilson, W.M. (1992) Voluntary dehydration and heat intolerance in cystic fibrosis. *Lancet*, 339, 696–699.
Ekblom, B. (2002) Assessment of fitness and player profiles. International Football and Sports Medicine Conference, Beverly Hills, CA, March 22–24.

Fogelholm, M. (1994) Vitamins, minerals and supplementation in soccer. *Journal of Sports Sciences*, 12, 523–527.

Gable, C.B. (1992) Hemochromatosis and dietary iron supplementation: implications from U.S. mortality, morbidity and health survey data. *Journal of the American Dietetic Association*, 92, 208–212.

Lemon, P.W.R. (1994) Protein requirements of soccer. *Journal of Sports Sciences*, 12, 517–522.

McArdle, W.D., Katch, F.I. and Katch, V.L. (1991) *Exercise Physiology: Energy, Nutrition and Human Performance* (3rd edn). Philadelphia: Lea and Febriger.

Meyer, F., Bar-Or, O., MacDougall, D. and Heigenhauser, G.J.P. (1992) Sweat electrolyte loss during exercise in the heat: effects of gender and maturation. *Medicine and Science in Sports and Exercise*, 24, 778–781.

Meyer, F., Bar-Or, O., Salsbury, A. and Passe, D. (1994) Hypohydration during exercise in children: effects of thirst, drink preferences and rehydration. *International Journal of Sports Nutrition*, 4, 22–35.

National Academy of Sciences (1989) *Recommended Dietary Allowances*. Washington, D.C.: National Academy Press.

Sizer, F. and Whitney, E. (1994) *Hamilton and Whitney's Nutrition: Concepts and Controversies* (6th edn). St. Paul, HN: West Publishing Company.

Snyder, A.C., Dvorak, L.L. and Roepke, J.B. (1989) Influence of dietary iron source on measures of iron status among female runners. *Medicine and Science in Sports and Exercise*, 21, 7–10.

CHAPTER EIGHT

ACQUIRING SOCCER SKILLS: EFFECTIVE PRACTICE AND INSTRUCTION

INTRODUCTION

In order to perform at the highest level, players have to spend many hours in deliberate, purposeful practice with the specific intention of improving performance. Although practice on its own does not guarantee success, there is no substitute for earnest endeavour in the pursuit of excellence. Some players may be more genetically predisposed to benefit from practice effects, but no players have reached the elite level without a significant commitment to the process of refining and developing their soccer skills. Ward and co-workers (2004) showed that those who are recruited by Premier League Academies in England at 16 years of age typically started playing the game at 6 years of age and over the next 10 years devoted an average of 15 hours per week, 700 hours per year (over 7,000 hours in total) to practice activities related to soccer. It is likely that at least 10,000 hours of practice are required before these players are ready for their debut in the first team. The academy players also considered practice, along with the motivation to succeed, to be the most important factors in becoming an elite player, whereas, in contrast, less skilled players considered skill and teamwork to be the key factors underpinning success.

Whilst acknowledging the importance of practice in developing skilled players, the nature of the practice activity undertaken and the type of instruction provided are at least equally as important. Practice on its own does not make perfect; rather, effective practice coupled with appropriate instruction is instrumental in defining and shaping the path to excellence (Williams *et al.*, 2003). In this chapter some of the key factors underpinning the practice and instruction process are reviewed. Initially, important differences between performance and learning are highlighted and a brief overview of the skill learning process provided. A model of instruction is then presented and some guidance as to what constitutes good practice at each stage within the model is proposed. An attempt is made to challenge traditional beliefs about the instruction process and to encourage coaches to reflect on current practice.

PERFORMANCE AND LEARNING

Performance is simply referred to as observed behaviour. That is, it is the behaviour demonstrated by a player during an individual practice session or match. The difficulty for the coach is that a range of factors such as fatigue, motivation or anxiety can affect performance. Learning is typically defined as 'a set of processes associated with practice or experience that leads to relatively permanent changes in the capability for movement' (Schmidt and Lee, 1999: 264). Learning, therefore, results in a permanent change in behaviour and an increased capacity for skilled performance.

Whilst learning is likely to lead to neurological changes in the central nervous system, these are not directly observable but rather have to be inferred from changes in performance. It is therefore essential for coaches to assess performance over extended periods of time (normally using some measure of retention) or to evaluate performance in a novel situation that requires some adaptation of the skill (a measure of transfer). The distinction between performance and learning has a significant influence on coaching behaviour. As discussed in the remaining sections of this chapter, some skills that have beneficial effects on performance influence learning in a negative manner and vice versa. For example, providing feedback on every trial during acquisition has beneficial effects on performance whilst, in contrast, less frequent feedback is better for learning. The difficulty therefore is that 'what you see is not necessarily what you get' as far as skill learning is concerned. Although players may be performing well in a particular session, this is not necessarily a good indicator of learning. The task is one of portioning out short-term performance effects from long-term learning.

A related issue is how coaches should assess performance. Typically, this is a fairly subjective process, relying on the opinion of one coach. Greater objectivity can be gained by using a panel of coaches to rate performance independently, possibly using Likert scale ratings for each skill. Video footage can be used to evaluate performance, particularly when coupled with quantitative data on the particular aspect of performance under investigation (e.g. accuracy of passing, quality of crosses). Soccer skills tests provide objective and reliable data on specific aspects of performance (e.g. dribbling, shooting, turning), but it may be difficult to generalise the findings to the more dynamic, match situation.

HOW DO PLAYERS LEARN SOCCER SKILLS?

Several theories have been proposed over the years to explain how players learn movement skills (for a detailed review, see Summers, 2004). The most prevalent theoretical approach has emerged from the field of cognitive psychology. The assumption is that with practice learners develop a generalised motor programme or schema for each skill (see Schmidt and Lee, 1999; Schmidt and Wrisberg, 2000). For example, the player may have a generalised motor programme for the soccer pass which contains all the relevant movement commands needed to execute the skill. These centrally stored movement schema are supported by various spinal and supra-spinal feedback loops that involve, amongst others, the muscle spindles, cerebellum and motor cortex. During early learning, the assumption is that movement is regulated mainly via conscious feedback loops involving, for example, vision and audition, whereas later in learning players develop larger and more refined motor programmes and rely on subconscious feedback mechanisms to refine the movement. This move from primarily conscious control of movement to more subconscious control via motor programmes and peripheral feedback mechanisms reduces the attention demand on performers, enabling them to focus on more strategic aspects of performance.

Various models have also been proposed to describe some of the changes that occur with skill learning. Fitts and Posner (1967) proposed the most popular of these models. They argued that players move through three stages as they acquire movement skills. The initial, cognitive stage of learning is relatively attention demanding. Players make many errors as they attempt to come to terms with the technical demands of the sport and its various rules and laws. Performance variability is high, but improvements are quite marked. In the intermediate or associative stage, players have mastered the basic skills of the game and are more concerned with trying to refine existing skills and develop a better mastery of strategic aspects of performance. Performance variability decreases and players begin to develop the ability to detect and correct their own errors. At the final, advanced or autonomous stage of learning, motor skills can be executed with only limited attention demand, performance errors are small and infrequent, and the focus is on strategic and tactical aspects of performance. Although performance variability is low, in relation to achieving the desired outcome, players may vary technique in order to try and solve the movement problem in a variety of different ways.

Newell (1985) proposed an alternative stage model of skill learning based on developments in the fields of ecological psychology and dynamical systems theory. In this model, three distinct stages of skill learning are outlined. In the coordination stage, learners are concerned with developing the fundamental movement pattern. In order to simplify this process, they may well 'freeze' motion around anatomical joints (i.e. freezing degrees of freedom). For example, young children learning to kick the ball typically try and reduce the motion around certain joints (e.g. hip, knee and ankle) by kicking with a 'stiff leg'. In the control stage, learners explore different ways of performing the task by refining and scaling movement parameters such as range of motion and joint angular velocity (freeing degrees of freedom). Finally, in the skill stage, learners continue to refine the movement producing smooth, efficient and skilful behaviour (exploiting degrees of freedom) (for detailed reviews, see Scott *et al.* 2003; Williams *et al.*, 1999).

THE INSTRUCTION PROCESS

The coach plays a fundamental role in helping players to acquire soccer skills and consequently the instruction process has attracted significant interest in recent years (for a detailed review, see Williams and Hodges, in press). A typical model of skill instruction is presented in Figure 8.1. The coach initially provides learners with information regarding the skill to be performed, normally using visual demonstrations and/or verbal cues. An opportunity to learn the skill is then provided by organising and delivering practice activities, followed by the provision of feedback as to how performance may be improved on subsequent practice attempts. The coaching philosophy underpins the extent to which the instruction process is very 'hands on' (i.e. focus on prescriptive guidance) or 'hands off' (i.e. focus on discovery learning). A brief review of the scientific research related to each stage within the instruction process follows.

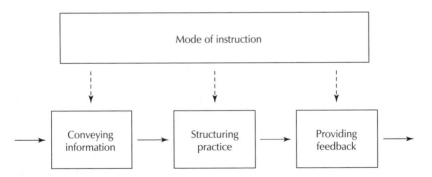

Figure 8.1 A model of instruction highlighting stages in the coaching process
Source: Adapted from Lavalle *et al.* 2003

Visual demonstrations and verbal instructions

Coaches rely heavily on demonstrations to convey information to the learner regarding the skill to be performed. Is this confidence in the importance of demonstrations misplaced? Are demonstrations always effective in facilitating the learning process? Can demonstrations occasionally have detrimental effects on skill learning? How should coaches use verbal cues to supplement or replace demonstrations? Coaches require guidance when attempting to answer such questions.

The process underlying demonstration is observational learning, which is defined as the learner's tendency to watch the behaviour of others and to try and mimic this behaviour (Williams et al., 1999). The presumption is that the demonstration provides a visual template or reference of correctness for the skill. The most prevalent theory in this area is Bandura's (1986) Cognitive Mediation Theory. This theory proposes that four inter-related processes are important for demonstrations to be effective. The learner must be able to *attend* to the important features of the model and the information extracted must be *retained* in some form of symbolic code or representation. The learner then has to have the necessary *motor reproduction* ability and *motivation* to continue to refine and practise the skill.

The processes of attention and retention have attracted most interest from scientists (for a detailed review, see Williams et al., 1999; Horn and Williams, 2004). Models that convey high status, such as a teacher or coach, have been shown to attract more attention than those of lower status, such as a student peer. Similarly, because observational learning is dependent on the learner attempting to copy the model, high skill models are better than low skill models. There is some evidence to suggest that learning models (e.g. a student from within the group) may be as effective provided the learner is able to hear the feedback given to the model by the coach. The typical routine of practising in pairs where one player acts as a model for the other may be useful. In a similar vein, it may also help the skill acquisition process if learners are able to view demonstrations from a number of different people so that they can appreciate subtle variations in technique.

Although Bandura's theory has received considerable research attention, the question of what information learners pick up from demonstrations has often been neglected. Scully and Newell (1985) attempted to address this issue with their 'visual perception perspective' on observational learning. They argued that the learner picks up the relative motion or global orientation between the major anatomical body segments/limbs involved in the skill. Consequently, the suggestion is that demonstrations are most effective earlier rather than later in learning (i.e. during the coordination stage). In the control and skill stages of learning, players are more likely to be concerned with refining or scaling the movement skill and this information is much harder to pick up through observation. For example, it may be hard for the learner to identify the important distinguishing factors between a short and long instep pass through demonstration. A simple verbal directive to transfer body weight more quickly through the ball or to have a faster follow-through may be more appropriate. In a similar vein, demonstrations may be no more effective than verbal instruction when the task requires learners to pick up important haptic or kinaesthetic information (i.e. a 'feel' for the task) rather than a clear movement strategy. For example, a demonstration showing players how to cushion the ball with the instep is likely to be no more informative than the simple directive to relax when the ball strikes the foot.

Verbal instructions can often be as helpful as a demonstration, particularly if the coach merely wishes to highlight the desired outcome. The simple verbal directive to play a lofted pass from the by-line into the near post area may be sufficient for learners to start practising the skill of crossing the ball. This approach encourages learners to practise the skill and to develop their own way of solving the movement problem. If progress is poor, demonstrations can then be introduced to help guide or constrain the learner. When providing verbal instructions, the language employed should not be too complex or technical, particularly when conveying information to young children. Wulf and colleagues (e.g. Wulf and Weigelt, 1997) have shown that verbal instructions that direct learners' attention towards external features such as the goal of the task (e.g. ball flight characteristics) are better than those that create an internal focus on the body. An internal focus of attention towards technical components of the skill may be at the expense of goal attainment (e.g. an accurate cross). In contrast, if the intention is to develop correct movement form, then coaches should consider reducing the emphasis placed on performance outcome (Horn and Williams, 2004). The feedback provided by the coach should also be compatible with the verbal instruction (e.g. if the emphasis is on ball flight characteristics then feedback should relate to this aspect of the skill and not to movement form).

STRUCTURING PRACTICE SESSIONS

Once learners have an idea of the skill in question the coach must then decide how best to structure the practice session to make most effective use of the time available. Three questions are of fundamental importance: How effective are variable practice conditions compared with specific practice schedules? Is it best to practise one skill in a blocked manner or a number of skills in a random practice schedule in each practice session? How much rest should be provided between practice attempts? Some guidance for coaches follows.

Variable practice conditions

A variable schedule requires that learners practise several variations of the same skill within the practice session. For example, when learning to play the instep pass, players would be required to vary the 'weight' (speed) and flight path of the ball. The alternative would be to employ constant, specific practice conditions requiring players to pass the ball back and forth in a repetitive fashion using, for example, a 10 × 10 m grid area. The research evidence indicates that whilst specific practice conditions produce better performance within each session, variable conditions are better for skill learning. The presumption is that variability within the practice environment helps to create a more flexible generalised motor programme that can cope with a variety of similar but different situations.

The positive effects of variable practice conditions are particularly marked with young children (Yan et al., 1998). It is therefore advisable for coaches to provide young children with a range of practice opportunities that mimic the competitive setting. Coaches can easily manipulate the practice session to ensure that players continuously vary how the skill is performed on each occasion. For example, the coach could manipulate the type of pass required from the learner by increasing or decreasing the distance between players and by introducing obstacles and targets to pass the ball through, around or over. The positive effects of variable practice may also be more pronounced when coupled with random rather than blocked practice conditions.

Blocked vs random practice conditions

In blocked practice schedules, players are required to practise a single skill such as passing, shooting or heading during the session. In contrast, under random practice conditions various skills are performed in a random, ad hoc manner in each session. The consensus of opinion is that blocked practice is better for short-term performance, whereas random practice conditions are better for skill learning. This phenomenon is referred to as the contextual interference effect and it is one of the most robust observations in the motor learning literature (for a detailed review of the literature, see Brady, 1998).

The important relationship between variability of practice and contextual interference is highlighted in Figure 8.2. Although there is some evidence to suggest that specific, blocked practice (e.g. practice of single skill in a 10 × 10 m grid) may be desirable very early in learning, particularly with young children, coaches should endeavour to move towards variable, random practice as early as possible (e.g. small-sided games). Whilst acknowledging that there may be nothing new in this proposal, the difficulty for coaches is that the decision as to how quickly to progress is often based on how players perform in any given practice session. Given the distinction between performance and learning highlighted earlier, coaches need to be encouraged to progress at a faster pace than is currently the case. A 'leap of faith' is required for coaches to try innovative practices that encourage players to take greater responsibility for their own learning. At the extreme end of the scale, there are those who suggest that youngsters should be confronted with variable and random practice conditions at the outset, perhaps mirroring the importance of 'street football' from previous generations.

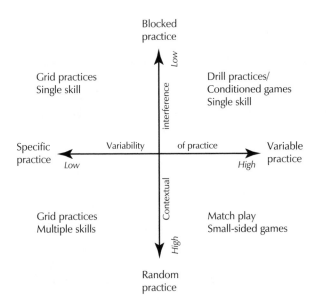

Figure 8.2 A model illustrating the relationship between variability of practice and contextual interference

Source: Author.

Notes: Specific, blocked conditions include practising a single skill (e.g. passing) in a specified grid area. Specific, random conditions involve practising a number of different skills in a random manner but under conditions of low variability such as encouraged by grid type practices (e.g. passing a ball over a set distance as marked by the grid or dribbling around set cone positions). Variable, blocked practice conditions involve practising a single skill under a variety of practice conditions involving drills and conditioned games where only one skill is emphasised. Variable, random conditions are best experienced in small-sided games or regular match play.

The challenge for the coach is to maintain a healthy balance between performance and learning effects. If the coach progresses to variable, random practice conditions too quickly then performance may be poor, perhaps reducing motivation and increasing potential drop-out in young children. On the other hand, if players spend too much time in drill-like situations with low variability and low contextual interference then learning will be negatively affected.

How much rest between practice attempts?

The answer to this question depends on the nature of the task. Skills that place heavy physiological demands on the learner and are complex may benefit from longer rest periods between practice attempts than those that provide a natural rest period after an attempt or are fairly simple. An important consideration, however, is that whilst practice when fatigued is detrimental to performance it may not have detrimental effects on skill learning. Moreover, most soccer skills are discrete activities (e.g. a shot on goal) that provide a natural break between practice attempts. Practice when fatigued allows the coach to make better use of the available time and replicates the demands placed upon the player during competitive matches. Clearly, coaches need to be careful to avoid overuse injuries, particularly with young players.

PROVIDING AUGMENTED FEEDBACK

An important aspect within the instruction process is the provision of feedback. Learners will already have access to performance feedback through their own sensory mechanisms (e.g. sight and feel of the movement). However, research indicates that learning occurs more rapidly when coaches provide augmented feedback, for example, in relation to technical execution of the skill, to supplement this intrinsic feedback. The provision of augmented feedback leads to more efficient learning and better skill development. Those who receive constructive feedback from significant others are also more interested in the task, put more effort into the learning process and persist longer after feedback is removed. These factors ensure that the provision of feedback is particularly important early in learning (i.e. during the cognitive stage), and with young children (Magill, 2003).

Although augmented feedback is important early in learning, it becomes less important as learning progresses. Players develop their own ability to detect and correct errors; consequently, the role of the coach becomes less prescriptive later in learning. An important challenge for coaches is to facilitate this transfer from reliance on augmented feedback to the more effective processing of intrinsic

Table 8.1 Some examples of how players' reliance on prescriptive feedback from coaches can be 'faded out' as learning progresses

Feedback	Feedback and effect
Bandwidth feedback	Provision of feedback only when performance falls outside agreed criteria or bandwidth for error tolerance
Descriptive vs prescriptive feedback	Provision of descriptive feedback rather than prescriptive guidance, thereby encouraging learners to find their own solutions to the movement problem
Summary feedback	Feedback provided as a summary of performance on the preceding block of practice attempts
Question and answer style	Asking learners to come up with their own solution through a question and answer approach (e.g. What could you have done better on that attempt?)

Source: Adapted from Williams, 2003.

feedback. The suggestion is that whilst feedback after every practice attempt is beneficial for performance it is detrimental for skill learning. Coaches must therefore resist the temptation to provide augmented feedback too frequently and must try and 'fade out' its influence as early as possible. Some techniques to facilitate this process are highlighted in Table 8.1.

The specific frequency of feedback provision will depend on a range of factors including the complexity of the task and the age and skill level of the player. Younger and less skilled players will require feedback more frequently than their older and more skilled counterparts, particularly when learning difficult skills. Guidance for coaches when considering the optimal frequency of feedback provision is provided in Figure 8.3.

It is also important for the coach to monitor the complexity and precision of the feedback provided. This is particularly the case with young children who are unable to summarise and simplify performance feedback in the same way as adults. Feedback must therefore be provided in simple non-technical language that is appropriate for the age and skill level of the learner. As learning progresses, players may require more detailed, technical information to refine the movement further. This suggestion appears somewhat at odds with the notion that the frequency of feedback should be decreased as learning progresses, but the distinction is that whilst the frequency of feedback may be reduced, the complexity can be increased.

Scientists have also explored how best to convey feedback to learners (for a detailed review, see Hodges and Franks, 2004). Whilst most augmented feedback

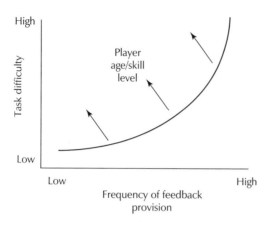

Figure 8.3 The frequency of feedback provision

Source: Author.

Notes: Some guidance as to how the frequency of providing feedback should vary with task difficulty and players' skill/age level. The curve would be moved to the left for younger or less skilled players.

is provided verbally, coaches now have greater access to video and other forms of technology that help provide technical information on skill execution. These techniques offer coaches a number of exciting opportunities for providing feedback in innovative and creative ways (for some examples of current technology, see www.quintic.com; www.siliconcoach.com; www.dartfish.com; www.pinnaclesys.com). It is not yet clear how best to integrate this technology into coaching practice.

PRESCRIPTIVE COACHING VS GUIDED DISCOVERY: THE UNDERLYING COACHING PHILOSOPHY

The philosophy employed by the coach underpins much of the discussion in the preceding sections. In particular, an important question is the extent to which coaches should be very prescriptive or 'hands on' in the instruction process as opposed to employing more 'hands off' guided-discovery learning strategies. Although less prescriptive approaches were advocated in the 1970s, the emphasis in recent times has been on more hands-on approaches, particularly in the United Kingdom. The learner receives large amounts of pre-practice information through demonstrations and verbal guidance, whilst detailed augmented feedback is provided post-practice. However, recently researchers have proposed that highly prescriptive instruction is likely to impose artificial constraints on learning, producing temporary and inefficient solutions to the movement problem. Skills learnt in this manner are also more likely to break down under pressure than those taught through less prescriptive methods (for a detailed review, see Masters and Maxwell, 2004). These concerns have resulted in a resurgence of interest in guided-discovery instructional approaches.

The renewed interest in less prescriptive approaches is partly due to the development of alternative perspectives based on ecological psychology and dynamical systems theory. These perspectives view the performer as a dynamic and complex system with the observed pattern of behaviour being a by-product of the unique constraints imposed on the learner. According to this viewpoint, movement coordination is achieved as a result of learners adapting to the constraints imposed on them during practice (for a detailed review, see Williams *et al.*, 1999; Davids *et al.*, 2003). The constraints that guide the learning process are determined by the individual characteristics of the learner, the nature of the task and the environmental conditions. The relationship between these constraints and the emergence of movement behaviour is illustrated in Figure 8.4.

The individual characteristics of the learner include the player's chronological and biological age, body morphology, fitness levels, perceptual and cognitive development, and emotions such as anxiety and self-confidence. Important task constraints include the rules and laws of the game, any conditions imposed by the coach and the equipment employed such as the size of the ball (i.e. scaling of equipment relative to body size). Finally, environmental constraints include the playing surface and weather conditions as well as access to different sources of sensory information such as vision and proprioception. Coaches are encouraged

Figure 8.4 The learning process guided and shaped by various constraints
Source: Adapted from Newell, 1985.

to manipulate these constraints such that the desired behaviour emerges through guided discovery rather than prescriptive coaching. Skills learnt via guided discovery are presumed to be more adaptable and unique and less likely to break down under pressure than those acquired through prescriptive approaches. Some examples of how coaches can manipulate constraints to facilitate skill acquisition are highlighted in Table 8.2.

OVERVIEW

The aim of this chapter was to provide guidance to those involved in the skill acquisition process in soccer. A model of instruction was presented as a conceptual framework around which to base the remainder of the chapter. It was proposed that demonstrations provide a convenient method of conveying information to the learner. Demonstrations may not always be effective, however, and verbal instructions may be equally as effective at least in instances where the information conveyed is fairly simple or the task requires the learner to develop a 'feel' for the movement. Demonstrations are most effective when used early in learning, after some initial practice on the skill and when 'faded out' over time. When structuring practice sessions, there is some evidence to suggest that specific, blocked practice is preferable early in learning and with young players. However, coaches should endeavour to introduce variable, random practice opportunities as early as permissible. The provision of augmented feedback is most important early in learning, but the frequency of providing feedback should be 'faded out' as quickly as possible. Players should be encouraged to take greater responsibility for their own learning by developing the ability to detect and correct errors in skill execution.

Perhaps the most important hurdle for the coach to overcome is appreciating the distinction between performance and learning. Highly prescriptive coaching with frequent use of demonstrations, specific, blocked practice conditions and copious amounts of augmented feedback produces better performance within a single practice session, whereas a less prescriptive approach to instruction coupled with variable, random practice conditions invariably produces better learning in the long term. The challenge for coaches is to find an effective balance between maintaining a reasonable level of performance during practice and promoting effective skill development. The process of manipulating constraints so as to help shape and guide learners' practice opportunities may provide innovative coaches with an important tool in meeting this challenge.

In conclusion, the intention in this chapter was not to present definitive guidelines about the skill instruction process but merely to encourage coaches and teachers

Table 8.2 Some examples of how the constraints of the learning environment can be manipulated to encourage certain types of behaviour

Constraints on behaviour	What can be manipulated?	Some examples	Emergent behaviour
Task	Conditions or rules	1- and 2-touch Score off a cross only 1-touch finish	Pass and move, awareness of other players Heading and volleying Positioning, sharp finishing, quick feet
	Pitch markings	Flank corridors No tackle zones Shooting zones	Crossing Containment, staying on feet Shooting and finishing
	Number of players	5 vs 3 defence vs attack 6 vs 4 attack vs defence	Playing out from back Width and penetration in attack
	Time	Restricting time in possession of ball	Fast counterattacking
	Equipment	Futebol de Salão (juggling practice and matches)	Encourages development of kinaesthetic touch/feel
Player	Coupling between limbs	Using rubber bands around the ankles with goalkeepers Tethering goalkeepers to the two goal posts using rope or elastic bands during 1 vs 1 situations	Goalkeepers move the feet together rather than cross the feet when moving across goal Greater awareness of goal position and angles during 1 vs 1 situations
Environment	Access to sensory information	Using special glasses to occlude sight of the feet during a ball control or dribbling task	Players rely on touch/feel rather than vision when orienting the foot to control the ball

Source: Adapted from Williams, 2003.

to reflect on current practice, particularly as it relates to the coaching of young children. The material should extend coaches' professional knowledge in this area. It is acknowledged that the instruction process is as much an art as a science, and consequently the skill of the coach is to blend this information with craft knowledge acquired through years of experience. Children learn at different rates and in varying ways and coaches therefore need to be flexible and adaptable to ensure that each individual benefits from the practice and instruction process.

REFERENCES

Bandura, A. (1986) *Social Foundations of Thought and Action: A Social-Cognitive Theory*. New York: Prentice-Hall.

Brady, F. (1998) A theoretical and empirical review of the contextual interference effect and the learning of motor skills. *Quest*, 50, 266–293.

Davids, K., Button, C. and Bennett, S.J. (2004) *Coordination and Control of Movement in Sport: An Ecological Approach*. Champaign, IL: Human Kinetics.

Fitts, P.M. and Posner, M.I. (1967) *Human Performance*. Belmont, CA: Brooks/ Cole.

Hodges, N.J. and Franks, I.M. (2004) The nature of feedback. In M. Hughes and I.M. Franks (eds) *Notation Analysis of Sport* (2nd edn). London: Routledge, 17–39.

Horn, R.R. and Williams, A.M. (2004) Observational learning: is it time we took another look? In A.M. Williams and N.J. Hodges (eds) *Skill Acquisition in Sport: Research, Theory and Practice*. London: Routledge, 175–206.

Lavalle, D., Kremer, J., Moran, A. and Williams, A.M. (2003) *Sport Psychology: Contemporary Themes*. London: Palgrave Publishing.

Magill, R.A. (2003) *Motor Learning: Concepts and Applications*. New York: McGraw-Hill.

Masters, R.S.W. and Maxwell, J.P. (2004) Implicit motor learning, reinvestment and movement disruption: what you don't know won't hurt you. In A.M. Williams and N.J. Hodges (eds) *Skill Acquisition in Sport: Research, Theory and Practice*. London: Routledge, 207–228.

Newell, K.M. (1985) Coordination, control and skill. In D. Goodman, R.B. Wilberg and I.M. Franks (eds) *Differing Perspectives in Motor Learning, Memory, and Control*. Amsterdam: Elsevier Science Publishing, 295–317.

Schmidt, R.A. and Lee, T.A. (1999) *Motor Control and Learning: A Behavioral Emphasis*. Champaign, IL: Human Kinetics.

Schmidt, R.A. and Wrisberg, C.A. (2000) *Motor Learning and Performance: From Principles To Practice*. Champaign, IL: Human Kinetics.

Scott, M.A., Williams, A.M. and Horn, R. (2003) The coordination of kicking techniques in children. In G. Savelsbergh, K. Davids, J. Van der Kamp and S. Bennett (eds) *Development of Movement Coordination in Children: Applications in the Field of Ergonomics, Health Sciences and Sport*. London: Routledge, 241–250.

Scully, D.M. and Newell, K.M. (1985) Observational learning and the acquisition of motor skills: towards a visual perception perspective. *Journal of Human Movement Studies*, 11, 169–186.

Summers, J. (2004) A historical perspective on skill acquisition. In A.M. Williams and N.J. Hodges (eds) *Skill Acquisition in Sport: Research, Theory and Practice*. London: Routledge, 1–26.

Ward, P., Hodges, N.J., Williams, A.M. and Starkes, J.L. (2004) Deliberate practice and expert performance: defining the path to excellence. In A.M. Williams and N.J. Hodges (eds) *Skill Acquisition in Sport: Research, Theory and Practice*. London: Routledge, 231–258.

Williams, A.M. (2003) Learning football skills effectively: challenging tradition. *Insight – The F.A. Coaches Association Journal*, 2(6), 37–39.

Williams, A.M. and Hodges, N.J. (eds) (2004) *Skill Acquisition in Sport: Research, Theory and Practice*. London: Routledge.

Williams, A.M., Davids, K. and Williams, J.G. (1999) *Visual Perception and Action in Sport*. London: E. & F.N. Spon.

Williams, A.M., Horn, R.R. and Hodges, N.J. (2003) Skill acquisition. In T. Reilly and A.M. Williams (eds) *Science and Soccer*, London: Routledge, 198–213.

Wulf, G. and Weigelt, C. (1997) Instructions about physical principles in learning a complex motor skill: to tell or not to tell. *Research Quarterly for Exercise and Sport*, 68, 362–367.

Yan, J.H., Thomas, J.R. and Thomas, K.T. (1998) Children's age moderates the effect of practice variability: a quantitative review. *Research Quarterly for Exercise and Sport*, 68, 362–367.

CHAPTER NINE

PERCEPTUAL AND COGNITIVE EXPERTISE: DEVELOPING GAME INTELLIGENCE

INTRODUCTION

The ability to anticipate opponents' intentions and to make appropriate decisions based on this information are essential components of skilled performance in soccer at youth and adult levels. Coaches and spectators often refer to elite players having superior 'game intelligence' when compared to their less elite counterparts. This enhanced 'awareness' of unfolding events provides skilled players with an air of having 'all the time in the world' as they move effortlessly to intercept an opponent's pass and initiate a counterattack. There is also widespread acceptance amongst coaches that at the elite level players are more often differentiated by these 'mental' or psychological factors rather than by physical or physiological characteristics (Williams and Reilly, 2000). Another common perception amongst coaches is that the ability to 'read the game' and to make appropriate strategic and tactical decisions are largely innate or, at best, far too difficult to improve through practice and instruction. The intention in this chapter is to remove some of the myths surrounding this area. The important factors underpinning game intelligence are highlighted and the issue of whether performance can be improved via various training interventions is considered.

HOW DO PLAYERS ANTICIPATE OPPONENTS' INTENTIONS?

The ability to determine what an opponent is likely to do before it actually happens is referred to as anticipation. The processes underlying anticipation skill are likely to be perceptual and cognitive in nature. Over the last 20 years or so scientists have been able to answer many of the mysteries surrounding this area. In the first part of this chapter, some of the important factors that contribute to skilled players' superior anticipation skill are outlined. Initially, an important myth about the nature of anticipation skill is dispelled.

Visual abilities

Coaches and spectators often use statements such as the player has 'great vision' or a 'superb eye' to describe a skilled individual. The perception is that skilled players are in some way blessed with superior visual function and that this ability contributes significantly to their advantage over the less skilled individual. Several researchers have examined this proposition by testing groups of skilled and less skilled players on a range of established tests designed to measure visual function. These tests, which are similar to those observed at a local opticians or an ophthalmology clinic, typically assess abilities such as depth perception, visual acuity, peripheral visual awareness and colour vision (for a detailed review, see Williams *et al.*, 1999).

The research evidence supporting the importance of visual abilities to high level sports performance is at best equivocal. Occasionally, skilled players outperform their less skilled counterparts, whereas on other instances the reverse finding has been observed (e.g. see Helsen and Starkes, 1999; Ward and Williams, 2003). In a study involving over 200 soccer players between the ages of 8 and 18 years from Premier League academies and local schools in England, there were no consistent differences between elite and sub-elite players on standard measures of visual function (see Ward and Williams, 2003). Moreover, using sophisticated statistical procedures, these measures accounted for no more than 5 per cent of the variance in anticipation skill across groups. Perceptual and cognitive skills accounted for the remaining 95 per cent of the variance and these are considered in greater detail in the sections that follow. Ward and Williams (2003) did report a significant effect of age on most of the measures employed, however, with visual function improving progressively from the age of 8 years reaching adult levels around 12 years of age.

Perceptual and cognitive skills

Since skilled players do not appear to have superior visual systems, the intriguing question is, how are they able to read the game more effectively than less skilled players? There is now a substantive body of literature to demonstrate that the expert's superiority over the novice is mainly due to refined and elaborate perceptual and cognitive knowledge structures that enable information to be interpreted in a more effective manner. The quality of the sensory information picked up by the eye is far less important than the manner in which this information is perceived and evaluated. Some of the key perceptual and cognitive skills are highlighted next.

Advance cue utilisation

Skilled soccer players are able to use information from opponents' postural orientation to anticipate their intentions. For example, using a variety of experimental techniques such as film occlusion, questionnaires and eye movement recording, researchers have shown that skilled soccer goalkeepers are able to use information arising from a penalty taker's run-up and body shape immediately prior to foot–ball contact to anticipate the destination of the penalty kick successfully (for a review of methodology, see Williams *et al.*, 1999). Figure 9.1 highlights the typical experimental paradigm employed to measure anticipation skill in the soccer penalty kick. A head-mounted eye movement registration system is employed to indicate where goalkeepers fixate their gaze.

The consensus of opinion is that the most important visual cues or clues include the orientation of the penalty taker's non-kicking foot, which tends to point in the

Figure 9.1 Anticipation skill and visual search behaviour at the soccer penalty kick

Source: Author (reproduced from Williams *et al.*, 1999).

Notes: The typical experimental set-up used to measure anticipation skill and visual search behaviour at the soccer penalty kick. The player is positioned on pressure sensitive mats to determine response time and a head-mounted eye movement registration system is used to assess visual point of gaze.

developing game intelligence

same direction as the ball's intended destination, the angle of the hips prior to ball contact, which tend to slope away from the goalkeeper when the ball is played to his/her right side, assuming a right-footed penalty taker, and the arc of the kicking leg as it approaches the ball (see Franks and Hanvey, 1997; Savelsbergh et al., 2002). It is likely that outfield players use the same visual cues to anticipate the intended destination of an opponent's pass, although, as yet, this assumption has not been confirmed empirically.

Sophisticated eye movement recording techniques have also been employed to identify differences in visual search behaviours between skilled and less skilled players. Skilled players search the display for relevant information in a more selective and efficient manner than less skilled players. They also make themselves aware of the positions and movements of players 'off the ball', whereas in contrast less skilled players tend to be guilty of 'ball watching' (Williams et al., 1994). Skilled players use peripheral vision to extract information from the display more than less skilled players. For example, in time-constrained situations near the penalty area skilled defenders tend to fixate gaze centrally on the player in possession whilst using peripheral vision to monitor the movements of opposing players (Williams and Davids, 1998). The suggestion is that skilled players are more attuned to the relative motion information evident in an opponent's postural orientation and in the movements of players 'off the ball'.

Pattern recognition

Skilled players are more accurate than less skilled players at recognising and recalling specific patterns of play during soccer matches. This skill is typically assessed using methodology developed in the field of cognitive psychology such as the recognition and recall paradigms (see Williams et al., 1999). Soccer players are presented with structured (i.e. taken directly from match play) and unstructured action sequences (teams warming up prior to a match or players walking on or off the field of play before or after the match) typically lasting a few seconds. After viewing each sequence, participants are asked either to recall the positions of the players presented on film (recall paradigm) or to indicate whether or not the clip had been viewed previously (recognition paradigm).

Typically, skilled players are more accurate than less skilled players on the structured viewing sequences only, with no differences being apparent on the unstructured trials. The presumption is that skilled players have developed through experience sophisticated knowledge structures and effective retrieval processes that enable them to recognise an evolving pattern of play at the outset, thereby facilitating anticipation skill (Ericsson and Kintsch, 1995). Recent research suggests that this ability to recognise patterns of play is the strongest predictor of anticipation skill in soccer players (Williams and Davids, 1995).

A priori expectations

The skilled soccer player's ability to pick up advance visual cues and to recognise patterns of play as the action evolves are essential to skilled anticipation. In addition to this ability to process 'contextual' information more effectively, skilled players have more accurate 'a priori' expectations of the events likely to unfold compared to less skilled players. This superior knowledge of 'situational probabilities' helps guide the skilled player's search for information when verifying initial expectations. For example, a skilled central defender might be aware of the fact that the opposition striker tends to make a diagonal run from central areas behind the right full back (a priori expectation), and consequently, when the opposition's left back is in a position to play the ball into this area, the centre back will attempt to pick up information from the player's postural orientation prior to making contact with the ball (advance visual cues) as well as the runs and movements of the attacking players (pattern recognition). These situational probabilities may be generic, applicable in a range of related scenarios involving different players and teams, or specific (relating to a particular team or player) in nature. The cyclical relationship between the player's initial expectations of what is likely to happen and the more effective interpretation of contextual information, presented in Figure 9.2, is the core foundation of anticipation skill in soccer (Williams, 2000).

Ward and Williams (2003) recently examined the importance of situational probabilities in soccer using elite and sub-elite soccer players between the ages of 8 and 18 years. Film sequences taken from youth international matches were paused immediately prior to the ball being passed and participants were required to assign probability values to the 'best passing options' available to the player in possession of the ball. The elite players were better than the sub-elite group at identifying those who were in the best position to receive the ball and were more accurate in assigning an appropriate probability value to players in threatening and non-threatening positions, as determined by a panel of expert coaches. It appears that the elite players were more adept than their sub-elite counterparts at assigning a hierarchy of probabilities to likely events. Moreover, there was a strong effect for age, with each of the older age groups outperforming their younger counterparts. These data are presented in Figure 9.3.

In summary, there is clear evidence to show that skilled soccer players have superior perceptual and cognitive skills than less skilled players regardless of age

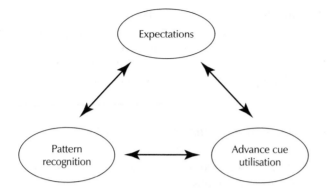

Figure 9.2 The relationship between players' expectations and the effective processing of contextual information

Source: Author.

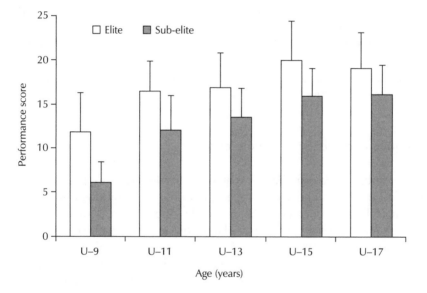

Figure 9.3 Mean performance scores on the situational probabilities test as a function of players' chronological age and skill level

Source: Data from Ward and Williams, 2003.

and that these skills contribute to their superior ability to 'read the game'. Skilled players have more accurate expectations of what is likely to happen in any given instance and are able to search the display more effectively than novices in order to pick up confirmatory cues from the postural orientation of the player in possession of the ball and the position and movements of players 'off the ball'.

HOW DO PLAYERS MAKE APPROPRIATE DECISIONS?

In the preceding sections the discussion mainly focused on players' ability to anticipate the opposition's likely intentions. Having determined the events likely to unfold, players must then make the correct decision as to what to do next. This decision may be based on several factors including the player's technical and physical ability, as well as that of the opponent, the current score and time remaining in the game, environmental and pitch conditions, and the strategic and tactical constraints outlined by the coach. Although skilled soccer players clearly make more appropriate decisions compared with less skilled players (e.g. see Helsen and Pauwels, 1993), relatively few researchers have attempted to outline the fundamental mechanisms underpinning the decision-making process. An exception has been the work of McPherson and French (and colleagues) using the knowledge-based paradigm and verbal protocol analysis (for a detailed review, see Williams *et al.*, 1999; McPherson and Kernodle, 2003).

Declarative and procedural knowledge

The knowledge-based paradigm is employed to identify more precisely the knowledge structures underlying skilled performance. Typically, researchers differentiate between procedural (i.e. knowing 'how to do' something) and declarative knowledge (i.e. knowing 'what to do' in a situation). For example, French and Thomas (1987) examined the involvement of these two types of knowledge in the development of skilled decision-making and overall performance in basketball. Basketball players aged 8 to 12 years and of low skill level completed a knowledge test to assess their declarative knowledge and shooting and dribbling skills tests to determine their procedural knowledge. The children's performance during match play was assessed using a subjective rating sheet to evaluate their control of the basketball, their decision accuracy and ability to execute specific skills. The skilled and older children possessed more basketball knowledge, scored higher on the shooting skills test and showed better performances during matches. The children's score on the declarative knowledge test was strongly related to their decision-making performance during matches, whilst performance on the dribbling and shooting skills was linked with these aspects of performance during matches.

In follow-up studies, McPherson and French (1991) showed that children's declarative and procedural skills improve with specific instruction over the course of a competitive season and that the increase in sport-specific knowledge is strongly related to improved decision-making in the sport. They also suggested that motor skills improve most effectively when instruction specifically focuses on these aspects of performance during practice, whereas in contrast, cognitive aspects of performance such as decision-making improve regardless of whether the instruction is oriented towards motor skill instruction or strategic aspects of performance. Although motor and decision-making skills improve more efficiently when these aspects are stressed within the instruction programme, players can learn tactical and strategic skills without specific instruction even when the focus in training is on developing technical skills, provided, of course, that the practice session mimics those situations experienced during regular match play.

Action plan profiles and current event profiles

Verbal report or 'think-aloud' protocols have also been employed to explore the breadth, depth and diversity of knowledge used during decision-making. Players normally view a schematic or video sequence representing a typical match scenario and are required to indicate what knowledge is important, and why, for strategic decision-making. Alternatively, in certain sports, such as tennis, players may be interviewed at the end of a specific point during match play and asked the question 'What were you thinking about during the last passage of play?' Skilled players possess more sophisticated knowledge structures than less skilled players with stronger, yet more flexible connections and linkages between concepts, enabling them to know when or under what conditions to apply particular actions. Skilled performers are able to represent problems at a deeper, more principled level, solving problems by using concepts, semantics and principles rather than the more superficial, syntactic elements employed by less skilled players.

McPherson and Kernodle (2003) argued that skilled players develop long-term memory adaptations to mediate performance. These adaptations are referred to as 'action plan profiles' and 'current event profiles' respectively. Action plan profiles are used to activate general sport-specific rules for decision-making. For example, when certain conditions apply (e.g. a particular game configuration such as a team mate getting in front of a defender on the near post) then the player must respond in a certain way (e.g. deliver a cross into the near post region).

The prediction is that skilled players possess an extensive library of action plan profiles and are more consistent then less skilled players in selecting the best response to make in any given instance.

Greater flexibility is provided by current event profiles. These contain tactical scripts and situation prototypes that guide the response process. Information relating to past, current and possible future events is stored in the memory and monitored during performance ready for activation or updating when the need arises. Current event profiles provide access to more recent information through specialised monitoring, encoding and retrieval processes linking together previous experiences with incidents from recent matches and those that have arisen during the current match. These current event profiles are also likely to be specific to a particular team or opponent, as opposed to action plan profiles that may be more general in nature. The presumption is that novice level, youth and adult players possess poor problem representations to guide decision-making, whereas intermediate level adult performers' and youth experts' response selection behaviours are guided by action plan profiles and advanced level adult players have access to both action plan and current event profiles. This model of skill development is presented in Figure 9.4.

In summary, with a few notable exceptions, there has been limited research on decision-making skill and its development in sport generally, and specifically in soccer. The research that does exist highlights the importance of elaborate and sophisticated problem representations that contain well-developed action plan and current event profiles. Further research is needed to determine how action plan and current event profiles develop amongst players varying in age and skill level and what type of instruction is most appropriate to facilitate the acquisition of these knowledge structures and effective processes for response selection.

HOW DO THESE SKILLS DEVELOP WITH AGE, PRACTICE AND EXPERIENCE?

Game intelligence develops as a result of the perceptual and cognitive adaptations that arise following many years of deliberate, purposeful practice in the sport (Ericsson, 1996). Although genetic predispositions and a player's chronological and biological maturity may impose certain constraints, these factors appear to be less important in the development of game intelligence than practice and experience within the sport. For example, Ward and Williams (2003) showed that perceptual and cognitive skills improve as a function of experience in groups of elite and sub-elite soccer players ranging from 8 to 18 years of age. The elite soccer players were superior to their sub-elite counterparts in predicting key

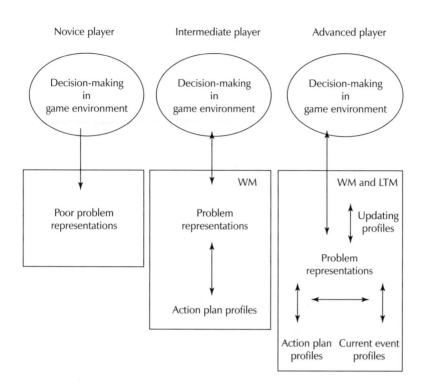

Figure 9.4 The decision-making model depicting problem representations at various skill levels

Source: McPherson and Kernodle, 2003.

Notes: WM = Working memory; LTM = Long-term memory.

player involvement when observing attacking plays and in assigning more accurate probability values to each player. The elite players were also able to use advance information available within emerging patterns of play and from postural cues more effectively than sub-elite players. Although skill-based differences were apparent as early as 8–9 years of age, the older age groups (i.e. 10–11, 12–13, 14–15, 16–17 years) generally showed better performance on various measures of perceptual and cognitive skill compared to their younger counterparts, regardless of skill level (e.g. see Figure 9.3).

A follow-up study indicates that differences in perceptual and cognitive skill between the elite and sub-elite 8–9-year-olds are more likely to be a function of accumulated practice hours rather than maturational or genetic factors. Semi-structured interviews and performance diaries were employed to determine the age at which players commenced participation in the sport and the typical amount

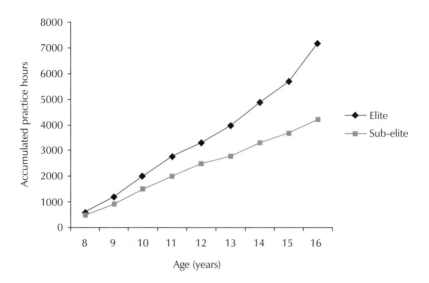

Figure 9.5 Accumulated practice hours for elite and sub-elite players

Source: Author.

Note: Accumulated practice hours for elite and sub-elite players as determined by retrospective recall using questionnaires and semi-structured interviews.

of time devoted to practice activities. Figure 9.5 indicates that although both groups of players commenced participation at a similar age, by 9 years of age the elite players had accumulated around an extra 200 hours of team/individual practice and match play. The difference in practice exposure between skill groups continued to increase with age such that by the age of 16 years the elite players had accumulated an extra 2500 hours of practice compared to their sub-elite counterparts.

Ward and co-workers (2004) provided further support for the notion that expertise is a by-product of specific adaptations to the performance context. Skilled soccer defensive and offensive players were asked to anticipate film sequences viewed from either the perspective of a defender or that of an attacker. The defenders showed superior anticipatory performance compared to the equally skilled forwards, particularly when viewing clips presented from a defensive perspective. The suggestion is that the superior anticipation skill of skilled defenders compared to the forwards could be a by-product of different accumulated in-game experiences and intricate idiosyncrasies in task-specific knowledge. It may be the case that defenders' in-game duties dictate that they experience anticipatory scenarios more frequently and retain more refined and relevant task-specific knowledge, thus facilitating the anticipation process.

CAN THE ACQUISITION OF GAME INTELLIGENCE SKILLS BE FACILITATED THROUGH PRACTICE AND INSTRUCTION?

An important question for coaches and scientists is whether the acquisition of game intelligence skills can be facilitated through practice and instruction (see Chapter 10). Coaches typically believe that these skills are somewhat innate and difficult to improve through structured interventions. Although there are few, if any, published studies focusing on the acquisition of decision-making skill, an increasing body of literature exists to show that perceptual and cognitive skills such as advance cue recognition, pattern recognition and knowledge of situational probabilities can be improved through practice and instruction (for a detailed review of this literature, see Williams and Grant, 1999; Williams and Ward, 2003).

The prototypical approach has involved using video simulation of the performance context coupled with instruction as to the important visual cues that players should be aware of when attempting to anticipate future events and feedback as to subsequent performance. Williams and Burwitz (1993) and Franks and Hanvey (1997), amongst others, have used this type of approach to improve goalkeepers' performance at soccer penalty kicks. In a similar vein, it would appear logical to employ this type of intervention to improve the ability of outfield players to pick up relevant information from an opponent's postural orientation prior to a pass. This type of simulation could easily be created using a video camera and basic editing facilities. Thus far, the majority of researchers have attempted to develop players' abilities to pick up postural information cues using relatively closed-play situations such as the soccer penalty kick, the penalty flick in field-hockey or the tennis serve. It is acknowledged that the process of training players to pick up important information cues in more dynamic, open-play situations may be more complex due to the variability inherent in such sequences of play. The aim when attempting to improve a player's ability to pick up advance visual cues in open-play scenarios may be to highlight general rules or relationships rather than to develop specific links between a particular cue and the desired response behaviour.

Although there is no research directly involving soccer, work using American football and volleyball suggests that pattern recognition skills can be improved through repeated exposure to a variety of related action sequences. It is suggested that exposure to specific patterns of play in soccer may lead to the development of specialised receptors or detectors that facilitate the pattern recognition process. These detectors develop and strengthen with exposure to the stimulus or stimuli resulting in increased speed, accuracy and general fluency with which stimuli are processed. Research is under way to determine whether repeated exposure to different types of offensive sequences (e.g. patterns of play involving overlap

149

runs, split runs or 'third man running') via video simulation can facilitate the recognition of similar patterns of play in soccer. Laboratory-based recognition and recall tests coupled with various measures of transfer are being employed to evaluate the effectiveness of such training programmes.

There are few published studies concerning the issue of whether knowledge of situational probabilities can be trained, despite its perceived importance in guiding the search for contextual information during anticipatory situations. An exception is a recent study by Williams and colleagues (2004) where novice, adult soccer players' ability to successfully predict an opponent's likely passing options improved following 45 minutes of video simulation, instruction and feedback on subsequent performance. It therefore appears likely that video technology, perhaps coupled with quantitative match analysis data, could be employed to improve players' knowledge of situational probabilities in soccer. Many soccer teams already use video to review recent performances and to scout forthcoming opponents. Although this is often a rather informal process that relies primarily on access to qualitative video sequences, players and coaches are now familiar with this type of intervention and may be amenable to a more structured form of practice. These structured training sessions may involve presentation of quantitative statistics regarding the moves and actions typically performed by forthcoming opponents. For example, analysis may reveal that the opposition typically plays to a certain pattern or that attackers are consistent (i.e. predictable) in their movement patterns. Awareness of such points markedly improves players' abilities to make accurate predictions regarding their opponents' actions. This information can also be built upon in training using specific coaching practices or drills.

Although preliminary findings are encouraging and highlight the potential of training programmes that attempt to improve perceptual and cognitive skill, there are several issues that need to be addressed before the use of such interventions becomes more widespread in soccer. The questions that need to be answered include: How effective is video and other forms of simulation such as virtual reality compared with on-field instruction? How should simulations be designed to mimic the performance environment? How should perceptual/cognitive training sessions be structured for effective learning? What type of instruction is most effective in facilitating training effects? At what age and skill level should coaches introduce this form of instruction? Whilst each of these issues is discussed elsewhere (e.g. see Williams and Grant, 1999; Williams and Ward, 2003), the question of whether there are key time windows for the acquisition of game intelligence skills is considered next.

Are there key 'time windows' for the acquisition of such skills?

An important question for coaches is, at what age or skill level is a player most susceptible to perceptual and cognitive training? Only limited research evidence exists to guide coaches when attempting to answer this question. As far as the chronological age of the player is concerned, the differences in perceptual and cognitive skill between elite and sub-elite soccer players are evident as early as 8–9 years of age (Ward and Williams, 2003). Marked improvements in performance on such measures, particularly pattern recognition skill, occur around 12 years of age. A suggestion therefore is that young players may be amenable to this type of instruction as early as 8–12 years of age. Certainly, according to the work of Piaget (1962) and others, this age bracket would appear important as far as children's general cognitive development is concerned. It may be difficult to provide more definitive guidelines to coaches on this issue because of the likely differences in perceptual/cognitive development across individuals.

The decision-making skills of 8–10-year-old tennis players can be improved following specific strategic and tactical instruction, whilst similar observations have been reported using 12–14-year-old soccer players (see Williams and Grant, 1999). Others have argued that the development of strategic and tactical knowledge should be closely related to motor skill development. For example, if players are unable to play a 40-yard diagonal pass, then they are unlikely to include this option as part of their decision-making strategy. The content and focus of practice sessions are therefore likely to determine development of the knowledge representations underpinning game intelligence as well as motor skill acquisition.

The majority of researchers have used novice players as participants in studies that attempt to improve game intelligence. Although novice players certainly have greater scope for performance improvement, it appears sensible for the learner to have at least a basic mastery of the important technical and strategic skills. It may be that this type of instruction is more beneficial with intermediate or expert players, where perceptual and cognitive skills are likely to make a more significant contribution to performance. Whilst the improvements observed at advanced stages of learning are likely to be small, the apparent benefits may nonetheless be substantial compared with the scope for improvement on technical or physical aspects of performance.

SUMMARY AND CONCLUSIONS

The aim of this chapter was to provide an overview of current understanding on game intelligence in soccer, particularly as it relates to youth players. The ability to read the game and to make appropriate decisions is important for performance at all levels of the game, but particularly at the elite level. The superior game intelligence of skilled players compared to less skilled counterparts is a by-product of more refined and elaborate perceptual and cognitive knowledge structures that help guide their search for relevant cues and ensure that this information is subsequently processed in the most effective and efficient manner. Perceptual and cognitive expertise in soccer, as in other sports, is the result of specific adaptations to the constraints imposed by the performance environment.

An important perceptual-cognitive skill is the ability to anticipate opponents' likely intentions. Skilled players are able to pick up information or visual clues from an opponent's body shape to help them anticipate pass destination and are able to recognise a pattern of play very early in its development. This ability to process information effectively from the display as action sequences unfold is coupled with more accurate and elaborate knowledge regarding the likely probabilities of certain events occurring. In a similar manner, skilled players develop elaborate knowledge structures, called action plan and current event profiles, to guide their strategic and tactical decision-making.

Whilst game intelligence is likely to improve with experience irrespective of coaching intervention, researchers have demonstrated that the effective acquisition of such skills can be facilitated through practice and instruction. In particular, video simulation of the performance environment coupled with instruction and feedback has shown considerable potential for performance enhancement in soccer. This type of instruction may be particularly useful with youth players of intermediate ability level, as well as with adults.

REFERENCES

Ericsson, K.A. (ed.) (1996) *The Road to Excellence*. New Jersey: Lawrence Erlbaum Associates.

Ericsson, K.A. and Kintsch, W. (1995) Long-term working memory. *Psychological Review*, 102, 211–245.

Franks, I.M. and Hanvey, T. (1997) Cues for goalkeepers: high-tech methods used to measure penalty shot response. *Soccer Journal*, May/June, 30–38.

French, K.E. and Thomas, J.R. (1987) The relation of knowledge development to children's basketball performance. *Journal of Sport Psychology*, 9, 15–32.

Helsen, W.F. and Pauwels, J.M. (1993) The relationship between expertise and visual information processing in sport. In J.L. Starkes and F. Allard (eds) *Cognitive Issues in Motor Expertise*. Amsterdam: Elsevier Science Publishing, 109–134.

Helsen, W.F. and Starkes, J.L. (1999) A multidimensional approach to skilled perception and performance in sport. *Applied Cognitive Psychology*, 13, 1–27.

McPherson, S.L. and French, K.E. (1991) Changes in cognitive strategy and motor skill in tennis. *Journal of Sport and Exercise Psychology*, 13, 26–41.

McPherson, S.L. and Kernodle, M.W. (2003) Tactics the neglected attribute of expertise: problem representations and performance skills of developing perceptual expertise in sport. In J.L. Starkes and K.A. Ericsson (eds) *Expert Performance in Sports: Advances in Research on Sport Expertise*. Champaign, IL: Human Kinetics.

Piaget, J. (1962) *Play, Dreams, and Imitation in Childhood*. New York: Norton.

Savelsbergh, G.J.P., Williams, A.M., van der Kamp, J. and Ward, P. (2002) Visual search, anticipation and expertise in soccer goalkeepers. *Journal of Sports Sciences*, 20, 279–287.

Ward, J., Williams, A.M., Ward, P. and Smeeton, N.J. (2004) The effects of playing position and viewing perspective on anticipation in soccer. *Journal of Sports Sciences*, 22, 575.

Ward, P. and Williams, A.M. (2003) Perceptual and cognitive skill development in soccer: the multidimensional nature of expert performance. *Journal of Sport and Exercise Psychology*, 25, 1, 93–111.

Williams, A.M. (2000) Perceptual skill in soccer: implications for talent identification and development. *Journal of Sports Sciences*, 18, 737–740.

Williams, A.M. and Burwitz, L. (1993) Advance cue utilisation in soccer. In T. Reilly, J. Clarys and A. Stibbe (eds) *Science and Football II*. London: E. & F.N. Spon, 239–244.

Williams, A.M. and Davids, K. (1995) Declarative knowledge in sport: a byproduct of experience or a characteristic of expertise? *Journal of Sport and Exercise Psychology*, 17, 259–275.

Williams, A.M. and Davids, K. (1998) Visual search strategy, selective attention, and expertise in soccer. *Research Quarterly for Exercise and Sport*, 69, 111–128.

Williams, A.M. and Grant, A. (1999) Training perceptual skill in sport. *International Journal of Sport and Exercise Psychology*, 30, 194–220.

Williams, A.M. and Reilly, T. (2000) Talent identification and development in soccer. *Journal of Sports Sciences*, 18, 657–667.

Williams, A.M. and Ward, P. (2003) Developing perceptual expertise in sport. In J.L. Starkes and K.A. Ericsson (eds) *Expert Performance in Sports: Advances in Research on Sport Expertise*. Champaign, IL: Human Kinetics.

Williams, A.M., Davids, K. and Williams, J.G. (1999) *Visual Perception and Action in Sport*. London: E. & F.N. Spon.

Williams, A.M., Davids, K., Burwitz, L. and Williams, J.G. (1994) Visual search strategies of experienced and inexperienced soccer players. *Research Quarterly for Exercise and Sport*, 5, 127–135.

Williams, A.M., Heron, K., Ward, P. and Smeeton, N.J. (2004) Using situational probabilities to train perceptual and cognitive skill in novice soccer players. In T. Reilly, J. Cabri and D. Arajuo (eds) *Science and Football VI*. London: Taylor & Francis.

CHAPTER TEN

PEDAGOGY APPLIED TO YOUTH SOCCER COACHING

INTRODUCTION

Effective soccer coaching is central to the optimal development of children's performance and development. The process of developing children's motor skills and game performance is undertaken by thousands of coaches, teachers and parents on a day to day basis. Coaching sport as a profession is relatively new, and now great emphasis is placed upon effective and professional coaching at all levels of sport. Coach education programmes are now central to all major sports in the UK and Western countries.

The promotion and success of soccer rely upon the effective education and development of its participants such as coaches and players (Potrac *et al.*, 2000). Consequently the study of coaching is breaking new ground and is helping to inform the coaching process. Whilst coaching science is very young as a subject of study rapid progress has been made in coaching practice since the Eastern European countries dominated many Olympic sports. Much was learnt from the professional and meticulous preparation of elite sports girls, boys, women and men in Eastern Europe. Both East Germany and the Soviet Union invested heavily in the production of academically and professionally equipped coaches. Sports teachers and coaches were required to study sport to degree level qualification. Entry requirements for these degree courses were rigorous and depended on academic education, fitness and sports performance. Furthermore, as with the East German system in the 1970s and 1980s, sports-related subjects from GCSE through to degree level are popular areas of academic study for students in the Western world. A vast array of teaching and coaching manuals have been published in almost every country affiliated to FIFA and most national associations have sophisticated development plans for coaches and players.

Until recently the other major influence on coaching practice prior to the development of a coach education system in the UK was the physical education profession. From the early part of the twentieth century physical educators have planned and delivered a curriculum using sport as a vehicle to educate school children. Coach educators are now using the well-developed practices and values used in physical education. Whilst the rationale for taking part in physical education is different to sport (one being by obligation, the other by choice) the ethical, moral and educational issues in teaching and coaching are similar. Despite debate over the strict definitions of teaching and coaching, both involve the same processes and should have similar goals for young people. Coaching and teaching should educate participants from a young age to become responsible for development in their sport and activity over a lifetime. The role of the physical educator is to provide a particular aspect of a broad and balanced school-based education. On the other hand, a coach of a single sport (such as soccer) is more concerned with the needs of the sport and aims to integrate psychological, physiological and sociological knowledge in the context of child development. Coaches with expert knowledge in these domains and extensive experience in coaching are likely to be more effective in helping young soccer players meet their potential.

COACHING COMPETENCES

Coaching competence can be separated into five stages of development. Being able to assist coaches during training sessions characterises the first stage whereas a complete mastery of the scientific basis of soccer coaching characterises the fifth stage. This classification highlights a progressive pathway towards coaching expertise. The successful navigation of this pathway requires the potential soccer coach to develop a vast array of coaching attributes. Coaching practitioners require not only an expansive technical knowledge of their sport, but also the pedagogical skills of a teacher, the counselling wisdom of a psychologist, the training expertise of a sociologist and the administrative leadership of a business executive. Coaches of junior soccer also require additional expertise in child development, educational psychology and parental guidance. Moreover, successful coaches have a detailed knowledge of desirable coaching behaviours deemed effective for enhancing player performance. The development of coaching attributes of planner, administrator, performer, psychologist, sociologist, physiologist, sports physician, developmentalist and teacher who is able to develop individuals and teams in youth soccer is an awesome task. This chapter aims to challenge coaches and students of football to develop the smorgasbord of attributes necessary to meet this challenge.

The IKEA principle

Recently the acronym IKEA (I: information; K: knowledge; E: expertise; A: application) has been used to describe the key principles of coaching soccer. We now live in the so-called information (I) age. Using the Google search engine to search for soccer on the Internet revealed 16,300,000 hits for 'football', 8,840,000 for soccer, 720,000 for youth soccer, 876,000 for youth football, 1,510,000 for women's football, 85,200 for girls' football. Access to information on soccer coaching is now almost unlimited. However, no amount of information guarantees knowledge (K).

Coaching knowledge is derived from knowing what to do and how to do it. As information is easier to acquire, more time should be available for coaches to acquire knowledge and expertise (E). As knowledge is refined and developed the coach becomes more expert. The effective application (A) of expertise by the youth soccer coach will result in young players meeting their aspirations and potential. Therefore, knowledge and expertise represent the basic building blocks for effective coaching of youth soccer players. In the next sections of this chapter, knowledge domains and their use are outlined to help youth soccer coaches understand the coaching process. Principles of expertise have been covered in Chapter 8.

KNOWLEDGE DOMAINS FOR COACHING

There are three main domains of knowledge required for effective coaching. A coach's knowledge of psychomotor (skills/fitness), affective (social, working with others) and cognitive (knowledge/understanding) domains is essential for the planning and delivery of a holistic soccer education for young players. Basic concepts and principles supporting these domains have been covered elsewhere in this text. An expert coach of youth soccer would be able to synthesise principles of growth and development with domain knowledge and then present activities and practices that are developmentally affordable and provide appropriate opportunities and experiences for young players.

Psychomotor domain

The psychomotor domain involves the development of complex motor skills as well as fitness outcomes. These may be promoted during coaching sessions that aim to increase skill and fitness. A long-term psychomotor goal for a child might be to be fit and skilful enough to play soccer at academy level.

Cognitive domain

The cognitive domain refers to aims and objectives that describe the knowledge and ability to process information. These are intellectual processes related to knowledge and understanding. Cognitive outcomes relate to what players should know, for example how to stretch the hamstring muscles before playing soccer and how to design an exercise programme to increase flexibility. A player's ability to problem-solve in a game context would allow the coach to assess knowledge and understanding. For example, a problem might be how to transfer the knowledge of defensive strategy from a 5-a-side to an 11-a-side game of soccer where space and time are different.

Affective domain

The affective domain describes a young player's feelings, values and social behaviour. These may be met through developing a player's ability to deal with success and failure, to understand sportsmanship and the behaviour that goes with it and to learn to wait for his/her turn. Also positive self-esteem and respect for others and their safety may also be affective aims.

The coach may plan to develop these aspects through single or multiple aims. For example, the coach asks the player to lean back more to achieve greater height on chipping the ball (psychomotor only). This task may be compared to one where players are asked to find out any number of ways to get height on the ball (psychomotor and cognitive). A coach developing all three domains together may ask one youngster to observe another pair chipping the ball to each other. The group next decides what needs to be done to achieve the highest and most accurate chip kick (psychomotor, cognitive and affective). The last experience is the richer experience as more coaching aims are met.

Expert coaches maximise the potential for learning and development in their young soccer players by carefully planning a balanced coaching programme. The programme aims not only to develop soccer ability but also to promote other general behaviours essential to sound and balanced growth and development in youngsters. Developing transferable life-skills is important as few players make a living out of playing soccer. Furthermore, those who do manage to become professional players have careers that are relatively short, mostly lasting 10 years or less. Whilst the focus is clearly on developing performance, other equally valuable aims could also be met through careful planning of coaching programmes. The highly successful coach ultimately utilises his/her expertise to promote a youngster's deep desire to 'play' the game.

COACHING SOCCER AS A GOAL-ORIENTED PROCESS

The attributes of the player and coach necessary for successful soccer performance are described in Winkler (2001). The essential ingredients for both the player and coach are incorporated in Figure 10.1.

Young players should be coached through the affective, cognitive and psycho-motor domains and these should be developed through long-term planning and regular assessment of player performance by the coach. If a coach has applied the range of knowledge outlined by the three domains then s/he will be adequately equipped to provide optimal soccer education for the developing young player. The arrows in Figure 10.1 reflect the fact that the process of learning is two-way. Expert coaches readily agree that they learn as much from their players as the players do from them. This two-way process differs depending on the age of the group being coached.

All coaching plans should have clear aims, goals and objectives. An aim is an overarching goal such as: 'this season our aim is to develop skills and strategies for attacking and defending from set pieces'. There would be multiple objectives such as left and right foot crosses, setting a defensive wall, getting free at throw-ins and so on. For each of these objectives, the coach would design a number of learning activities. Finally, performance against these aims and objectives should be recorded.

The aims of each coaching plan should include objectives related to each domain of knowledge. A session on ball skills with 9-year-olds will have a psychomotor goal. Observation of a video highlighting the offside trap with 15-year-olds will have a mainly cognitive goal. A combined session starting with a video and then applying this to a practice will have both cognitive and psychomotor goals.

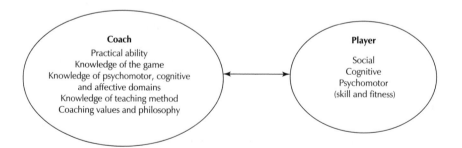

Figure 10.1 Basic attributes of coaches and players
Source: Adapted from Winkler, 2001.

Procedural and declarative knowledge

The principles of procedural and declarative knowledge for players have been discussed in Chapter 9 (perceptual and cognitive expertise). These principles may also be applied to the coach. Coaching as a 'goal-oriented process' suggests that coaches develop their 'declarative knowledge' ('what') compared to 'procedural knowledge' ('how'). Players and coaches bring their accumulated declarative and procedural knowledge to every coaching session and these are supported by knowledge from the psychomotor, cognitive and affective domains. The coach then engages young players in soccer activities that reinforce existing or develop new knowledge through the solution of new problems. The quality of the engagement is dependent on the knowledge of the coach. Many coaches when they start out have sound declarative knowledge as ex-players. However, the ability required to organise and plan coaching sessions requires detailed procedural knowledge. Coaching knowledge should therefore be organised into two main types: procedural and declarative.

Procedural knowledge is knowledge about how to do things; it is often kinaesthetic in nature. Coaches aim to master many instructional skills just as youngsters master playing skills. Once mastered, these skills are stored and recalled. Sound procedural knowledge helps coaches design practice sessions within the structure of a practice season. *Declarative* knowledge is concerned with facts, e.g. a young soccer player understands the strengths and weaknesses of a 3-4-1 compared to a 4-4-2 team formation. Players may also use their declarative knowledge to solve problems in game-related situations.

For players and coaches, procedural knowledge and declarative knowledge take time and effort to acquire. The adage 'use it or lose it' tends to apply. However, once a coach develops a sound procedural approach to efficiently organising a group of 30 players (for example, into six grids for 3 vs 2 passing practice, or organising appropriate space and distance to coach the chip pass to 10-year-olds), this knowledge remains for a lifetime.

A good example of procedural knowledge is how to teach and organise an activity using the IDEA procedure. First the coach will introduce (I) the activity to the players, s/he will demonstrate (D), then explain (E) the demonstration and finally apply it (A) to the game context. Coaches may use this 'procedure' when coaching 'any' particular skill or strategy.

The problem with the procedural and declarative knowledge system is that it may be over-simplistic and relies too much on recall. Critics suggest that as much time as possible should be spent using declarative knowledge in *problem-solving activities*. There may be a core of soccer-specific declarative knowledge. Five categories of knowledge relevant to soccer players are worth noting: rules of the game, on-the-ball skills, off-the-ball movements, communication and teamwork, and game strategies. Both the coach and young player need to be in harmony to integrate these aspects of knowledge into overall performance. The coach needs to think of methods to teach declarative knowledge whilst players need to be receptive in receiving and developing their knowledge through observation (watching game play) practice and game play with coach, parents, friends or significant others. Some research has been undertaken on knowledge in the pedagogy of youth soccer. In a review of Australian coach education courses (Australian Sports Commission, 1997) results suggested that too much time was given to procedural at the expense of declarative knowledge. Evidence suggests that coaches are clear about 'how' to coach soccer drills such as dribbling, whereas they are less clear as to 'why' the drills are good at improving dribbling. Furthermore, coaches with immature declarative knowledge tend to analyse games at a superficial level.

Consider a scenario where a midfielder misses a tackle and the opposition scores. The coach subsequently decides that tackling practice (procedural) is essential in future practices. Perhaps the more mature coach would have looked at how possession was lost in the first place. This coach may then consider activities for the team as a defensive unit (declarative knowledge) in addition to the skill of tackling itself.

APPROACHES TO PLANNING COACHING SESSIONS AND PROGRAMMES

In addition to the IDEA principle, coaches may also plan to follow the *analysis, practice, attention-management* approach to instruction listed below.

1   *Analysis* – thinking about what you are doing, how you are doing it, and how you could do it better.
    Example: I am working on crosses, but seldom seem to get players to deliver with accuracy. Perhaps I should reduce the distance and place scoring targets on the floor and award points if the players hit them. More points will be awarded for crosses of greater length.
2   *Practice* – to the point where the skill becomes automatic. This can be achieved through progressively increasing the difficulty of the drill.
    Example: During the under-15s season, include a regular routine of keep the ball up football as the introductory start to every coaching session for 12 weeks.
3   *Attention-management* – getting and maintaining attention.
    Example: Ensure the right motivational climate by praising and rewarding where appropriate. Make sure that there is visual and auditory contact

160

between players and coaches during instruction. Longer attention spans and less direct control are required with increasing age and maturity.

The difference in approach when the coach uses procedural and declarative learning is that the former requires high levels of arousal and intense effort whereas the latter requires a quiet relaxing environment and large amounts of attention from players. Coaches will recognise the potential to increase declarative learning with age as players become more receptive, have greater levels of concentration and can cope with abstract principles (e.g. if *you* were in situation x as the defender in a 2 vs 1 encounter what would you do?) as well as concrete (e.g. *you* are in situation x as the defender and the two attackers are moving towards you, try and maintain your space between the two attackers and stay goal side) principles. As young players mature, they become more able to create general concepts from fragmented experiences. Fragmented experiences come from many hours of practice and game play. These learning experiences build conceptual knowledge of soccer. Conceptual learning can come from declarative, procedural, and domains of knowledge. Nevertheless, general concepts may be influenced by cultural behaviour and individual values. Brazilian flair, German organisation, British endeavour represent metaphors for cultural and individual values.

SOCCER CONCEPTS

Developing knowledge in young players also requires correct use of language. The language used should be understood by all participants and should be directly related to the activity being coached. In order to facilitate understanding, movement concepts have been proposed (Rink, 1985). Action words, qualities, principles, strategies, effects and affects are concepts that relate to the coaching content of soccer.

Soccer concepts should be considered while planning every coaching unit or session. Inclusion of all concepts in all sessions is possible with careful planning. Coaches are likely to focus on two or more concepts in a single session. This approach ensures that each concept can be covered in depth. Coaches will consider these concepts alongside the needs of the players. If a youth soccer team is receiving an excessive number of bookings or suspensions, the expert coach may combine an analysis of the skills that lead to fouls and an analysis of social behaviour towards officials and opposition players. The coach will then use 'soccer affects' activities to develop positive social behaviour alongside soccer strategies to identify the positional limitations of team units that may contribute to individual players committing fouls. Soccer coaches should use concepts to plan and develop

Table 10.1 Action words used while coaching youth soccer

Concept	Description	Example
Action words	Turn, spin, jump, kick, volley, balance	Increasing the size of the base stabilises movement
Qualities	Quickness, directness, levels, shape, body awareness	Quality of effort and appreciation of skilled movement
Principles	Follow-through, basic mechanics, force production and reduction, spin	Kinetic chain. More body parts, more force produced
Strategies	Attack and defence strategies Cooperation with others	Cooperation: a ball should be passed so that the receiver can control it
Effects	Short- and long-term effects of exercise on heart, flexibility and strength	Increasing body temperature is essential for increased flexibility prior to performance
Affects	Relationships with others, expressions, feelings, teamwork, behaviour and sportsmanship	Behaviour: good social behaviour enables positive team relationships to develop

Source: Winkler, 2001.

coaching units throughout a season. This will help coaches define the content of their soccer programmes and identify essential aspects required for the age and stage of their playing group.

Coaches who aim to become expert practitioners need to use soccer concepts and declarative knowledge regularly. Advanced use of soccer concepts and declarative knowledge will help coaches develop breadth and depth to their work. Furthermore, coaches who can influence young players' conceptual knowledge can make learning more exciting and long-lasting. Coaches who have an understanding of child development will be able to design activities that promote procedural and declarative knowledge and match these to players' age and stage of development.

PSYCHOLOGY OF CHILD DEVELOPMENT

While a chapter of this nature cannot deal in detail with the extensive research into child development a number of basic principles will be covered. These principles are mainly from Piaget's theory of cognitive development and Ericsson's theory of psychosocial development. Piaget described four main developmental stages; these are sensory motor, pre-operational, concrete operational and formal operational stages.

The sensory motor stage is described as the build-up of basic movement schema into complex movement patterns that provide the major means for communication during the first two years of life. The pre-operational stage describes development between 2 and 4 years of age. At this age, the child has significant thoughts and representations through the exploration of the environment. This period is the essential exploratory phase. Between 8 and 11 years of age the concrete operational stage appears. During this stage children develop logical thought and can relate both themselves and objects to the world around them. Children develop rational thinking after the age of 12 and are able to think hypothetically. This stage is described as the formal operational stage.

Piaget's work emphasises the mental activity that children engage in when exploring their environment. Ericsson on the other hand mapped the development of the child into the complete self, using a staged approach similar to Piaget's. Like Piaget's system, each stage builds upon the previous one. In the trust stage between birth and 2 years the child learns about the physical environment and becomes familiar with routines. The autonomy stage develops between 2 and 4 years of age when the child recognises the existence of free will and choice. Between 4 and 6 years of age children experience the imitation stage when they imitate the world around them. Here the influence of role models cannot be overestimated. The competence stage occurs between 6 and 12 years of age when children need to be able to demonstrate competence in front of their peers. The identity phase applies between 12 and 18 years of age and is the critical time of development between childhood and adulthood. Awareness of these developmental theories and stages is important for coaches to understand the nature of the child they are coaching. All good soccer coaching programmes should consider these stages.

AIMS AND OBJECTIVES OF SOCCER COACHING

From an early age soccer players require careful nurturing in a planned and systematic fashion. To plan performance and attainment levels for youngsters coaches require knowledge of educational, developmental and performance goals. These may involve perception of visual and behavioural messages, understanding and knowledge about tactics, techniques and skills, and social interaction of team members. Wein (2001) proposed a detailed soccer development model for both

Table 10.2 Soccer development model

Level	Age (years)	Content	Games
1	7–8	Main activities based on skill development	For basic abilities and capacities
2	8–10	Develop skills and correct in 2 vs 2 activities. Prepare for games. No goalkeepers	Mini-soccer
3	10–12	Mini-soccer games. Correct in 3 vs 3 activities. Introduce goalkeeping. Indoor 5-a-side	7 vs 7 soccer
4	12–15	7 vs 7 games. Individual and group tests. Correct in 4 vs 4 and 5 vs 5 games	8 vs 8 soccer
5	>15	8 vs 8 games. Collective training especially standard situations. Individualised training focused on positions. Detailed attacking and defensive strategies	11 vs 11 soccer

Source: Wein, 2001.

girls and boys based on age and stage. This model consists of five levels as outlined in Table 10.2.

Within the soccer development model, training and competition are clearly linked and training activities and preparatory games are not viewed as separate from games and matches. Whilst Wein's soccer development model focuses mainly on game performance and soccer play, other more strategic models have also been added to the area of youth sport. These models outline general aims and objectives for coaching young soccer players during each stage of their development.

Aims and objectives for soccer programmes related to stages of development

For some time now there has been a healthy debate over an appropriate model for developing young sports people. These models set the overall philosophy for coaching at each stage of a young person's development. Development as opposed to performance is key to any long-term approach. Perhaps the most widely known model is the *long-term athlete development model* (LTADM) proposed by Balyi and Hamilton (2000). This model encompasses lifelong development and engagement in sport. In this section, the LTADM will be interpreted in the context of football. Progression by the young football player through this plan requires dedication, patience and a burning desire to achieve excellence and success in players and coaches. The time commitment to achieve this goal is significant (see Chapter 8).

From a young age, essential aspects of training lie in the promotion of fundamental movement skills and the acquisition of technical, tactical and fitness skills. These generic skills do not have to be sport specific but can be acquired through a variety of movement activities. The premise here is that multisports and activities are more effective in developing the range of children's fundamental movement skills than a single sport such as soccer. Within the LTADM structure, these generic skills are promoted in a developmentally appropriate model. Soccer coaches will adapt their activities to suit the developmental stage of the youngster where training is driven by individual needs and the fundamentals of movement (running, jumping, hopping, throwing, skipping, bounding, balancing, sliding, sending, receiving and so on). More specialisation occurs when the fundamental movement skills become automatic.

Description of the LTADM model

Coaching in each phase of the LTADM model has generic overarching aims that are outlined in Figure 10.2. *Fundamentals* represents the foundation phase where youngsters sample a range of sports that develop basic movement skills such as jumping, hopping skipping, rolling, balancing, throwing, kicking, catching and striking. *Training to train* is the next stage where participation is promoted above winning. Third comes the *training to compete* phase where performance is more important, and finally the *training to win* phase where excellence is the key criterion for success. Each phase describes these aims and the model provides a clear direction for player development. Figure 10.2 reviews the focus of each phase of the LTADM. Each phase is described by age, gender, programme description and degree of participation. The change from fundamentals to increased specificity and intensity increases with age and stage. The LTADM outlines this progress in four phases. These phases are intended to clarify athletic development for the sporting community, including parents, teachers and coaches, in schools, sports clubs, recreation and leisure services and soccer academies. An understanding of the LTADM is an advantage for coaches of children who take part in a number of other sports. The aims for coaching all sports are similar during the fundamental phase. Coaching in the first phase of the

165

Phase	FUNdamentals	Training to train	Training to compete	Training to win
Age and gender	Male/Female 6–10 years	Male 10–14 years Female 10–13 years	Male 14–17 years Female 13–17 years	Male 18+ years Female 17+ years
Programme	• Programme typified by fun activities promoting fundamental movement skills and basic rules	• Fundamentals of tactical appreciation • Fundamentals of specialised skills • Fundamentals of physical and mental fitness	• Advanced tactical appreciation in sport-specific situations • Individualise specialised skills • Advanced knowledge in physical and mental fitness preparation	• Maintenance or improvement of physical capacities • Refinement of tactical and technical skills • Frequent recovery breaks • Ability to model all aspects of performance
Participation level	• Sports participation 5–6 times per week (with variety)	• Sports-specific training 4 times per week and participation in other sports	• Sports-specific training 6–9 times per week	• Sports-specific training 9–12 times per week

Figure 10.2 The long-term athlete development model

Source: Adapted from Balyi and Hamilton, 2000.

166

LTADM may be more effective if coaches work together to develop youngsters' fundamental skills through a balance of generic and sport-specific activities. It is therefore an advantage to participate in a range of physical activities that promote running, jumping, skipping, throwing, hitting, kicking, catching, rolling and so on during this phase. During the fundamentals and 'training to train' phases footballers learn the basics of game skills and, more importantly, learn how to train properly. Competition is less important than a sound sports education, but a healthy engagement in competition does feature in the initial two phases. The ratio of competition to training increases in the training to compete and training to win phases. The training to train phase results in the young footballer learning how to taper training and compete under the full range of performance conditions. The training to win phase takes this a little further and enables the player to maximise performance and aim to peak for significant competition.

The LTADM proposes an overarching approach to soccer development including the organisation of essential aspects over time. The guiding philosophy of fundamentals, training to train, training to compete and training to win will guide the content and structure of soccer development programmes for young players. This model should assist coaches in prioritising important aspects during each of the four phases. These aims will have been met when young footballers are able to diagnose their own strengths and weaknesses and develop optimal strategies for their own improvement in partnership with the coaching team. This approach will result in higher levels of achievement and greater degrees of excellence than would otherwise be the case. The language of the LTADM is significant. At all phases except for fundamentals each phase is based upon training. This language is important when setting aims for each phase. Coaches should communicate with players, parents and significant others that training is the key ingredient for successful performance and competition. Together with the soccer development model (Wein, 2001), the LTADM provides an excellent approach to coaching young soccer players.

COACHING SOCCER FOR UNDERSTANDING

In relation to training and playing Winkler (2001) proposed two main aspects to coaching youth soccer – 'training forms' and 'playing forms'. The training forms relate to the planning and implementation of playing forms. Detailed procedural and declarative knowledge is essential if training forms are used to design the playing form and structures suitable for players. Winkler (2001) suggested five content groups for youth soccer training.

Content group 1
'Training forms' on ONE goal:
'Playing forms' attack and defence.
Example: 3 vs 1: Attackers aim to score by keeping width and depth, defender tries to channel ball away from goal. Change defender every 3 attacks

Content group 2
'Training forms' on TWO goals:
'Playing forms' attack and defence.
Example: 3 vs 2: 3 Attackers aim to score by using width. After an attempt on goal the 2 defenders change to attack on the break with one attacker reverting to a defender trying to recover to prevent a score

Content group 3
'Training forms' on goal shots.
Example: Goal shots mixed with goalkeeping

Content group 4
'Training forms' with the ball but without goals.
Example: Skill and grid type activities out of the context of the game

Content group 5
'Complementary training forms' for improvement of coordination and conditioning.
Example: Fitness and conditioning

Winkler's approach to junior soccer coaching complements both the soccer development and LTADM models. Moreover, Winkler's description of general content for youth soccer provides guidance for coaches wishing to build and design programmes with increasing complexity from the fundamental through to the training to win phase. The type of learning occurring here is described as 'situated'. Situated learning occurs when training takes the form and context similar to that found in a game; the training form is reflected in the playing form helping young soccer players to learn and develop in the game environment. In physical education, situated learning has been evolving since the early 1980s when a 'teaching games for understanding' (TGFU) approach was proposed (Bunker and Thorpe, 1982). Bunker and Thorpe claimed that TGFU provided an alternative approach to traditional games teaching that was dominated by skill improvement through drill-type activities. Furthermore, Bunker and Thorpe (1982) argued that some groups of games shared common characteristics. Invasive games such as soccer have:

1   Tactical features to create space in attack.
2   The containment of space in defence.
3   The use of a goal for scoring.

Throughout its evolution, TGFU has sometimes been called 'games centred games' which reflects the nature of coach delivery. Whatever the case, the three components of invasive games listed above are central to a TGFU instructional model. In other words the majority of practice time is spent in game-like contexts and less time in a traditional 'skill-drill' approach. Figure 10.3 illustrates the place of the learner in the centre of the TGFU model.

Young soccer players learn more about time and space if they play games in addition to practising soccer skills and techniques. The promotion of game understanding and performance is reflected in the 'making appropriate decisions' part of the model. The model should also help coaches explain to young players what their role is, whether they are in possession of the ball or not. The principles of maintaining and regaining possession of the ball are difficult to coach without playing small or large type games. In the TGFU model, expert coaches and teachers place various conditions on the game to draw out the principle of play that they are looking to develop.

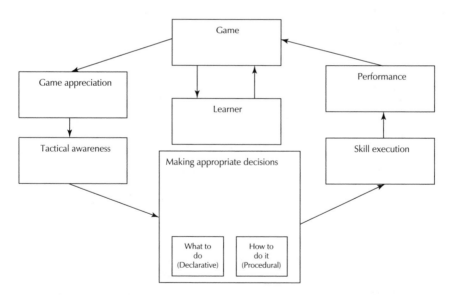

Figure 10.3 Teaching games for understanding model
Source: Adapted from Bunker and Thorpe, 1982.

Consider the principles of width and depth. A game here might start in a 10-metre square grid where the game is conditioned to exclude dribbling and tackling. The aim of the attacking team is to stop the ball under the sole of the foot and on a pre-designated sideline of the grid. The game principle is one of forming triangles. The game is conditioned to maximise success and develop vision by removing tackling and dribbling. Attackers may then have as long as they want to look up and position the body so that they can get a pass to a colleague. Colleagues have time (3 vs 1) to move into a space and signal when they want to receive the pass. With increased technical ability and age, activities may increase in difficulty, e.g. by reducing the size of the grid, only using half the width of the grid line to stop the ball on, playing 'two touch' football and so on. A similar core task can be adapted to suit the TGFU model yet still be matched to the stage of development of the players.

The important concept of the TGFU model is that an invasion game is defined by having at least one defender, and that the activity develops technique in the context of chaos and changing time and space. Players will therefore develop game-related techniques 'in situ'. Expert coaches who understand how learning takes place are best able to maximise the potential of TGFU to use situated learning. Other similar games-instructional models are the 'tactical games model' (Griffin et al., 1997) and 'game sense' (Australian Sports Commission, 1997). Given that this represents a seemingly straightforward explanation of game behaviour, the following example might suggest that issues are more complex than they first appear.

An 8-year-old soccer player who knows that he has difficulty in crossing the ball dribbles the ball into a position wide and to the right of goal. He knows that, first, he cannot cross and, second, his team mates find it difficult to add power to their headers. Therefore, the player decides to try to continue dribbling the ball to a point where he can pass the ball along the ground to a colleague. He loses the ball. These players know that crossing the ball into the box may be the best option, but based on skill they decide not to do so. Playing games develops this game sense whilst proponents of this approach argue that skill-drill dominated activities do not. In this case the player has decided the best course of action to affect performance positively.

The coach then decides on the next course of action: that is how s/he can promote the skills of crossing and heading in a game context. The approach where the individual actively engages in learning in the environment neatly describes 'situated learning'. The coach who understands this principle develops teaching and coaching strategies where young players are regularly engaged in soccer game activities, thereby enhancing the holistic game development of players. The 'parallel development' of skill (knowing how) and game understanding (knowing what) during coaching sessions and activities is arguably the most effective way of developing young soccer players into intelligent and expert performers. Whilst this is an established concept in physical education, the TGFU approach only seems to have an intuitive and tacit basis and it has not been empirically tested in youth soccer coaching.

LEARNING AND PERFORMANCE

Different learners approach tasks with different objectives, orientations or motivations. This vocabulary should help the coach realise that there are important differences between learning and performance. Table 10.3 outlines the key characteristics of learner and performance oriented players.

For the soccer coach the fact that good learners do not focus directly on performance may be a paradox. Evidence from research into learning suggests that those with a 'learning orientation' as opposed to a 'performance orientation' are more likely to have higher levels of motivation, stick with the task, practise and improve. It does not suggest that performance is unimportant as the outcome of soccer is measured in the performance. However, far more time is spent in practice than performance and coaches should emphasise 'improvement' during practice. The emphasis on 'training' is also central to the LTADM. Tasks also need

Table 10.3 Learner and performance oriented players

Learner oriented players	Performance oriented players
Are concerned with improving their performance	Are concerned with proving their ability
Believe that effort is linked to success	Believe that ability leads to success
Prefer tasks that are challenging	Have sense of achievement when doing better than others
Provide their own guidance when involved in a task	Avoid difficult tasks, feel helpless and have 'can't do' attitude to difficult tasks
Have a sense of accomplishment from personal success in difficult tasks	Emphasis is on being better than everyone else, competition and comparison to others
Believe in ability to improve and learn	Want to be judged as able, and 'can perform'

Source: Author.

to be challenging and set at a level where success can be achieved, but not 'too easily'. The approach or style of coaching can dictate whether soccer practice sessions are learner or performance oriented. Practice sessions that involve problem-solving, self-evaluation and time for questions and reflection are more likely to promote good learners. In a simple analysis, the sum of better learners would ultimately mean better performance.

COACHING AND TEACHING STYLES

There is no single style of instruction and the aim in this part of the chapter is to provide a synopsis of current thinking on styles of coaching. Modern pedagogists refer to the use of teaching styles or approaches. In a similar vein coaches may also use a variety of instructional styles or approaches. The intention of these approaches is to cater for children of different ages, abilities and needs. The key issue to consider here is that coaches instruct individuals who take part in groups. No two individuals will respond in exactly the same way to the same task. Therefore, coaches need to consider individual differences when coaching groups of young soccer players who range in maturity and experience.

The use of a variety of teaching styles provides the coach with opportunities to individualise teaching and learning. Teaching approaches make use of different tasks and contexts. Styles A–E are defined as *reproductive*, whereas styles F–G are defined as *productive* (see Mosston and Ashworth, 1986 for further detail). A description of the styles is set out in Table 10.4.

Table 10.4 A description of reproductive and productive teaching styles

Style	Category	Description
Command	A	All decisions are made by the coach
Task	B	Players execute movement tasks on their own
Reciprocal (Partner)	C	Partner helps in one or more coaching functions
Small groups	D	Player roles are divided into doer, observer and recorder
Individual	E	Individual programmes are organised for players
Guided discovery	F	Coach provides clues to solving problems
Problem-solving	G	Players discover their own answers to problems

Source: Adapted from Mosston and Ashworth, 1986.

Productive and reproductive coaching styles

The reproductive and productive styles of coaching are differentiated by the amount of decision-making given to the player. Reproductive styles are best suited to coaching basic skills and the replication of models and procedures, where most of the decisions are made by the coach. Using reproductive styles A–B the coach might demonstrate the Cruyff turn and then ask players to copy it. Style C might involve the same Cruyff turn but this time the player has a partner who gives feedback about the quality of the turn. The coach communicates directly with the partner observing, not the performer. This way the coach is measuring the observation and understanding of the skill by the observer and has passed responsibility for coaching the skill to the observer. Style D is similar to C but involves a larger group of participants who take on different roles. In style E the coach gives different versions of the Cruyff turn to individuals within the group. Styles A–E are reproductive, that is players reproduce what the coach asks them to do. Productive styles enable the learner to have more control over the decision-making process, allowing creativity and discovery and multiple outcomes. Style G 'guided discovery' can be further split into convergent and divergent. In the convergent style, a guided discovery approach allows the coaches to provide clues that lead to one outcome or performance. In the divergent, guided discovery approach, the coach provides clues that may lead to multiple outcomes. The following tasks are examples of how a coach may use convergent and divergent styles in coaching ball control. When using the convergent style the coach might ask: 'How do you bring the ball to a stop using your foot?' Coach A requires players to use their instep and guides them toward this technique (single outcome). Coach B on the other hand uses a divergent style and asks the players to show as many ways of stopping the ball as possible (multiple outcomes). A coach who uses style G would ask a player to develop a turn that could wrong-foot a defender.

These examples clearly illustrate that reproductive and productive teaching styles place different emphases on *how* the young soccer player learns and *what* the young soccer player learns. For coaching skills and techniques, styles A and B as opposed to inclusion style E are generally more effective. On the other hand Griffey (1983) found that high ability students and girls performed more effectively with the practice style B compared to children of low ability who performed better with the command style A. Pellet and Harrison (1995) reported that low-skilled learners performed better with the command style A for the volleyball spike and practice style B for the set. Byra and Jenkins (1998) found that inclusion E and self-check D styles promoted more decision-making opportunities than the practice style. There is limited empirical evidence on the use of productive styles of coaching. Few data are available on coaching styles in youth soccer and there is little evidence to suggest that one coaching approach had a better long-term effect on performance than another. Furthermore, a number of approaches to games teaching (e.g. TGFU) use style G and place decision-making at the centre of the learning process. A balanced approach to coaching probably results in a variety of coaching styles being used in the same session. Expert coaches suggest that this is the most effective way of promoting soccer performance.

DIFFERENTIATION

Every player brings a different level of knowledge to each session and coaches regularly experience problems when trying to meet the needs of every individual through a process of 'differentiated coaching'. Tasks are varied to allow for different abilities and stages of development. This variety is an essential principle given the changes in maturation of players during their growing years. Youngsters need to be 'included' as opposed to 'excluded' because of their stage of soccer development. A perfect session of differentiation and inclusion would have each participant working to his/her potential all the time. This is extremely difficult to achieve in most coaching contexts. However, coaches should strive to differentiate as much as possible and coach activities that aim to include all participants.

Activities can be differentiated by 'task' or by 'outcome'. Differentiating by task requires the coach to set appropriate tasks for different individuals. In its simplest form, a coach may request some players to shoot with their preferred foot whilst the more able use their non-preferred foot. A coach differentiates by outcome by setting the same task for the group, but adapting it for individuals during the session. The task is made more difficult for the more able and easier for the less able. To differentiate, coaches need a depth of experience that allows them to interact with youngsters, quickly assess their attainment and have practice activities stored in memory ready for immediate delivery. This requires a real depth of declarative, procedural and domain knowledge as well as an ability to assess performance immediately and adapt activities according to attainment. Competent use of assessment techniques is central to effective differentiation.

MONITORING, ASSESSING, RECORDING AND REPORTING IN YOUTH SOCCER

Whilst assessment can be used as a tool in talent identification it is not the intention of this section to discuss it in this way. Monitoring, assessing, recording and reporting youth soccer performance are central to the successful development of young players. Assessment is one of the most powerful methods for judging performance in any sport. Furthermore, appropriate use of assessment can lead to better coaching, learning and performance. Many theories and approaches are applicable to assessment in youth soccer. A selection of these will be outlined in the following sections. Whilst TIPS (technique, intelligence, personality, speed) has been used in youth soccer this is not central to a youngster's overall development. The most recent English national curriculum for physical education (NCPE 2000) assesses pupils' learning in four key aspects:

1 Evaluating and improving performance.
2 Developing, selecting and applying skills.
3 Tactics and compositional ideas.
4 Fitness and health.

These categories are also directly applicable to youth soccer. They not only assess the product of performance during competitive matches but also allow assessment to take place more effectively during training.

Assessment approaches

There are two main categories for the assessment of both coaching and performance: formative and summative.

Formative assessment

During formative assessment the coach observes and assesses during each minute of each coaching session. The assessment of the 'here and now' is used to make judgements about current coaching and whether coaching approach and style need adaptation. Short notes are suitable for recording formative assessments.

Summative assessment

All the pieces of formative assessment may be used to produce a summative assessment report. Summative assessment may also be used at the end of coaching schools or specific periods of coaching that have measurable outcomes. This method may involve end of course assessments that are used to enhance the formative process.

Measurement-related factors in assessing performance

There are many approaches to assessing children's soccer development. In order to make a considered decision on how best to assess performance, a number of measurement-related factors need to be addressed. In this section issues related to assessment, measurement of knowledge and understanding related to soccer performance are reviewed.

Purpose of assessment

Assessment may be used for three main reasons: to categorise or identify; to plan an intervention or instruction strategy; and to evaluate change over time.

To categorise or identify

The purpose of categorising or identifying the developmental stage at which an individual is currently performing is to provide a benchmark relative to some predetermined criterion or normative measurement. This criterion is often used to establish the typical age at which an individual should reach a given stage of development. Although there is little evidence to support its use, this method has also been used for talent identification purposes. Admission to a development programme may be dependent on a child's score in relation to a normative group. For example, if a 10-year-old ran 100 shuttles in the 20-metre multistage-shuttle run test, or could use alternate feet to keep the ball in the air for 50 touches, this may indicate a talent in soccer.

To plan an intervention or instruction strategy

When planning an intervention, a baseline measure (i.e. assessment prior to intervention) should be conducted to identify the developmental stages of soccer performance. Specific points can be highlighted within the assessment that permit the coach to target the intervention toward the needs of the individual or group. By using this approach, soccer coaches can establish clear programme objectives. Therefore, if a coach aims to detect areas for improvement in a young soccer player, a number of soccer-specific assessments will take place to detect specific strengths and weaknesses.

To evaluate change over time

When evaluating a long-term programme for youth soccer players it is necessary to assess before and after its implementation. The effectiveness of the programme can then be measured according to the difference between the two assessments. If the same group of players aimed to improve strength and balance after the programme, this achievement would be detected by using robust measures of these skills before and after the coaching programme. Similar measures may be used for assessing knowledge and understanding of soccer strategies and systems – comparing a TGFU model to a traditional model of coaching, for example. Whatever the reason for assessment it is clear that a longitudinal approach to development provides a more appropriate and absolute method of monitoring change in performance over time.

OVERVIEW OF TYPES OF ASSESSMENT

Assessment is usually split into two distinct categories; these are norm-referenced and criterion-referenced.

Norm-referenced

Norm-referenced assessment compares an individual or group score with a normal population. The player is compared against the norm resulting in above average, below average or average performance. These types of measures are used to identify developmental deficiencies, determine eligibility for a service or programme (e.g. talent development) and evaluate the effectiveness of a programme. The measured value is typically outcome/product focused (e.g. distance, time), thus escaping the complexities and subjectivity of measuring a process.

Norm references may be linked to distances thrown, reaction times, 30-metre sprint times and so forth. The average number of shuttles for the above example might be 65. This is the quantitative score.

Criterion-referenced

Criterion-referenced assessment compares an individual's form against a standardised version of the movement/skill. When the movement/skill meets the criteria, it is scored in absolute terms, e.g. yes/no, or rated according to a sliding scale (e.g. 1 = poor, 2 = adequate, or 3 = good/mature). These data are qualitative and this form of assessment is used to judge the effectiveness of an intervention on predetermined process criteria. There are three typical components of a criterion-based assessment: these are the movement to be performed, the task conditions, and the performance criteria that are being employed. After the initial assessment, criteria are developed according to the key performance components. These standard criteria represent a minimum skill level expected for that movement in various contexts. A typical application of criterion-referenced assessment is over-arm throwing or kicking. Within each criterion, an ideal point of view is provided for the assessors, a record of the task conditions, and graded criteria to which the movement can be matched (see Haywood and Getchell, 2001).

Criterion-referenced assessment focuses overall on the body, or the various limb segments. The approach described as 'total body configuration' uses one criterion-referenced value to describe the fundamental movement skill. Although a person's body parts may not develop in parallel, sufficient congruence is shared between body parts in a particular stage of development for a movement to be considered by one common set of criteria. Simple developmental stage norms can be constructed using a one-point assessment. This construct combines both the criterion-referenced measures of the skill and norm-referenced methods of comparison.

The major advantage of the criteria over normative assessment is the focus on individual performance. Information is provided that highlights what an individual is able to do, not how members of a group compare with one another. The assessment will also indicate how an individual can improve. However, there are drawbacks to this approach. First, the specific environment in which the criteria were developed, and the list of criteria itself, may not be specific to an individual's needs. Second, there is no agreed level of mastery comparable across populations. For example, what is considered competent for an 11-year-old may be considered impressive for a 7-year-old. Third, the method of assessment is not always sensitive to the subtle changes in movement across attempts or individuals, making trial to trial comparisons difficult. The second and third types of measurement are concerned with generalising the assessment results.

Coaches who are competent at assessment are able to plan effectively as well as think about what they have coached and how youngsters developed over a period. In contemporary coaching 'reflective practice' has assumed an important role in coach development. Reflection is an essential part of the coaching cycle. Reflection enables the coach to evaluate player progress and adapt the coaching plan according to experience and context. This approach to coaching is part of a much more systematic framework for progression.

THE REFLECTIVE SOCCER COACH

The development of coaching expertise is influenced by the definition of learning. Learning can be defined as a reflective activity that enables the coach to use previous experience to understand the present and shape the future (Watkins *et al.*, 1996). The reflective coach is therefore the learning coach. Reflective practitioners are able to review what they have done, and how to apply this learning to future coaching activities. This can be best represented by Kolb's (1984) 'process of learning' model (Figure 10.4).

In the process of learning, coaches should make connections to other coaching experiences. This involves reflecting on learning and coaching performance. Reflective coaches understand how the context is linked to effective learning for players and how the adjustment and adaptation of coaching plans can account for other learning goals. Motivated coaches apply this model to their own learning and engage in dialogue with other coaches to develop their coaching practice. When players are mature enough, coaches are able to expose them to the 'do-review-learn-apply' model. Players themselves will then become more responsible for their own soccer development and this 'learning to learn' approach fits with the start of the 'training to train' aspect of the LTADM.

OVERVIEW

Many junior soccer coaches are enthusiastic and energetic and have the best interests of their youngsters at heart. Coaches with a detailed knowledge of principles of child development, growth and maturation, soccer skills, strategies and game play, and coaching principles will undoubtedly be best placed to promote excellence and participation in soccer. Maintaining a balance between these principles helps players and coaches understand the unpredictable nature

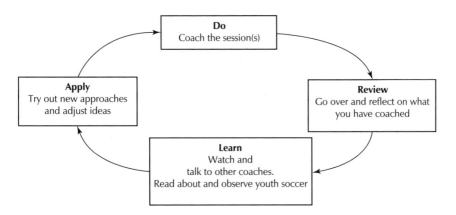

Figure 10.4 Process of learning model
Source: Adapted from Kolb, 1984.

of junior soccer performance and allows for technical, spontaneous and inspirational behaviour in training as well as in match play. Furthermore, a major aim of any youth soccer programme should be the development of independent learners. This chapter has clarified the position of the youth soccer coach as the primary influence for children's independent learning and continued involvement and participation in the sport. The quality of coaching practice should not be underestimated in maintaining participation and promoting excellence. Finally, the scope and extent of competence required of the modern coach suggest that junior soccer may be best managed by a group of coaches. Whilst the development of soccer knowledge as outlined in this chapter is complex, the most effective approach to promoting excellence in young soccer players is to develop teams of coaches with the necessary expertise to optimise performance.

REFERENCES

Australian Sports Commission (1997) *Game Sense: Developing Thinking Players*. Belconnen: Australia Sports Commission.

Balyi, I. and Hamilton, A.E. (2000) Long-term athlete development. The FUNdamental Stage™: Part One. *Sports Coach*, 23, 10–13.

Bunker, D. and Thorpe, R. (1982) A model for the teaching of games in the secondary school. *Bulletin of Physical Education*, 10, 9–16.

Byra, M. and Jenkins, J. (1998) The thoughts and behaviors of learners in the inclusion style of teaching. *Journal of Teaching in Physical Education*, 18, 26–42.

Ericsson, K.A. (ed.) (1996) *The Road to Excellence*. New Jersey: Lawrence Erlbaum Associates.

Gervis, M. and Brierly, J. (1999) *Effective Coaching for Children: Understanding the Sports Process*. Marlborough, UK: Crowood Press.

Griffey, D.C. (1983) Aptitude × treatment interactions associated with student decision making. *Journal of Teaching in Physical Education*, 2, 15–32.

Griffin, L.L., Oslin, J.L. and Mitchell, S.A. (1997) *Teaching Sports Concepts and Skills: A Tactical Games Approach*. Champaign, IL: Human Kinetics.

Haywood, K.M. and Getchell, N. (2001) *Lifespan Motor Development* (3rd edn). Champaign, IL: Human Kinetics.

Kolb, D.A. (1984) *Experiential Learning: Experience as the Source of Learning and Development* (2nd edn). Englewood Cliffs, NJ: Prentice Hall.

Mosston, M. and Ashworth, S. (1986) *Teaching Physical Education* (3rd edn). Columbus, OH: Merrill.

National Curriculum for Physical Education (NCPE) (2000) http://www.nc.uk.net/servlets/NCFrame?subject=PE accessed 28/6/02.

Pellet, T.L. and Harrison, J.M. (1995) The influence of teacher's specific, congruent and corrective feedback on female junior high school students' immediate volleyball success. *Journal of Teaching in Physical Education*, 15, 53–63.

Potrac, P., Brewer, C., Jones, R., Armour, K. and Hoff, J. (2000) Toward an holistic understanding of the coaching process. *Quest*, 82, 186–199.

Rink, J.E. (1985) *Teaching Physical Education for Learning*. St. Louis, MO: Times Mirror/Mosby.

Stratton, G. (2002) A knowledge based structure for coaching young football players: steps to acquiring expert knowledge. *Insight – The F.A. Coaches Association Journal*, 2, 37.

Watkins, C., Carnell, E., Lodge, C. and Whalley, C. (1996) *Effective Learning. School Improvement Network*. Research Matters. No. 5. London: Institute of Education, London University.

Wein, H. (2001) *Developing Youth Soccer Players: Coach Better with the Soccer Development Model*, Champaign, IL: Human Kinetics.

Williams, M. and Davids, K. (1995) Declarative knowledge in sport: a by-product of experience or a characteristic of expertise? *Journal of Sports and Exercise Psychology*, 17, 259–275.

Winkler, W. (2001) Motor skills and cognitive training for junior soccer players. *International Journal for Performance Analysis in Sport*, 1, 91–105.

CHAPTER ELEVEN

SOCIAL-PSYCHOLOGICAL CONSIDERATIONS OF ELITE YOUTH PLAYER DEVELOPMENT

INTRODUCTION

The introduction of the English Football Association (FA) Technical Department's 'Charter for Quality' (1997) has placed a firm emphasis on the young player's development. The central figure within the Charter is the player. The objective is to ensure '. . . quality experiences for all young players . . .' (Football Association Technical Department, 1997: 1). Soccer clubs required increased access to young players to allow them more time to develop. The Charter (implicitly) emphasised the need for a more holistic approach to young player development. The FA Technical Department's Charter for Quality (1997: 1.3) stated that:

> Quite properly the player's match programme should be developed in the best interests of the player's educational, technical, academic and social needs, by the parents in conjunction with the player's school and Football Academy Education and Welfare Officer.

In this sense, the tenets of *talent identification, talent development, education* and *personal development* embrace a more *global* concept of youth player development (or production). A brief synopsis of the concepts of talent identification and development is presented in this chapter before focusing on the more social-psychological considerations of elite youth player development. Due to the more systematic development of boys' soccer Academies, the chapter focuses predominantly on the development of young male players. However, the authors recognise that some of the areas discussed are also relevant to the development of girls' soccer.

The soccer world has traditionally relied upon the soccer-specific (or craft) knowledge of experienced coaches and talent scouts to 'spot' talented youngsters. The ability to identify talent primarily involves a conceptual understanding of soccer ability (i.e. craft knowledge) and an ability to make (appropriate) decisions concerning a player's potential. Such potential exists in terms of possibility rather than actuality. One can only measure, assess or validate what exists in reality (i.e. current performance, not soccer potential). In this sense, talent identification is reliant on the experience of the 'spotter' who makes a subjective assessment (guided by craft experience) as to whether or not a young player should be offered a trial and/or signed by the soccer club. The process is further complicated by the dynamic nature of soccer performance in addition to the fact that *individuals* are generally identified within the context of a *team* performance.

Talent identification systems have been influenced by the Ajax FC talent acronym model, namely TIPS (technique, intelligence, personality, speed). The success of the Ajax model has been envied, and thus mirrored by some English FA Premier League clubs with 'similar' acronyms, such as TABS (talent, attitude, balance, speed) and SUPS (skill, understanding, personality, speed), emerging as the primary benchmarks for talent identification. Considering the complexity of talent identification and development, it could be argued that the processes underpinning the identification of talent should match the complexity of the end product. In this sense, it appears that the TIPS model espoused by Ajax FC also consists of a further ten sub-components for each category (Ajax FC, 2003).

The complexity of talent identification and development has been well documented (Bloom, 1985; Régnier *et al.*, 1993; Williams *et al.*, 1999; Reilly *et al.*, 2003). Talent detection concerns the prediction of the potential development of an individual's performance in a particular sport over various periods of time. This process may draw upon psychological, physiological, sociological, behavioural and performance attributes either alone or in combination. In this sense, talent detection concerns the 'matching' of a variety of individual characteristics, which may be innate or subject to the effect of learning, training and development, to the core tenets of sports performance (e.g. technique, speed). Talent selection refers to the identification of an appropriate individual who can best carry out the given sporting activity within a specific context, such as a soccer tournament. Thus, talent selection may be viewed as 'short-term' talent detection (i.e. those that will perform best 2 weeks, 2 months or even 12 months from now) (see Régnier *et al.*, 1993)

Talent identification aims to identify participants with the ability to progress to 'elite' status within a given sport. Talent identification is therefore a prerequisite for the process of talent development. Talent development is predominantly associated with the provision of a suitable environment from which potential talent can be realised. In this context, development is a much broader concept and incorporates social, environmental, intellectual, educational, welfare, physiological, physical and psychological factors and motor competence.

The different disciplines of sports science have (traditionally) been constrained within their own particular boundaries (i.e. physical considerations, physiological considerations, psychological considerations and sociological considerations) when associated with the concepts of talent identification. More holistic (Williams *et al.*, 1999) and humanistic (Richardson, 1998) approaches toward talent identification and development have emerged. Endeavours to establish clear criteria for the identification and development of talent have generally acknowledged the facets of sociological, educational and welfare (emotional and psychological) considerations as the poor relations within the overall 'talent map'.

Sociological and psychological considerations tend to place an emphasis on the nurturing of talent, environmental factors and the availability of opportunity. For example, the sociological and social-psychological perspectives recognise that the talented young soccer player may be subjected to certain (performance and circumstantial) pressures and these, particularly during childhood, may be detrimental to development. Consequently, potential talent may not be realised and talented individuals may drop out of their chosen sport (see Figure 11.1). The social-psychological characteristics would suggest that potential talent could not be nurtured without the appropriate environmental and support mechanisms.

Psychological characteristics are regularly espoused as the primary distinguishing factors that differentiate between successful and unsuccessful players (Régnier *et al.*, 1993). Psychological elements exist within a number of multidimensional sports talent identification models, but these have not been accepted as a means of reliable talent identification (Régnier *et al.*, 1993). Researchers have yet to advocate clear and consistent links between a player's 'psychological make-up' (e.g. personality, coping mechanisms) and expert performance (Morris,

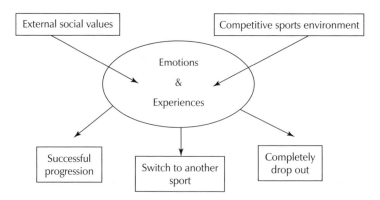

Figure 11.1 Potential developmental and/or attrition consequences of sport participation

2000). Similar frustrations are evidenced within the soccer world. Kees Zwamborn (cited in AjaxUSA, 2001), former Director of Youth Development (and former player) at Ajax FC, identified *personality* (i.e. self-confidence, anxiety control, motivation, attitude and concentration) as the most complex aspect of a player's talent characteristics for mentors to establish, understand and hence develop. Indeed, this understanding is important not only for the coach but also for the player. In this sense, the player should be encouraged to recognise his/her personal attributes and/or deficiencies, and hence (with appropriate support) be empowered to take responsibility for his/her soccer development.

The problems associated with matching identification programmes to specific sporting demands are more complicated in team games than individual sports, as there are no clear and consistent objective measures of performance (Reilly et al., 2000). In that sense, psychological researchers have yet to identify a specific personality characteristic and/or profile that can be associated with success in sport (generally) or in soccer (specifically). Consequently, no solitary inventory exists to aid the talent identification and development process.

Orlick and Partington (1988) used an athlete interview guide with elite Canadian athletes (n = 75) specifically identifying mental skills (i.e. total commitment, quality training, including setting daily goals, engaging in regular competition simulation, imagery training and quality mental preparation) to be developed and refined for consistent high-level performance at high-profile events such as the Olympic Games. Their work has enhanced knowledge in applied sports psychology and subsequent understanding of top performers and their qualities. In this sense, the value (and need) of engaging in *elite* athlete research must be recognised and practised across all athletic domains (including soccer). Orlick and Partington (1988) suggested that mental skills are a critical part of success in high-level performance sport that need to be refined and developed for those in pursuit of excellence. These authors recommended that researchers should explore the mental links to excellence in a variety of disciplines in order to understand the human pursuit of excellence, gain valuable insights into the critical components of excellence in sport, and allow them to develop within a structured psychological development programme. Later work hints towards a more covert development of these skills. Further, the notion of achieving performance excellence within any life arena (e.g. working and/or sporting arena) has been associated with the concepts of *resonance* (Newburg et al., 2002). More specifically, those individuals who engage in activities that enable them to pursue, and subsequently live, their dream are consistent with the contemporary notion that expert performers seek resonance in their everyday lives. It would appear appropriate to explore the contemporary notion of resonance within elite youth soccer players.

Professional coaches from varying sports suggest that it is the *superstars* who can handle constructive criticism and cope with unfair criticism. If they make a mistake they acknowledge it and do everything they can to ensure that they do not make the same mistake again (Orlick, 2000). Morris (2000) advocated the development of wide-ranging psychological skills among young players. Although personality traits are primarily inherited, it appears that relevant psychological attributes may be developed through specialised training. Motivation, coping mechanisms, concentration, self-confidence and attentional style have also been identified as potential areas for development through appropriate training (Morris, 1997).

Perceptual-cognitive skills such as anticipation and decision-making provide an alternative approach to talent identification (Williams *et al.*, 1999). Consistent differences have been detected between skilled and less skilled players when tested on their anticipation and decision-making skills. Such tests, which typically employ film-based simulations of match situations, have been used successfully with both adult and junior players (Williams, 2000). The superior performance of skilled soccer players during these tests reflects their greater knowledge and experience as a result of specific practice and instruction as opposed to any initial differences in visual skills such as acuity, colour vision or depth perception (Reilly *et al.*, 2003). It is not clear what proportion of perceptual skill is genetically determined compared with that developed through purposeful practice. It may be that talented players are predisposed to acquiring the knowledge structures underlying perceptual and decision-making skill in soccer (Williams, 2000).

Morris (2000) identified two additional cognitive measures for consideration, namely intelligence and creative thinking. At present the concept of intelligence is difficult to define and measure. It appears to incorporate elements such as analytical, creative and practical ability that may or may not be relevant to soccer. Skilled players have been reported to possess a 'game intelligence' that allows them to analyse major features of their opponents' play (see Singer and Janelle, 1999). It is not clear whether this game intelligence is linked to academic intelligence (Reilly *et al.*, 2003).

The developmental and social consequences of participation in soccer vary from one child to the next. The consequences may be associated with the internal emotions and experiences of children as well as the external societal values and meanings allied with soccer, and the resultant conditions in which participation occurs (Richardson and Reilly, 2001).

An important determinant of success is socialisation into the particular sport culture (Carlson 1993). McPherson and Brown (1988) (cited in Brustad, 1992: 267) stated that socialisation is a '. . . process whereby individuals learn skills, traits, values, attitudes and knowledge associated with the performance of present or anticipated social roles'. The possible implications of this statement may determine a child's development in his or her particular sport. Ultimately, a child's level of success is influenced by his/her ability to adapt and develop socially, and cope psychologically, within his or her chosen sporting domain.

Brustad (1992) clarified socialisation into three primary components: socialisation *into* sport, socialisation *via* sport and socialisation *out* of sport. Such components take shape across a period of time, which begins with a child's first participation in sport up until the period of discontinuation. Throughout a child's sport life-cycle, he or she will experience a host of different relationships and learning environments, which he/she may embrace or reject. In this sense, embracing or rejecting a particular sporting arena may depend on the child's personal aspirations, experiences and subsequent willingness to continue participation.

ENGAGING IN COMPETITIVE SPORT

Many children may participate in competitive sport at an early age. In some cases the children may be as young as 3–4 years of age, but on average a child is exposed to competitive sport from the age of 6–8 years (Cahill and Pearl, 1993). Readiness to learn within the sport setting generally occurs following an accumulation of events and/or experiences that enable the learner to acquire additional information, skills or values. The concept of readiness suggests that learning (and development) is accelerated and more enjoyable when readiness exists. As a child reaches the age requirement for participation in a given sport, it is (generally) assumed that he or she is 'ready' (e.g. under 8 years, under 10 years of age) to participate. However, an essential prerequisite of a child's readiness for competitive youth sport is a match between a child's stage of growth, maturity and development and the level of demand presented by competitive sport (Cahill and Pearl, 1993). The demands of athletic competition are numerous. The potential for stress exists in youth soccer as players may question whether their own physical and/or skill capability matches the demands made upon them. The fear of failure is a primary concern for young players in addition to the fear of social evaluation (i.e. not meeting the 'expected' performance targets) (Cahill and Pearl, 1993). Although the process of social comparison is witnessed in early childhood, most children under the age of 12 years have a minimal concept of the requirements of competitive sport. Young children tend not to compete if they feel incapable of, or uninterested in, social comparison. Nevertheless, these children should not be denied participation. Moreover, the game structures and adult (e.g. parent, coach) expectations of performance should be modified to meet the developmental capabilities of the child. In this sense, the non-competitive, small-sided games (i.e. 3 v 3, 4 v 4, 8 v 8) advocated by the Football

Association's Technical Department (1997) and experienced by young Academy players (i.e. 12 years and below), provide an ideal opportunity for young players to develop their *technical skills* in a *non-pressurised* environment, thus promoting fun.

Implicit within the concept of readiness is the process of self-selection. A child's chosen sport(s) may be influenced by the child's own interest, his or her parents' interests and aspirations, a teacher, a coach, or a combination of all four. Self-selection is a critical factor in a child's sporting development. The child is the one who must practise, be receptive to coaching and, ultimately, compete. The motivation of a child to practise and compete is an essential prerequisite for successful performance (Richardson and Reilly, 2001). The key to success in sport does not lie in how early a child is exposed to competitive sport, but in the fact that the child concerned is 'optimally' ready to be involved in the sport. This optimisation must also account for the readiness to accept failure within that particular sport (Cahill and Pearl, 1993).

SIGNIFICANT OTHERS

> Children's sport, education and life experiences are mediated through relationships, especially those relationships which are described as 'significant others'.
>
> (Richardson and Reilly, 2001: 88)

Implicit within a child's sporting, educational and life experiences are the influences of significant others (i.e. key relationships that are peculiar to a child's individual development). Consequently, these relationships may have an impact and/or influence on a child's values, beliefs, emotions, attitude and dedication to sport (i.e. decision-making and thought processes in relation to sport participation, individual goals and performance expectations). These relationships are highlighted in Figure 11.2. Further to the significant others identified in Figure 11.2, the inception of the soccer Academy structure in England has introduced another (potentially) 'significant other', namely the Head of Education and Welfare (see latter part of this chapter).

Children have traditionally been viewed as empty vessels into which childhood can be socially constructed (i.e. shaped by cultural and structural contexts of their developing experience) (James and Prout, 1990) and into which families can pour their social values, customs and cultures (Hill and Tisdall, 1997). As a result children's actions have been depicted as the result of effective or ineffective parenting (Hill and Tisdall, 1997). Numerous research groups have explored

social psychology and elite player development

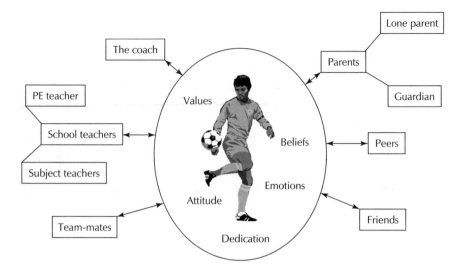

Figure 11.2 The influence of significant others on young players

Source: Adapted from Richardson, 2000.

Note: Significant others who may influence a young player's values, beliefs, emotions, attitude and dedication toward sport performance at any given time.

the influential role of parents and the associated support mechanisms that they provide (Bloom, 1985; Brustad, 1992; Hellstedt, 1988). Kay (2000) suggested that the family was the *key agent* in the process of nurturing talent. Hellstedt (1988) identified a parental involvement continuum ranging from under-involved, to moderate, to over-involved. Although this model offers a fairly simplistic synopsis of parental involvement, Hellstedt suggested that moderate levels of involvement promoted the best interest of the children. The level of parental involvement may also be attributed to certain social and economic factors. Considerable financial support is often required to enable children to participate in intensive training routines. Further, intensive (elite) training programmes tend to be time consuming, and demand an element of parental occupational flexibility. In this sense, the greater mobility of middle-class families may allow parents more time to take their children to and from training and competitive matches.

Bloom (1985) offered a social context to the three main stages of development, namely initiation (i.e. joyful, playful, excited, special), development (i.e. hooked, committed) and perfection (obsessed, responsible). Similarly, Côté's (1999) research concerning familial influences categorised three main chronological 'stages of sport participation'. These stages included the 'sampling years' (age

6–13), the specialising years (age 13–15) and the investment years (age 15 and over).

Significant others may modify their behaviour depending on their individual perception of the child, their relationship with the child, their feelings toward children in general and their knowledge of influences such as age, gender and birth order. The introduction of the coach exposes the child to a new type of authority. It has been argued that the behaviour of coaches and their involvement with a child are more important in the development of talent than initial ability levels (Carlson, 1988, 1993). Expert coaches know when to push players and when to reduce the intensity of training and their expectations. No real evidence has been established to guide the coach (or the player) on how far they should/could push a young player (legitimately) (i.e. provide an appropriate level of intensity). Moreover, the tolerance levels and subsequent benefit (or detriment) to individual young players may require individual attention (e.g. physiological and psychological requirements). In this sense coaches tend to be (over) reliant on personal craft knowledge and experience. Moderation of effort and potential 'drop out' may occur if harmony does not exist between coach and player. Some effort should be made to prevent this loss of talent by encouraging the player to gradually return to systematic training. Elite players are more likely to think highly of their coaches from early years of involvement (Carlson, 1993). The relationship is based on shared interests in accomplishing a task (e.g. soccer performance) rather than on a personal or emotional issue. Talented youngsters may see the coach as 'the gatekeeper' to future progression, achievement and success within their sport. The potential impact of the coach on the child's socialisation, development and progression invites further attention.

A child's social development may be greatly enhanced by the experiences and opportunities afforded by competing in top-level sport. If the appropriate support mechanisms are not in place (i.e. determined and provided by significant others) then the child's social development may be impeded. Knowledge regarding the child's initial socialisation into sport is required to further the understanding of the importance of the social influences that shape a child's initial attraction to sport and, in particular, soccer. This period of a child's life may be referred to as the *early years* (ages between birth and 8 years), or early childhood (2–6 years), with middle childhood being 6 to 11 years of age. Consequently, these periods can determine the participation and future success of the child's sporting career. It appears that the process of sport socialisation begins in the early years of childhood. During these early years children spend large amounts of time with close family, including time in physical activity (Greendorfer et al., 1996). During this period of socialisation children are strongly influenced by the prevalent attitudes and values within the family or associated peer group (Brustad, 1992; Jambor, 1998; Côté, 1999).

Quantifying the influence of significant others in the early years of children's lives has presented methodological problems to researchers. An absence of research on younger children has led to fragmented research in the areas regarding children *not yet* involved in sport, and the consequent effects of significant others and the extent to which they influence the socialisation process. Reports from adults and children already involved in sport have been the only sources of evidence. In this sense, when researching the influences upon children, it is essential that children are included in the investigation.

It seems that children are more likely to participate in sport if their parents have been participants (Kay, 2000). Moreover, the level of performance of the parent (i.e. recreational through to elite) appears to be strongly associated with the level the child would achieve. Similarly, Rowley (1992) reported that of the fathers of children involved in soccer, 70 per cent had played before with 59 per cent of them quoting their involvement as serious. In contrast, Jambor (1998) found that parental sport participation and consequent child participation were indifferent. This latter study reflected the results from two sets of parents, one with children involved in youth soccer programmes and one without. However, only 13 parents had played soccer before, which may be attributed to the delayed development of soccer in the United States and as such may be misleading.

Perhaps more significantly, Jambor (1998) suggested that parents were the individuals who were instrumental in determining whether a child participated in sport. Furthermore, they may often be the key socialisers in children's sport participation (Greendorfer et al., 1996). Rowley (1992) reported that the majority of children identify themselves as the main instigators of sport participation (46 per cent), due predominantly to an individual sense of motivation and commitment to the sport. Thirty-three per cent of children identified their father as being the person who introduced them to soccer. Fifteen per cent of children were influenced by their immediate peers (i.e. teacher or coach). Not surprisingly, only 3 per cent of the children were involved in soccer due to their mother's influence, a further 3 per cent being influenced by both parents.

When the influence of participation in soccer as suggested above emanates from the parents and the children themselves, it must be recognised that to some extent the cultural and ideological values, which are innate in the family, are highly responsible for the consequent involvement. Such involvement is initiated after the early years of participation and moves towards Côté's (1999) *sampling years* where the influence of the family becomes coherent with the influence of further significant others.

The responsibility and impact of these significant others toward the social, academic and sporting development of talented youngsters invite further investigation. A child's social (including welfare) development may be impeded by his or her involvement in high-level sport. Social restrictions and authoritarian structures embedded within a child's talent programme may restrict peer relationships, development opportunities outside of their sport and ultimately affect sport participation and performance.

Similarly, children's behaviour patterns, emotions and attributes may be affected by their environment (e.g. school, home, club), the nature of the environment (e.g. supervised, unsupervised, structured or unstructured) and the culture of the environment (Hill and Tisdall, 1997). Children's perception of themselves within such environments may affect their decisions, behaviour and ultimately performance. For example, high-level performance may occur within the familiar surroundings of a school soccer team but may diminish in the unfamiliar surroundings of a soccer club and a perceived 'superior' group of players. The intimidation of the 'new' or unknown must be recognised and considered when assessing the talent characteristics or performance attributes of young players.

EDUCATIONAL CONSIDERATIONS

Soccer within the UK, traditionally the preserve of the working classes, is undergoing great change. An increase in the number of players from 'middle-class' backgrounds has social and academic implications. The game is attracting players from different backgrounds, or as Revell (1999: 2–3) remarked:

> soccer recruitment has moved out of the backstreets of the industrial north and into the middle-class suburbs . . . Some insiders talk of the gentrification of the game, with everything from seat prices to recruitment policies aimed at a middle-class market.

Competitive sport and interscholastic/academic achievements are perceived predominantly as separate entities. Time allocated to one area is viewed as diminished time in the pursuit of success within the other. Establishing a professional playing career in tandem with academic success is a difficult proposition. Furthermore, there is no guarantee that a young player will make a successful career out of soccer.

The Football Association (FA) advocated the educational development of young soccer players within the aims of its former National School at Lilleshall. However, the educational emphasis of a young player's development on signing a one- or two-year professional contract at the age of 16 was limited. Bourke (2002) suggested that the presumption that young players disliked school (or education) was unsubstantiated. The FA sought to redress this imbalance by promoting an increased emphasis on the educational (and holistic) development of young players. More specifically, The FA Technical Department stressed:

> A fundamental aspect is the [player's] match programme, to be provided by the Football Academies. It is, therefore, proposed that the key individuals in the make-up of the player's match programme should be the parents. Quite properly the player's match programme should be developed in the best interests of the player's educational, technical, academic and social needs, by the parents in conjunction with the player's school and Football Academy Education and Welfare Officer.
>
> (FA Technical Department, 1997: 3)

The establishment of Soccer Academies was accompanied by the mandatory appointment of a full-time Academy Education and Welfare Officer [now referred to as the Head of Education and Welfare (HoEW). The HoEW was identified as a prerequisite within the Charter's 'Criteria to operate an Academy'. The education and welfare remit was outlined as:

2.4   To recognise and maximise the potential of exceptionally talented players whilst not compromising their overall education and welfare.

(FA Technical Department, 1997: 8)

. . .

4.7.1   Each Academy to ensure that appropriate and adequate educational provision (as determined by the Technical Control Board Academy Sub-Committee) is available for each Academy player including primary, secondary, further and higher educational provision. The player's technical and academic potential must be catered for and not compromised.

4.7.2   The Academy Education/Welfare Adviser [is] to ensure that adequate liaison is made with all schools and colleges where Academy players are enrolled.

4.7.3   Commitment to screening, profiling, monitoring and recording key aspects of the players' physiological growth and development, as determined by the FA Technical Control Board.

4.7.4   The interchange of research data and information between the Football Association and Academies and between Academies. This process will not compromise the individual rights to confidentiality.

4.7.5   Adequate player insurance.

(FA Technical Department, 1997: section 4.5)

Although the introduction of the HoEW was identified as a mandatory prerequisite for Academy status, it appears that the FA fell short of identifying specific guidance

193

for the person specification and/or explicit action of the role. The HoEW is (usually) an educational professional charged with monitoring the educational provision and developing a relationship with the individual student, his parents and his school. Clubs and players are encouraged to develop a productive partnership, especially in terms of personal, technical, social and academic development. The Football Association has established an Education and Welfare Committee including representatives from the professional leagues, PFA, English Schools' FA, Secondary Heads Association, Head Teachers' Association and Association of Chief Education Officers. In addition, the Football Association appointed an Education and Welfare Adviser who, in conjunction with staff from the FA Premier League and Football League, ensures the development of good practice, particularly in respect of education, welfare and child protection issues. The Football Association also provides regular in-service training for staff within the Academies to ensure the education of young soccer players in *all spheres* in order to equip the young players for the future. The Charter for Quality places the emphasis on Academies to enter into a 'Code of Conduct' with young players and their parents where each party acknowledges and agrees to its responsibilities in the partnership. Furthermore, the Football Association and FA Premier League have also developed detailed policies on child protection, where each club will be expected to produce its own child protection policy, procedure and practice.

Professional soccer cannot guarantee young players a successful professional playing career. Given this lack of security, it is now accepted that failure to 'make the grade' (i.e. gain a professional contract) must not hinder a young player's social and/or educational development. Soccer is moving into an era in which parents and young players are beginning to demand an educational 'exit route' (Richardson and Reilly, 2001). The seductive nature of the soccer environment may dilute the desire for educational development, particularly if individuals see their careers being shaped by soccer and not by academia. The pursuit of sporting excellence, and its perceived rewards, have created an educational dilemma concerning the context of academic versus sporting success. The HoEW has been introduced to provide support for young players (FA Technical Department, 1997). Consequently, the Head of Education and Welfare may alleviate such anxiety through the coordination of the young player's academic, social and technical development. Tradition dictates that education provides an *exit route* for players if they do not succeed as a professional player. Elements of the educational package should be viewed as an integral component of the youth player development package. For example, Fulham Football Club's Academy (2003: 4) advocates that:

> a player's education is essential. The ability for a player to be receptive
> to information is an important part of their development on and off the

field of play. We view a positive attitude towards school and education as a big advantage.

Moreover, clubs should provide an educational package in case the player *succeeds* in gaining a professional contract. Soccer education should ensure that the successful player is equipped to cope with life as an elite player. In this sense, a synthesis between the player's soccer development and his or her educational programme would enable a more 'performance based soccer education' (i.e. lifestyle, behaviour, diet, nutrition, fitness, conditioning, coping strategies, reflective practice) to be undertaken. Furthermore, this would enable the HoEWs, in association with the coaches and Academy staff, to provide a more coherent educational, welfare and performance package for the development of elite young players.

OVERVIEW

Psychological and sociological player characteristics in addition to environmental and cultural considerations ought to be more readily recognised within the development and nurture of (elite) young soccer players. Personality (i.e. self-confidence, anxiety control, motivation, attitude and concentration) has been identified as one of the most important yet complex components of the talent map. As such, no psychological tests (e.g. player profiling) can provide comprehensive measurements or indication of elite player performance. It is more appropriate for professional clubs (i.e. including Academy Directors, coaches, HoEWs) to provide an inclusive, appropriate and supportive environment that draws on elements of psychological and sociological support such as reflective practice, counselling, lifestyle and behavioural skills. The development of young talent cannot rely solely on the physical, technical and tactical attributes of young players. A talented young player requires a supportive network of influence (i.e. parent, coach, teacher, HoEW, Academy Director) to enable his/her potential to be realised. Clubs have embraced the responsibility of investing in youth development programmes, at least for boys. Talented young players are afforded access to appropriate facilities and opportunities for meaningful practice. However, clubs should embrace a more inclusive responsibility toward player development. For example, a soccer performance educational and welfare programme that includes elements of diet, nutrition, fitness, conditioning, emotional and behavioural skills (i.e. pertinent to life as a soccer player and appropriate for an educational exit route), which includes the coaches, will encourage players to become more responsible for their own soccer development. In this sense, players will become active in their own development rather than being passive receivers of knowledge. The clubs must supplement this ethos with an investment in appropriate coach education opportunities.

The young player's overall development and general well-being should be the concern of all those involved in the process of player development (i.e. including coaches). The pursuit of excellence should not occur at the expense of the child's physical and emotional health, growth and development. An appropriate, inclusive and supportive familial, educational, welfare and socio-cultural environment is an essential ingredient in a balanced youth development programme.

REFERENCES

Ajax Football Club (2003) Ajax Youth. http://ajax.nl (accessed 12/5/03).

AjaxUSA (2001) Interview with Kees Zwamborn. http://www.ajax-usa.com/ajax/youth/kees_interview042601.html (accessed 12/5/03).

Babkes, M.L. and Weiss, M.R. (1999) Parental influence on children's cognitive and affective responses to competitive soccer participation. *Paediatric Exercise Science*, 11, 44–62.

Bloom, B.S. (1985) *Developing Talent in the Young*. New York: Ballantine.

Bourke, A. (2002) The road to fame and fortune: insights on the career paths of young Irish professional footballers in England. *Journal of Youth Studies*, 5 (4), 375–389.

Brustad, R.J. (1992) Integrating socialisation influences into the study of children's motivation in sport. *Journal of Sport and Exercise Psychology*, 14, 59–77.

Cahill, B.R. and Pearl, A.J. (1993) *Intensive Participation in Children's Sports*. Champaign, IL: Human Kinetics.

Carlson, R. (1988) The socialization of elite tennis players in Sweden: an analysis of the players' backgrounds and development. *Society of Sports Journal*, 5, 241–256.

Carlson, R. (1993) The path to the national level in sports in Sweden. *Scandinavian Journal of Medicine and Science in Sports*, 3, 170–177.

Côté, J. (1999) The influence of the family in the development of talent in sport. *The Sports Psychologist*, 13, 395–417.

Football Association Technical Department (1997) Football Education for Young Players: A Charter for Quality. London: Football Association.

Fulham Football Club (2003) What is the Academy? http://www.fulhamfc.com (accessed 16/3/03).

Greendorfer, S.L., Lewko, J.H. and Rosengren, K.S. (1996) Family and gender-based influences in sport socialisation of children and adolescents. In F.L. Smoll and R.E. Smith (eds) *Children and Youth in Sport: A Biopsychosocial Perspective*. London: Brown and Benchmark, 89–111.

Hellstedt, J.C. (1988) Kids, parents and sports: some questions and answers. *Physician and Sportsmedicine*, 16 (4), 59–62, 69–71.

Hill, M. and Tisdall, K. (1997) *Children and Society*. New York: Longman.

Jambor, E.A. (1998) Parents as children's socialising agents in youth soccer. *Journal of Human Movement Studies*, 34, 83–94.

James, A. and Prout, A. (1990) *Constructing and Reconstructing Childhood*. London: Falmer Press.

Kay, T. (2000) Sporting excellence: a family affair? *European Physical Education Review*, 6, 151–169.

Morris, T. (1997) *Psychological Skills Training: An Overview* (2nd edn). Leeds: British Association of Sport and Exercise Sciences.

Morris, T. (2000) Psychological characteristics and talent identification in soccer. *Journal of Sports Sciences*, 18, 715–726.

Newburg, D., Kimiecik, J., Durand-Bush, N. and Doell, K. (2002) The role of resonance in performance excellence and life engagement. *Journal of Applied Sport Psychology*, 14, 249–267.

Orlick, T. (2000) *In Pursuit of Excellence: How to Win in Sport and Life Through Mental Training*. Champaign, IL: Human Kinetics.

Orlick, T. and Partington, J. (1988) Mental links to excellence. *The Sports Psychologist*, 2, 105–130.

Régnier, G., Salmela, J.H. and Russell, S.J. (1993) Talent detection and development in sport. In R. Singer, M. Murphy and L.K. Tennant (eds) *A Handbook of Research on Sports Psychology*. New York: Macmillan, 290–313.

Reilly, T., Bangsbo, J. and Franks, A. (2000) Anthropometric and physiological predispositions for elite soccer. *Journal of Sports Sciences*, 18, 669–683.

Reilly, T., Williams, A.M. and Richardson, D. (2003) Identifying talented players. In T. Reilly and A.M. Williams (eds) *Science and Soccer* (2nd edn). London: Routledge, 307–326.

Revell, P. (1999) Golden goal. *The Guardian*, Education, 2–3, 12 January.

Richardson, D. (1998) Reducing the 'relative age' advantage. *Insight – The F.A. Coaches Association Journal*, 1(2), 46.

Richardson, D. (2000) The influence of 'significant others' in the development of talented young football players. *Insight – The F.A. Coaches Association Journal*, 4(3), 28–29.

Richardson, D. and Reilly, T. (2001) Talent identification, detection and development of youth football players – sociological considerations. *Human Movement, Polish Scientific Physical Education Association*, 1 (3), 86–93.

Rowley, S. (1992) *Training of Young Athletes Study: Identification of Talent*. London: The Sports Council.

Singer, R.N. and Janelle, C.M. (1999) Determining sport expertise: from genes to supremes. *International Journal of Sport Psychology*, 30, 117–150.

Williams, A.M. (2000) Perceptual skill in soccer: implications for talent identification and development. *Journal of Sports Sciences*, 18, 737–750.

Williams, A.M., Reilly, T. and Franks, A. (1999) Identifying talented football players: a scientific perspective. *Insight – The F.A. Coaches Association Journal*, 3, 20–25.

CHAPTER TWELVE

THE ROLE OF THE SOCCER ACADEMY

INTRODUCTION

In recent years there has been a keen interest in the development of young talent (Franks *et al.*, 1999). Across many sports investing in youth is viewed as a vehicle to ensure the continuous production of elite sports performers. Both soccer coaches and club management appreciate that identifying young talented soccer players at an early stage and exposing talented players to specialised coaching and training may accelerate (and enhance) the talent development process (Williams *et al.*, 1999). The primary objective of a soccer club is success on the playing field. In this sense, success is inextricably linked with sound management, effective coaching, appropriate facilities and support mechanisms and, fundamentally, good quality players. The nature and function of elite youth player development are captured in this chapter. More specifically, by drawing on examples of good practice from different countries, some fundamental mechanisms and requirements of a successful Soccer Academy are outlined.

In England formal structures for the development of young talent have been set up to enhance the development of talent within the soccer environment. Schemes such as Youth Opportunities (YOP) and the Youth Training Scheme (YTS or YT) offered young players a platform to develop their soccer talent in conjunction with the added 'incentive' of engaging in alternative academic and/or vocational pursuits. The establishment of the Footballers' Further Education and Vocational Training Society (FFE and VTS) by the Professional Footballers' Association (PFA) has ensured that educational and/or vocational pursuits are an integral part of youth soccer development programmes in England. Since the emergence of the English Football Association's National School in 1984, soccer 'Centres of Excellence' have materialised as a mechanism to enhance player development (and production). More recently, the FA Technical Department's Charter for Quality (1997) instigated more formal managerial structures through the introduction of the Soccer Academy. The effect of such structures on the development of talent invites further exploration.

The English Football Association (FA) proposed regulations for the soccer season 1998/1999, more commonly referred to as 'Football Education for Young Players: A Charter for Quality'. The overriding principle of the 'Charter' was to 'attempt' to provide quality experiences for all young players at all levels. Clubs have expressed a need for increased access to young players to allow them more time to develop. In association with this objective, the underlining principle of the Academy structure is to produce players for the first team:

> The purpose of the FA Programme for Excellence is to identify players of outstanding ability and place them in a technical and educational programme designed to produce football excellence in conjunction with personal development.
>
> (FA Technical Department, 1997: 1)

THE SOCCER ACADEMY – AN EVOLVING PROFESSIONAL DOMAIN

The more humanistic and holistic concepts of development emphasise a more caring and nurturing environment in order to encourage the development of the 'whole' individual. Educational elements of the developmental process not only provide opportunities for life after soccer, but also facilitate the production of a more *intelligent* player. 'The production of an intelligent player can provide "added value" to an increasingly valuable commodity (e.g. an understanding of lifestyle management, self-awareness, an ability to respond to complex tactics, media relations)' (Richardson, 1999: 19). Although no real evidence exists as to how this added value is realised within individual club settings, the Academies themselves espouse the production of a more well-rounded individual.

> You get one or two players coming through. You look at them, watch how they transport themselves on the playing field and how they do in their ordinary life and you say to yourself, 'he's well brought up'.
>
> (Sir Alex Ferguson cited in Premier League, 2003: 1)

The inception of the FA Premier League in 1992 and the introduction of the FA Premier Academy Leagues witnessed a transformation in youth development. The general *mission* of the Soccer Academy is to create an appropriate environment for the development of elite players (see Ajax FC, 2003; Fulham FC, 2003).

200

Table 12.1 Financial investment per annum in youth development programmes

	Ajax FC	FC Barcelona	Parma	Inter Milan	Sao Paolo FC
Declared financial investment in youth development per year	£1 million	£3.2 million	£1 million	£2 million	£1.8 million

Source: Adapted from FA Technical Department, 1997.

In this sense, Academies aspire to develop players for the first team or (at least) generate income through the sale of 'marketable assets'. For example, Fulham Football Club (2003) believed that the Academy has the potential to save the club millions of pounds because of the (theoretically) reduced need to engage in *major* transfer transactions. In this sense, the difference in cost between operating a *successful* Academy and entering the inflated transfer market justifies the initial outlay and continuing investment in the Academy structure (see Table 12.1).

> Fulham Academy graduate Sean Davis is an England under-21 inter-national . . . his estimated transfer value is around *six* times more than it costs to run the *entire* Academy system for *one year*.
> (Fulham Football Club, 2003: 2)

In this sense, the production of one or two players every six years could be viewed as a successful venture and ensure the Academy (at least) broke even financially. Further, La Masia, the historic residence of Barcelona's youth development programme established in 1979, claims that 30 youngsters (an average of 1.25 per year) have graduated to Barca's first team. The role of honour includes players such as Amor, Guardiola, Sergi, De la Peña, Puyol, Xavi, Reina Víctor Valdés and Gabri, many more establishing careers with other leading Spanish clubs (FC Barcelona, 2003). Similarly, Manchester United's youth programme (i.e. pre-Academy status) yielded Scholes, Butt, Gary and Phil Neville and Beckham as well as successful products such as Robbie Savage (Birmingham City and Wales), Keith Gillespie (Blackburn Rovers and Northern Ireland) and Ronnie Wallwork (West Brom). The successful development of these players has saved, and generated, substantial amounts of money for the parent club.

> It's difficult to assess, but you can't put an estimate below £20 million. It would have to be above that. That's a safe prediction.
> (Sir Alex Ferguson, cited in Premier League, 2003: 1)

Furthermore, whilst trying to produce a player for the first team, the clubs are also aware of the 'safety-net' that a successful Academy can provide. In some instances the Academy players are considered as an insurance policy for the club that may safeguard the club's future (Sulley, Academy Director, Bolton Wanderers FC, cited in Premier League, 2003).

The Academy system is now an established cornerstone of elite youth player development. Soccer clubs recognise the need to provide more effective coaching and sophisticated development programmes than previously existed for their young players. The importance of producing talented young players is not only the concern of the clubs, but also a national concern. The national concerns in England centre on the limited production of technically gifted young players. Moreover, there is a concern that English players are (traditionally) unable to match the technical ability of their international counterparts (Waddington, 2001). Nevertheless, the general philosophy of a soccer club must be to produce a successful first team, not a successful national team. The increased emphasis on youth development will undoubtedly reap *some* future national rewards, even if indirectly.

THE ACADEMY STRUCTURE

Although various discrepancies in the structure of Academies undoubtedly exist (e.g. within England and throughout other countries) the following section offers an insight into the basic organisational mechanisms and philosophies that exist across different clubs. Figure 12.1 offers an organisational diagnostic, which depicts a 'typical' Academy structure.

Figure 12.1 evidences the clear investment in elite youth player development by *most* soccer Academies. Furthermore, Sulley (cited in Premier League, 2003) claimed that the Academy facilities and structures that exist in England are equivalent, if not better, than anywhere else in the world. In this sense, these Academies are providing an appropriate environment and opportunity for young talent to be realised.

Figure 12.1 shows the overall position of the Academy Director who is responsible for the day-to-day running of the Academy. He, in turn, may be responsible to the first team manager and/or a member of the club's Board of Directors (i.e. with explicit responsibility for youth development). Most Academies will have at least one coach per age group from under-19s down to under-9s. In some cases, clubs may employ specialist youth coaches or even specialist skills development coaches (i.e. technical development for under-12s and below) who possess critical child development knowledge (i.e. an understanding of skill development, growth, maturation and an empathy with elite young players; see Chapter 10).

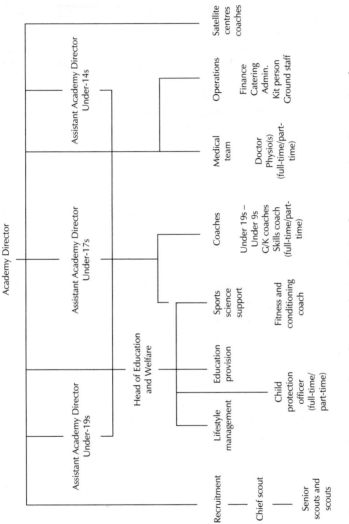

The Academy structure

Academy Director

Assistant Academy Director Under-19s

Assistant Academy Director Under-17s

Assistant Academy Director Under-14s

Recruitment

Chief scout

Senior scouts and scouts

Head of Education and Welfare

Lifestyle management

Education provision

Child protection officer (full-time/ part-time)

Sports science support

Fitness and conditioning coach

Coaches

Under 19s – Under 9s G/K coaches Skills coach (full-time/part-time)

Medical team

Doctor Physio(s) (full-time/part-time)

Operations

Finance Catering Admin. Kit person Ground staff

Satellite centres coaches

Figure 12.1 Representation of a typical organisational structure in a Soccer Academy

Source: Author.

Investment in technical skills at this early stage of a player's development is essential for players to develop a fundamental relationship with the ball.

The medical needs of the Academy personnel are serviced by the Academy doctor or (at least) a part-time doctor, ideally with no explicit responsibility to the first team, in association with (at least) one full-time chartered physiotherapist, and a therapist who holds the FA Diploma in 'Treatment and Management of Injuries'. The medical teams in England are required to conduct cardiovascular screening on all players 'on entry' to the Academy (i.e. 9 years and upwards), with further cardiovascular and orthopaedic screening 'on entry' to the scholarship scheme (i.e. under-17s). The medical team is also required to maintain secure, confidential and up-to-date medical records for all Academy players. In addition, all coaches should possess an Emergency First Aid qualification. Further to the general medical care provided, the FA (2003) also stipulated that the medical staff should be actively engaged in the FA's Medical Research Projects. Such projects include:

6.1 *An Audit of Injuries in Academy Football – Longitudinal Study*
■ To identify the prevalence of injuries in specific age-group Academy players.
■ To identify potential injury risk factors of young players.
■ To reduce the prevalence of injury through preventative strategies.
■ To correlate injury patterns with measurements in 6.2 below.

6.2 *Orthopaedic Musculo-Skeletal Evaluation Research – Longitudinal Study*
■ To establish age specific measurement norms and ranges.
■ To identify orthopaedic/biomechanical abnormalities in young players that may predispose injuries in specific age groups in Academy football and later in professional football.

(Football Association, 2003: 3)

Further to the longitudinal research concerning the incidence of injury, the FA also restrict the number of games that young players can play due to concerns of 'overuse' and general incidents of injury. The under-12s engage solely in small-sided games and can play no more than 30 games per season. The under-13s and above play 11-a-side soccer but are restricted to a maximum of 30 games and a minimum of 24 games per season. These figures are dependent on the club's and players' circumstances (e.g. injuries) but provide further evidence of the FA's commitment to youth development.

In addition to the coaching and medical support provided by the Academy the clubs are also responsible (or have a responsibility) for the educational development of the young player. It is suggested that the education of the player should not be compromised by the player's soccer development. This concept was originally espoused by the FA, and is epitomised by the following statement from Fulham Football Club:

> The [Fulham] Academy aims to develop each player technically, academically, personally and socially . . . Fulham Football Club Academy acknowledges and accepts its responsibility towards the education of its registered students [players]. The Academy has a 'holistic' approach to education. The development of the 'whole boy' is taken into consideration and this will not be compromised by the focus placed on his technical development.
>
> (Fulham Football Club, 2003: 5)

Generally, players between 9 and 16 years will train at an Academy between two and four times per week. *Most* Academies provide 'homework' clubs, appropriate tutors and learning resources for young players to ensure that their schoolwork is not affected. In addition, the club's Head of Education and Welfare will liaise with parents and school to ensure that the player's academic potential is maximised.

The educational provision is continued through into the scholarship scheme (i.e. under-17s to under-19s) under the guidelines of the Footballers' Further Education and Vocational Training Society. Scholars are required to engage in 10 hours per week of a vocational and/or academic qualification plus two hours per week of core or competency skills (see Figure 12.2 for examples of such skills).

RECRUITING ELITE YOUNG PLAYERS

The onset of the Academy structure and the perceived expectation to produce talented players for the first team have further fuelled the competition to attract young talent to the Academy. Young players usually attend the club's premises for a trial period of up to 6 weeks (one or two nights per week). The FA stipulates that boys under 12 years of age must live within one hour's journey to the Academy premises, with the under-13s to under-16s living within a journey time of 90 minutes. Players who are successful are offered a 'registration' as an Academy player. Registered players do not *normally* play games or organised soccer outside the Academy programme unless agreed by the club. For example, Fulham Football Club actively encourage their boys to play for their school and representative teams to enable them to continue mixing with their peers (e.g. Fulham Football Club, 2003). Furthermore, the FA provides guidelines for the registration of players. Players under the age of 12 years must be offered a registration on an annual basis. Under-14 players are offered a 2-year registration, and at the age of 14 years players can be signed until the end of the under-16 season. When a player reaches his 14th birthday the club may offer him a full-time Academy scholarship to cover him up to his 19th birthday. This will normally include an option to extend the registration up until the player's 21st birthday.

It would appear that the key to a successful Academy lies in the recruitment process (the new word for scouting). The majority of clubs would agree that without identifying, accessing and attracting the best young players available, even the most experienced and talented coaches would struggle to equip players with the necessary skills to compete at an elite level (see Celtic FC, 2003). The talent identification (and recruitment) process, in most soccer clubs, now starts with players aged 7 years and upward. The emphasis is then placed on the provision of effective and appropriate coaching and support structures that enable players to realise their potential. Academies now present young talent with a *complete* soccer development package. More specifically, this package includes the technical, tactical, physical, and (increasingly) social and psychological considerations (see Chapter 11) of talent development. Ultimately, talented young players can be nurtured, and schooled in the coaching philosophy of each club, to become future first team players. For example, Ajax Football Club (2003) employs the talent identification acronym TIPS, which stands for technique, intelligence (or insight), personality and speed. Kees Zwamborn, former Director of Youth Development at Ajax's youth academy, De Toekomst (now Academy Director at Sunderland AFC), described the intricacies of the acronym:

> The 'T' is for 'technique', what you can do with the ball. 'I' is for 'intelligence', tactics. You can read the game. 'P' is for personality – the 'P' is very important. It's difficult to scout . . . a very young player. It's difficult to see. Because when you come here and you must be a grown-up player, it's a very hard way, so you have to be a fighter, a winner. Very, very important, but difficult to see when you are a kid of seven years old. And the 'S' is for speed, because in the play of Ajax it is important, not only speed like in the running of 100 metres, but also it is very important that you are fast with the ball . . . Because we are playing – it's one of the most important things of our system.
>
> (Cited in AjaxUSA, 2001: 1)

Each aspect of the TIPS model is further broken down into 10 sub-components. Personality and intelligence are *generally* perceived as innate properties whereas technique and speed can be developed further. Ajax also espouses a *club* style of play (4-3-3), training and behaviour which are practised throughout the club structure (i.e. first team through to under-9s). Furthermore, 'Ajax strives to keep the way of playing football recognisable; attractive, offensive minded, creative, fast, fair and preferably away from their own goal in the opponents' half' (Ajax Football Club, 2003: 1–2). As identified in Chapter 11, similar talent acronyms have also emerged in England such as TABS (technique, attitude, balance and speed) and SUPS (speed, understanding, personality, skill). However, whilst these criteria recognise certain attributes for success, the judgements of coaches and talent scouts can be speculative and subjective. More recently, these criteria (craft judgements) are being supplemented with objective measures offered by sports science techniques (see Chapter 10). Academies are, however, beginning to invest more readily in the benefits offered by sports scientists within their talent identification and development programmes.

Whilst dreaming of becoming the stars of tomorrow, it is all too easy for identified young talent to neglect their educational interests. The Academy bears a responsibility not only for the player's soccer development (education) but also for their academic education. The Football Association Technical Department (1997) stressed the importance of providing a more 'holistic' approach to player development in the Charter for Quality.

Consequently, today's elite young players are generally exposed to an Academy curriculum that offers an extensive education in soccer. The Academy curriculum usually consists of technical, tactical, physical, social, behavioural, psychological, nutritional, educational and welfare considerations of talent development (see Figure 12.2).

THE ACADEMY CURRICULUM

The following text offers a brief synopsis of what is (potentially) available to elite young players within a typical Academy curriculum. Each club, although sometimes constrained by the guidelines of their respective governing body, may offer a slightly different package. Each package may be dependent on the values, perceptions, aspirations, finances (and hence resources) ascribed to each component by individual clubs, Directors, managers, Academy Directors and coaches.

The technical and tactical components

The technical component of a player's development is critical to elite performance. Recently, more emphasis on technical development is concentrated in the early years of player development. Increasingly, Academies are utilising skills development coaches to enhance technique at an early age. Furthermore,

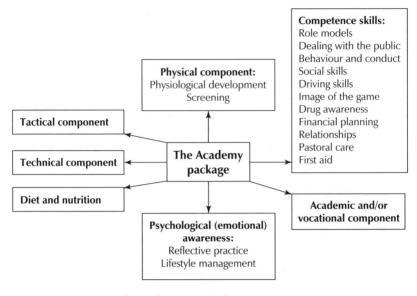

Figure 12.2 A typical Academy curriculum

Source: Adapted from Celtic FC, 2003.

Academies employ a range of strategies that enable new and experienced coaches to develop their coaching skills (e.g. in-service training, guest coaches). Some clubs stipulate a philosophy of play that is embraced throughout the club and the Academy (e.g. Ajax's 4-3-3 system). Although not all clubs employ such philosophies (as such, philosophies are often dependent on the management or the Academy Director), players are schooled in tactical awareness (i.e. positional awareness, systems of play) from an early age. As players progress through the Academy the emphasis on tactical awareness increases with elements of notational/match analysis being employed to evaluate both individual and team performance.

Diet and nutrition

There is a need for players to understand the performance benefits of a balanced and appropriate diet. Some Academies educate their young players and (importantly) their parents about dietary intake. The demanding training and match schedules of a typical Academy player require that optimal fuel (and re-fuel) intake is provided in order to maximise performance. Players (and parents) require education and (in some cases) counselling in order to establish an appropriate performance-enhancing diet.

Physical component

The physical component of an Academy structure is generally dominated by the physiological development of young players. Elements of physiological development include flexibility, power, strength, speed and range of motion. The full-time scholars are generally subjected to more rigorous physiological testing (e.g. $\dot{V}O_{2max}$, high intensity recovery tests, anaerobic thresholds) (a fuller description can be found in Chapter 6). Such tests provide the Academy staff and coaches with a comprehensive assessment of a player's physiological capabilities and hence test results can be utilised to guide individual training programmes.

Psychological (emotional) awareness

Clubs are slowly beginning to recognise the benefits of developing the psychological and emotional awareness of young players. The psychological practices tend to place a greater emphasis on the nurturing of players. Players are being encouraged to become more responsible for their own development. For example, 'The Reflective Practitioner' module in the new BTEC Performance and Excellence qualification (see Premier League Learning, 2003) encourages players to reflect on their own development, skills, technique and subsequent performance. Kees Zwamborn (cited in AjaxUSA, 2001: 2) alluded to personality (and emotion) as being the most complex component of young player development:

> that's [personality] the problem. It's a thing that's not only hard to describe, but it's hard to develop, as well. You have to wonder if you can train 'P' [personality]. When you don't have the 'P' in your body, in your brain, then it's very difficult. And it's a problem . . . It's the most difficult thing when you are developing players, because you say, 'Ah, they are young, they can learn a lot.' But when we have difficulty with their behaviour, it's of course hard to send them away when they are little boys.

The complexity of developing the emotional and psychological development of young players invites further attention. In addition, elements of goal setting and performance profiling are becoming more commonplace within the Academy setting.

Academic and/or vocational component

The academic and/or vocational component of a player's soccer development has traditionally been perceived as irrelevant. The installation of the Head of Education and Welfare (as a mandatory requirement for Academy status) and a growing appreciation of the benefits of producing a well-rounded and receptive individual by *most* clubs have ensured that education is part of all Academy players' soccer development. Educational support is often provided by the Academy for all its players. The predominant educational responsibility lies with the player, the parents (and/or guardians) and the school until the player signs a full-time Academy scholarship (i.e. 16–19 years of age).

Competence skills

In addition to the educational programme, Academy players should engage in a range of competence or life (management) skills. These are usually delivered and/or coordinated by the Head of Education and Welfare and/or appropriate support staff (e.g. lifestyle consultant, sports psychologist). Such a programme provides players with a range of diverse skills (including social and behavioural) that can be utilised both inside and outside the club.

OVERVIEW

It is clear that the emphasis on elite talent identification and development has increased in recent years. Today's elite young player is exposed to a range of support mechanisms that can enhance both his soccer and his personal development. The introduction of the Academies and the development of 'other' (e.g. European) youth programmes suggest that clubs are (increasingly) taking their responsibility for the development of young players more seriously than ever before. The development of elite young players through the Academy and into the first team is the fundamental aim of all Academies. It may still be too early to judge their success. It appears that the Academies are embracing a more holistic development of today's young player. As they continue to develop they will reap the rewards in the production of exceptional, technically gifted, physically and emotionally equipped well-rounded 'home-grown' players.

REFERENCES

Ajax Football Club (2003) Ajax Youth. http://ajax.nl (accessed 7/7/03).

AjaxUSA (2001) Interview with Kees Zwamborn. http://www.ajax-usa.com/ajax/youth/kees_interview042601.html (accessed 7/7/03).

Celtic Football Club (2003) *Development Pools: The New Youth Development Programme.* http://celticfc.co.net (accessed 16/5/03).

FC Barcelona (2003) La Masia. http://www.fcbarcelona.es (accessed 19/8/03).

Football Association (2003) Medical Criteria Governing Football Academies. http://www.thefa.com (accessed 15/3/03).

Football Association Technical Department (1997) Football Education for Young Players: A Charter for Quality. London: Football Association.

Franks, A., Williams, A.M., Reilly, T. and Nevill, A. (1999) Talent identification in elite youth soccer players: physical and physiological characteristics. *Journal of Sports Sciences*, 17, 812.

Fulham Football Club (2003) What is the Academy? http://www.fulhamfc.com (accessed 16/3/03).

Premier League (2003) 'Youth Saved United Millions'. http://premierleague.com (accessed 28/5/03).

Premier League Learning (2003) *BTEC Course Summary.* http://premierleaguelearning.nescot.ac.uk (accessed 15/3/03).

Richardson, D. (1999) Responsibility of the coach in the academic development of the young player. *Insight – The F.A. Coaches Association Journal*, 3 (2), 19.

Waddington, I. (2001) *Singer and Friedlander Football Review 2000–01 Season.* In association with The Centre for Research into Sport and Society: University of Leicester.

Williams, A.M., Reilly, T. and Franks, A. (1999) Identifying talented football players: a scientific perspective. *Insight – The F.A. Coaches Association Journal*, 3, 20–25.

INDEX